Time-Life Books Inc. is a wholly owned subsidiary of
TIME INCORPORATED

Founder: HENRY R. LUCE 1898–1967
Editor-in-Chief: HENRY ANATOLE GRUNWALD
Chairman and Chief Executive Officer: J. RICHARD MUNRO
President and Chief Operating Officer: N. J. NICHOLAS JR.
Chairman of the Executive Committee: RALPH P. DAVIDSON
Corporate Editor: RAY CAVE
Executive Vice President, Books: KELSO F. SUTTON
Vice President, Books: GEORGE ARTANDI

TIME LIFE BOOKS INC.

Editor: GEORGE CONSTABLE
Executive Editor: ELLEN PHILLIPS
Director of Design: LOUIS KLEIN
Director of Editorial Resources: PHYLLIS K. WISE
Editorial Board: RUSSELL B. ADAMS JR., DALE M. BROWN,
ROBERTA CONLAN, THOMAS H. FLAHERTY, LEE HASSIG,
DONIA ANN STEELE, ROSALIND STUBENBERG,
KIT VAN TULLEKEN, HENRY WOODHEAD
Director of Photography and Research:
JOHN CONRAD WEISER

President: CHRISTOPHER T. LINEN
Chief Operating Officer: JOHN M. FAHEY JR.
Senior Vice President: JAMES L. MERCER
Vice Presidents: STEPHEN L. BAIR, RALPH J. CUOMO,
NEAL GOFF, STEPHEN L. GOLDSTEIN, JUANITA T. JAMES,
HALLETT JOHNSON III, CAROL KAPLAN,
SUSAN J. MARUYAMA, ROBERT H. SMITH,
PAUL R. STEWART, JOSEPH J. WARD
Director of Production Services: ROBERT J. PASSANTINO

EDITORIAL OPERATIONS

Copy Chief: DIANE ULLIUS
Production: CELIA BEATTIE
Quality Control: JAMES J. COX (DIRECTOR)
Library: LOUISE D. FORSTALL

Valuable assistance was also provided by: LIZ BROWN,
CHRISTINA LIEBERMAN (NEW YORK)

THE TIME-LIFE BOOK OF CHRISTMAS
Publisher: PAUL STEWART
Assistant to the Publisher: JUDITH HARLEY
Art Director: DON SHELDON

PRODUCED BY THE COMPAGE COMPANY

Executive Editor: KENNETH R. BURKE
Project Editor: JESSIE WOOD
Designer: BARBARA ZILLER
Assistant Project Editor: CAROL HENDERSON
Lead Writers: CHRISTINA NELSON, PAUL SCIAVO
Additional Writing: KARIN BREUER, MARLENE SPIELER
Lead Photo Researcher: LINDSAY KEFAUVER
Additional Photo Research: VILETTE HARRIS,
REBECCA HIRSCH
Text research: ELINOR LINDHEIMER
Copy Editor: ALICE KLEIN
Art Production: DEBRA HOWARD
Indexer: FRANCES BOWLES
Typography: TERRY ROBINSON COMPOSITION SERVICES

Reviewers and Consultants: DOLPH GOTELLI,
SHARRON UHLER, RACHEL BOLTON, ANN CULLEN,
JAN NIX

Library of Congress Cataloging-in-Publication Data
THE TIME-LIFE BOOK OF CHRISTMAS.
    Includes index.
    1. Christmas—United States.   I. Time-Life Books.
GT4986.A1T55   1987b   394.2'68282'0973   87-14566
ISBN 0-8094-6725-9

For information about any Time-Life book or music series,
please write, or call:
Reader Information
Time-Life Customer Service
P.O. Box C-32068
Richmond, VA 23261-2068
Telephone: 1-800-621-7026

THE TIME-LIFE
BOOK OF CHRISTMAS

Norman Rockwell

Time-Life Books, Alexandria, Virginia

THE TIME-LIFE BOOK OF CHRISTMAS

CHRISTMAS IN AMERICA

Christmas! As the ancient poem reminds us, it comes only once a year, but what a warm, colorful, and joyous occasion it is. No other holiday in America boasts such a wealth of traditions and customs. Christmas is gifts and greeting cards, sumptuous dinners, familiar songs. It is brightly lit trees and red-ribboned wreaths, Santa Claus and stockings. It's a season hectic with shopping and preparations, yet at its heart lies an inspiring message of hope, peace on earth, and good will to all.

Not only do we enjoy our uniquely American traditions—Christmas dinner with roast turkey, stuffing, and cranberry sauce; electric lights strung on doors and entrance ways; plump Santa Claus with his red suit and jolly laugh—but we also celebrate in ways that reflect the diverse backgrounds of our immigrant ancestors. Their holiday traditions, transplanted here from many countries, have taken root and thrived.

Christmas came to America with the first European settlers, who observed the holiday in the New World much as they had in their homelands. To the first English colonists who arrived in Virginia in 1607, Christmas was both a holy day and a festival, and they celebrated it here with the same merriment and feasting that had marked the occasion in the British Isles. Those early Virginians also began the practice of exuberant noise-making, with horns, drums, and firecrackers, that is still part of Christmas in the South, and the chief way of welcoming the New Year throughout the country.

Christmas celebrations were necessarily simple in the new land. Life offered few luxuries, and most families struggled just to survive. But some immigrants had other reasons for not observing Christmas. The Puritan Pilgrims who landed in New England in 1620 took a dim view of the singing and dancing, feasting and drinking that characterized the Yuletide celebration back in England, and in the Virginia colony. For the Puritans, Christmas was strictly a religious matter, and merrymaking on this holy day was an unwelcome reminder of pagan winter rites. Furthermore, they said, it had never been proved that December 25 was the day on which Christ was born. So the Pilgrims who landed in Massachusetts in the winter of 1620 spent the twenty-fifth of December erecting their first building, refusing to make the day special in any way.

The bans imposed by the Puritan fathers were enough to dampen the most vibrant spirit. They insisted on a full day's labor on December 25, forbade Christmas greetings, and even outlawed the traditional mince pie. Nevertheless, most families managed some small observance. Rebellious homemakers still baked mince pies, disguising them by varying the ingredients and cooking them in pans of various shapes.

The harsh laws remained in effect well into the 1700s, but with the break from England—and its all-too-merry Christmas—the Puritans began to lift their bans. Still, a few laws persisted even after the Revolutionary War, and it was not until 1856 that Massachusetts recognized Christmas as a legal holiday.

Christmas was cheerier elsewhere in the colonies. Four years after the Pilgrims landed at Plymouth Rock, an expedition of the Dutch East India Company arrived in what is now New York Harbor. On Christmas day, 1624, they went ashore to the island that now bears the name of its first inhabitants, the Manhattan Indians, and gave thanks with a merry feast. As more colonists arrived from Holland, they brought their Christmas customs with them: the gift-bearing St. Nicholas, the stocking filled with treats, and the spirit of family closeness that is so much a part of Christmas today. The Dutch leaders even adopted St. Nicholas as the patron of New Amsterdam, as they called their settlement.

Other immigrants along the Atlantic seaboard joined the Dutch in keeping a merry Christmas, but they did so according to their own traditions. With the Scandinavians who settled in Delaware in 1638 came the legend of gift-giving elves, as well as the custom of hanging a wreath of fir or pine boughs on the front door as a sign of welcome and a symbol of good luck. A century or so later, German colonists introduced the practice of decorating evergreen trees with candles, cookies, and ornaments.

Christmas in the southern states was a convivial affair, the American counterpart of the English Yuletide revelry. It was not so much an occasion for gift giving as for friendship and hospitality. In Williamsburg, Virginia, people lit the Yule log as the foundation of the traditional Christmas Eve fire, and gathered to sing carols. The next morning they attended church services, and then the festivities began in earnest—with banquets, dances, games, hunts, and fireworks sometimes continuing until the New Year.

On plantations all over the South, the Yule log played a special role in holiday observances. As long as it burned, usually throughout Christmas week, no one was expected to work. Not surprisingly, people went to great lengths to keep the giant log ablaze.

In the huge expanse of country beyond the thirteen original colonies, other traditions took hold. From the Great Lakes to Louisiana, French settlers attended a midnight mass on Christmas Eve, then sat down to a special supper called a *reveillon*. Children left their shoes by the crèche before going to bed, in hopes that the infant Jesus would fill them with gifts. For most French-American families Christmas was a time of peace and contemplation. The secular celebration waited until New Year's Eve, which was celebrated with a town festival complete with parades, masquerades, and noise making.

Spanish communities in what is now Texas and in the mission settlements of the Southwest had a special ritual—they reenacted the journey of Mary and Joseph on the first Christmas. Called *Las Posadas*, this combination procession, play, and pageant was followed by a lively celebration. At the height of the festivities a *piñata*, a brightly colored pottery container filled with treats, was hung from a roof beam. Children swung at it by turns with a large stick, and when it broke scrambled wildly after the toys and sweets that spilled out. In many Hispanic communities, *Las Posadas* and the *piñata* are still central to the celebration of Christmas.

As the tide of immigrants swelled in the nineteenth century, new Christmas customs appeared throughout the land. It was at this time, too, that Christmas assumed national importance. In 1831, Louisiana and Arkansas became the first states to declare December 25 a legal holiday. By the 1840s, Clement C. Moore's classic poem "'Twas the Night Before Christmas" was a family favorite from New York to Chicago.

By 1860 a Christmas celebration with parties and gift giving, Santa Claus and ornamented trees was common to the whole country. In parts of Maryland, Kentucky, and Alabama, where English Yuletide mirth combined with French New Year's gaiety, Christmas week took on a carnival atmosphere. On the Texas plains, cowboys celebrated with barbecues and square dances. Prospectors in California donned their holiday best and enjoyed puddings made of dried fruits, raisins, and a good measure of wine. In the mining towns of Montana, eastern European families joined Norwegian and Cornish immigrants in a celebration that combined fragments of many traditions—from masquerading in costume to carrying a small tree decked with candles and ornaments down into the mines. Even in the old Puritan stronghold of New England, the Christmas spirit was strong; garlands of holly and evergreen boughs decorated doorways, and bands of carolers and bell ringers filled the streets with music.

The Civil War may have inhibited Christmas celebrations, especially in the South, but it could not prevent them altogether. With husbands and sons on the battlefield and food and other goods rationed or held up in blockades, women fashioned children's gifts from scraps and saved every penny to buy candy and fruit for the stockings. It wasn't easy. As the wife of a Confederate officer described, "Every crumb of food better than the ordinary, every orange, every apple or banana, every drop of wine went straightway to the hospitals."

When peace came, it brought with it a more festive and abundant Christmas. By the 1890s, the height of the Victorian era, Christmas had acquired many modern trappings. Thanks to Thomas Nast, the famed illustrator, Santa Claus had become familiar to nearly every man, woman, and child in the country. The decorated tree, long admired in the homes of German-American families, was now a holiday fixture everywhere, including the White House, which displayed its first Christmas tree in 1889. And the Christmas card, practically unknown before 1870, was so popular that the postal service was urging its patrons to "mail early." Christmas gift giving had become a vast enterprise, with stores and street vendors open for business until midnight.

But there was also a spiritual side to the Victorian celebration. Then as now, Americans remembered the true meaning of Christmas through generosity and charitable deeds. While they made merry with family and friends, they also recalled the origin of this once-a-year event, exemplified in star-topped trees, Nativity scenes, performances of Handel's *Messiah*, and above all the sharing of joy and reverence. 🎄

CHRISTMAS ACROSS THE COUNTRY

The sky grows dark in the late afternoon along Fifth Avenue in midtown Manhattan, but the deepening twilight is spangled with color. From office buildings and fashionable shop windows, a million lights cast their glow into the street. Up and down the avenue shoppers hurry from store to store, clutching packages and consulting gift lists. There's not a moment to lose; only hours remain to prepare for the most eagerly awaited holiday of the year.

As pedestrians hurry between 49th and 50th Streets they pass a magnificent sight: the great spruce tree that arrives each November in the plaza at Rockefeller Center. Draped with lights and rising nearly a hundred feet into the sky, it towers majestically over the shoppers and over the skaters circling the ice rink at its feet. The tree is dwarfed by the surrounding skyscrapers, yet seems somehow more imposing than any of them, its silent grandeur a striking contrast to the pervasive noise and bustle.

Not everyone has last-minute shopping to do. In a Maine farmhouse, preparations for Christmas are all but complete. The tree is decorated, presents are wrapped and in place. Cranberry bread, a special holiday recipe, bakes in a cast-iron oven, its sweet aroma spreading from the kitchen through the house. Wood has been cut and stockpiled; already a small blaze dances in the fireplace. In front of the fire sit the providers of this scene of peace and plenty, quietly watching the flame and enjoying its glow. Tomorrow will bring children and grandchildren, laughter and a hearty dinner. But as evening descends over the snow-covered hills the words of the old carol could not be more true: "All is calm, all is bright."

In the nation's capital, an altogether different scene is taking place. At Washington's National Cathedral, thousands gather for the annual Children's Pageant, a vivid commemoration of the birth of Jesus. At the center of the celebration is a *tableau vivant*, a living crèche. The players who bring this Nativity scene to life include a young couple and their new-born child, chosen from the community this year to represent the Holy Family. Shepherds, angels, and live animals complete the portrayal of that first Christmas.

This is Christmas Eve in America—the happiest, holiest, nearly the longest, and surely the most beloved night of the year. As dusk races westward across the continent, people everywhere repeat the time-honored rituals of the evening—hanging stockings, trimming the tree, singing carols, and exchanging kisses beneath sprigs of mistletoe.

Christmas Eve, a night like no other, marks the culmination of a season filled with holiday activity. Many Americans have already spent a month or more shopping, writing Christmas cards, and attending parties in offices and schools. They have selected their trees and brought them home, and retrieved boxes of ornaments from the dark recesses of closets. As December progresses, homes fill with holly boughs and poinsettias. Distant family members make travel plans and dream of white Christmases. Children are escorted to Nativity play rehearsals, and special holiday dishes are prepared.

Throughout America, the approach of Christmas is marked by strolling choirs of carolers. Bell ringers take up their stations on city sidewalks, and Santa Claus is everywhere—in stores, on street corners, at children's parties. Kids who miss Santa in other places are sure to find him at Christmas Village—the Torrington, Connecticut, park modeled after Santa's North Pole residence—or in dozens of similar sites across the country. Or they can speak to "Mr. or Mrs. Claus" by calling the Ho-Ho-Hotline, an organization of senior citizens who enjoy playing Santa by phone in over forty states.

In most cities, the sights and sounds of Christmas include special holiday entertainment. The New York City Ballet's lavish *Nutcracker* and the dramatization of *A Christmas Carol* by the American Conservatory Theater in San Francisco are only two of the season's traditional offerings. Orchestras present annual programs of Christmas music, and the strains of Handel's *Messiah* fill churches and concert halls across the land.

And there are the lights. They shine from the National Community Christmas Tree and from the windows and eaves of homes in every city and town. They glimmer on the water in Sitka, Alaska, as boats parade across the harbor, their masts and rigging aglow, to usher in the holiday. In Boston, Massachusetts, they illuminate the Commons, and in southern California they light up Christmas Tree Lane in Altadena, where each year 120 deodar cedars are arrayed with over ten thousand bulbs. In Salt Lake City, Utah, lights shine from virtually every branch in Temple Square, revealing the shape of each tree and bush in a lacy filigree of luminous color. The huge Zilker Christmas tree in Austin, Texas, on the other hand, is formed entirely of wire strung with lights and shaped into a giant evergreen.

Many of these Christmas scenes are common throughout America. Others, however, are decidedly regional and reflect the variety of cultures to which our nation is home. In New Mexico, as in other parts of the Southwest, Christmas has a distinctly Hispanic flavor. Seasonal fixtures include *luminaria*, the delicate paper lanterns, and processions commemorating Mary and Joseph's search for an inn in Bethlehem.

In Pleasant Hill, Kentucky, inhabitants observe Christmas as the original Shaker settlers did, with a simple holiday dinner, steaming punch, and the singing of traditional hymns by an unaccompanied choir. This restrained celebration is in contrast to one in Boise, Idaho, home of the nation's largest community

of Basque immigrants. Here the Sheepherders' Ball, a rousing Christmas party held each year since 1928, attracts hundreds of Basque revelers from across the western part of the country. They welcome the holiday with singing, dancing, and cries of *"Gabon on bat eta urte Bari Asi!"*—"Merry Christmas and Happy New Year!"

Nowhere is Christmas more meaningful, or more lovingly observed, than in Bethlehem, Pennsylvania, known as "America's Christmas City." The town that bears the name of Jesus' birthplace was established on Christmas Eve in 1741 by Moravian Church missionaries, and their descendants have preserved their traditional Christmas customs to this day. Lights and music are the heart of the celebration. Windows all across town blaze with white candles (most now electrified) that symbolize purity. The lights in the windows are meant to welcome the Christ Child, who according to Moravian legend wanders the earth on Christmas Eve. No less beautiful are the twenty-six-pointed Moravian Advent stars that decorate the town. But the most spectacular sight is the nearly hundred-foot-tall Star of Bethlehem, which shines down on the town from atop South Mountain.

Christmas music is provided by members of the Moravian Church, all of whom sing or play instruments, and by the renowned Moravian Trombone Choir, the oldest musical ensemble in the nation.

Community displays and public celebrations aside, for most Americans the night before Christmas is above all a time to spend with family. Those not at home rush to get there; late travelers throng airports, train stations, and bus terminals. In households throughout the country familiar scenes unfold. Parents wrap gifts in bright paper and ribbons and lay them beneath the tree. Some families exchange part or all of their presents at this time, but most let them brighten the room a bit longer, a tantalizing prospect for the following day.

Christmas Eve is also a time for visitors—friends, neighbors, and relatives who come to share the warm spirit of this special night. A group of carolers may drop by to spread Christmas cheer, glad to accept a cup of hot chocolate for their efforts. Many people attend midnight services, celebrated this night in churches all across the land. Whether in great city cathedrals or small country parishes, these yearly observances continue a centuries-old tradition of candles, carol singing, and shared feelings of peace and communion. Afterward there may be hot cider and Christmas cookies, but then it's home again, where bed and warm covers await, and for a few still hours it is indeed a silent night, holy night, throughout America.

Christmas morning begins, for many families, with children tugging at their sleeping parents so that the long-awaited exchange of gifts may begin. A headlong assault on ribbons and bows follows. Soon the packages have been conquered and their secrets revealed. The colored paper that had so carefully concealed the contents is scattered in gleeful disarray, and the youngsters are lost to their new playthings.

Other traditions fill Christmas day as well. Bells ring in steeples from coast to coast as church services commemorate the origin of the holiday. In recent years, Christmas morning rites at the National Cathedral

have been nationally televised. All across America families gather for Christmas dinner, a feast second only to Thanksgiving's in most homes.

Not everyone is lucky enough to enjoy the holiday among family, however. For thousands of American servicepeople, Yuletide cheer comes only through letters, phone calls, and USO programs. The Military Mail Project, a volunteer organization, each year distributes Christmas cards and gifts to nearly fifty thousand military personnel stationed overseas. Closer to home, thousands of our less fortunate citizens—the homeless, the poor, the lonely—take their Christmas dinners in shelters and community kitchens across the country. Los Angeles' Union Rescue Mission sometimes attracts television and film stars as volunteers, but at similar facilities in Atlanta, Chicago, and other large cities, unsung Samaritans serve the meals, happy to donate part of their Christmas day to bring a measure of comfort and joy to those who need it most.

On Christmas afternoon many people enjoy some form of recreation—in Wisconsin it might be a sleigh ride through snow-filled woods; in Hawaii, a walk along a sunny white beach. Some folks just sit back in comfort to read a new book, watch TV, or doze. This period of easy relaxation often seems the perfect antidote to all the celebrating and feasting. Nightfall brings an end to the holiday, along with fatigue. Even the children are ready for bed. If there is a sense of relief that another Christmas has come and gone, there is also the glow of happiness given and received—and the sure knowledge that the next Christmas is only 364 days away! ❄

Above: Though their leaves have long since vanished in the winter wind, these trees in Salt Lake City's Temple Square have acquired new foliage in the form of lights draping every branch during the Christmas season.

Opposite page: Even the traffic along Park Avenue contributes to the special holiday atmosphere as lights from cars and decorated trees combine to produce a festive glow.

Right: The City and County Building in Denver, Colorado, blazes with Yuletide glory, thanks to the multicolored lights that decorate its ornate clock tower.

Pages 12–13: Angels fashioned from wire and electric lights salute the towering Christmas tree in New York's Rockefeller Center.

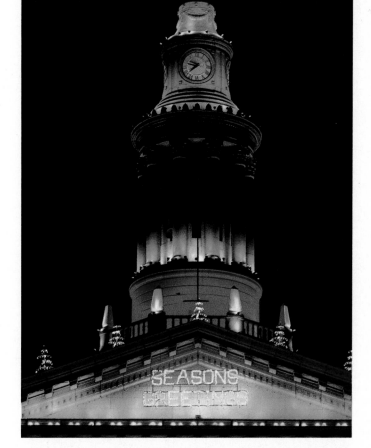

Right: The Country Club Plaza is Kansas City's most spectacular Christmas attraction. The lights, which brilliantly outline the Spanish-style buildings, are turned on each year on Thanksgiving night.

Left: There may be little chance of a White Christmas, but the holiday spirit is very much in evidence in San Francisco's marina, where masts and riggings are strung with colored lights.

Left: The holiday cheer radiating from these lights in a Massachusetts park seems doubly bright reflected in the nearby water.

Holiday displays in the fashionable stores of midtown Manhattan attract throngs of shoppers and sightseers every Christmas season. Many New Yorkers make a point of strolling with their children along Fifth Avenue, where the most lavish displays are found, simply to enjoy the colorful and ingenious exhibits.

Left: While most merchants content themselves with window displays, the famed jewelry firm Cartier uses its entire building to create a giant holiday package.

Below left: The paper fold-out Santa in the window of this card shop seems well pleased that the holiday season is once again at hand.

Opposite page: All the magic and enchantment of Christmas are reflected in the faces of these two young window-shoppers.

Below: A trio of dolls serenade passing shoppers with carols. Machinery allowing mannequins to move, as well as the use of recorded speech and music, creates illusions that delight children and adults alike.

Every year Wanamaker's Department Store in Philadelphia puts on one of the most spectacular "light shows" in the country. Ranged around the luminous, colorful, ever-changing tree, the moving figures include a locomotive with Santa as engineer, reindeer, snowmen, trumpet-playing birds, clocks, and festive figures from the "Nutcracker" ballet.

The tree alone is 56 feet high, not including the star, and uses 22,000 lights. The total height of the display is 120 feet from the floor to the top of the star. The panel of over 57,000 lights is controlled by a computer, one of the earliest of its kind, built in 1964 specifically to control this display.

Above: A stunning combination of electric lights and candle-lit lanterns, called *luminarias*, borders the driveway and outlines the contours of this house in El Paso, Texas. Decorating with *luminarias* is an old southwestern tradition, originally introduced by the Mexican families who first settled the area. *Luminarias* are simple to make at home by weighting paper lunch bags with sand, for stability and safety, and nestling a votive candle firmly into the sand.

Christmas decorations across the country are indescribably varied and individual.

Above right: A full moon adds a note of luminous mystery to simple strands of lights adorning this York, Maine lighthouse and outbuildings.

Right: A flock of jolly Santas, a Nativity scene, stars, snowmen—not an inch is wasted or a Christmas symbol missing in this yard in Springfield, Ohio.

Left: Fir trees can be hard to find in Arizona. But a saguaro cactus, decked with colored lights, makes a picturesque substitute, silhouetted against the desert sky.
Opposite page: A dazzling display in New Ulm, Minnesota captures the festive Christmas spirit in small towns across the country.

CHRISTMAS MEANS FAMILY

PAUL ENGLE

One December 23 I spent the day at Kennedy International Airport in a snowstorm. The runways were nearly all blocked with snow, but now and then a plane would leave. It was this occasional sound of engines which kept many thousands of half-hopeful people there, because that sound meant one plain and yet magical word—*home*, to the family.

Over and over, as I walked past little groups sitting with their luggage, or standing at the windows staring forlornly out the windows at the swirling menace, I overheard the same phrase—"home with the family by Christmas." It was all the hope for all of us. The mere chance of reaching their families in every far corner of the USA in time for the great holiday at the end of the year, kept restless crowds of weary people waiting in discomfort many hours. And yet, unlike other crowds I have been with at airports when weather imposed delays, this was a patient and cheerful crowd, for the hope of home and family kept them so.

This is only true of Christmas. We do not try desperately to rush home for the Fourth of July. Only Christmas has this live power of family attraction. This is as it should be, for the original event on a cold desert night of conspicuous stars was a family affair. Indeed, what could be more like our own day than the reason for Joseph and Mary making that trip in an uncomfortable season—they had gone to pay their taxes. Childbirth and taxes—are these not our own life also?

Christmas was always a close family matter for us. It began months before, and was no matter of hasty shopping for some slick present a few days earlier. Our children, two daughters, always made by hand several presents for their parents and for each other. One year Mary, then five, made a doll for Sara, then one. Friends in for Christmas Eve were a little startled to hear Mary, when I told her it was time for bed, reply firmly, "But I can't go now. I have to stuff a leg."

Mary slashed off a hank of her own hair before we knew it, and stitched it onto the doll's head, so that part of her was forever a part of it. The doll was taken to bed every night by Sara, and was clutched by her for comfort in the long, dark hours. Mary's left hand was in Christmas colors that day. Holding the doll as the unskilled fingers of her right hand worked the needle, she pricked the skin several times. The red blood was covered with a green bandage, to her great pride.

Of course, all planning of gifts for small children has to be done without illusions about the unpredictable choices they will make. One year we had found a wonderful wooden train of gaily painted cars on wheels which could be pulled in a curving line over the floor. The cars were unpacked, each held up eagerly, and the whole train hooked together pulled once around the room, and left. A few minutes later Sara came in dragging by an old string a line of wooden blocks and cakes of soap which she had laboriously put together herself months before. All day she pulled this home-made thing while the gleaming gift sat in a corner; naturally,

she preferred the cherished and familiar object to the bought toy. Her own life was mixed with it.

Sara also made gifts as soon as she could use her hands. They were largely for the animals which she acquired in as large quantities as we would allow. (With some animals, alas, acquiring one was only the first innocent step to the astonishment of coming down one morning and finding five small new ones.) Her first effort was a winter blanket for a tiny Chihuahua dog. The stitches were far apart, the blanket hung down on one side so far the poor dog tripped on it, but it actually had a crude fastener in front and the pooch became very attached to it. The cloth had been the tail on an ancient wool shirt of mine, so that I knew intimately just how warm it could be. The dog trotted proudly off through the snow in his uneven garment as if it had been tailored at Brooks Brothers. He also used it for sleeping on cold nights.

The whole family made things. The children's mother sewed beautifully, often making miniature clothes for the dolls which matched the dresses she had made for Mary and Sara. The girls were as happy, in fact, at receiving a box of little hats, shirts and blouses for their favorite dolls, as they were at receiving the same items for themselves. These were sensibly made with big snaps which the small fingers could really work. The dolls were always carefully prepared on Christmas Eve, just as if they were live children, properly dressed, then shown the lights on the Christmas Tree, carried around the neighborhood to view other trees, outdoors or seen through windows. Then they were undressed and put to bed with warnings not to peek before morning. In this way, the girls doubled their own pleasure by sharing it with their dolls. How dull Christmas next door seemed, where there were only boys, crashing around with hockey sticks and wind-up toy automobiles!

Mary received a "bake-with-mother" cooking set one Christmas, from our friends Owen and Leone Elliott, and in the following years, being an instinctively domestic child, she always prepared her own tiny cookies, the sort which my own sisters a long time before had called "thimble cookies." We had some old-fashioned houses of heavy paper, assembled to make a little village under the tree. Mary would always refer to these as the Brownie houses, and leave a pile of her cookies by each one for the nourishing of whatever Brownies had been out all night stuffing children's stockings with gifts, obviously an exhausting and hunger-making job.

One Christmas I found a second-hand wicker doll carriage, battered but sturdy. I painted it in a neighbor's garage. My wife sewed a perfectly-fitting pad, some small blankets, and even made from some wool a "snuggle-bunny" which would hold a doll. On Christmas morning I brought it over, where it was radiantly accepted as the one gift which could contain everything the girls most loved. First they put all of their dolls in, wheeling them rapidly around the room, and then shoving it back and forth between them. Later I found

Mary pushing Sara in it, the smaller child fitting exactly into the doll carriage. (This sisterly devotion went on until Sara's legs had grown so long her feet hung down over the front of the carriage.) Mary was very proud to wheel her live doll down the street with neighborhood friends who had only ordinary dolls. Of course, she would sometimes run with the sleeping girl bouncing over the rough spots, turning corners on two wheels.

Sara took over the carriage when she was older and would put her two tiny dogs in it, tucking them under the blankets with only their wrinkling noses and uneasy eyes peering out. She said her dolls didn't scratch afterward, no matter what jokes Mary made about that.

One of the great Christmases happened the year I brought home a used hobby-horse. It was a beautiful animal, with a miniature saddle and bridle, strong enough for Sara to get on and ride. This she did all day, putting the horse into mad gallops which sometimes went so fast the frame on which the horse was suspended would lift from the rug. There was one sad lack—the tail had been lost. We agreed with Sara that it disfigured the lovely creature, so I went to a friend who had horses and persuaded him to cut some from one of his animals which was the proper color.

It was winter, the horse had been rolling in the barnyard, it had not been brushed. First the cleaning, so we put the mess into a pan of hot water along with soap powder. Soon the gay cinnamon scent of our Christmas baking faded from the air and in its place the whole house was permeated with the most revolting animal stench. Turning our too delicate city noses away from the pan, we sudsed that foul wad of

hair. Then it had to be dried by a hot air register, which effectively stank up whatever far corners had escaped the odor of cooking horsehair. But by the end of Christmas Day the new horse had a long tail, holding it high with the help of some glue which Sara managed to spread over her hands and face. Sara took the hair which was left over and made herself a tail out of it, wearing it gaily behind her for years of cantering from room to room with a fine whinny.

We always made strings of fresh white popcorn to scatter through the green tree like ropes of snow. There was Indian corn of many colors, and we could string that if we got it soft, before the kernels hardened and became too flinty for a needle in the hands of children. Many of the ornaments would be homemade, too—paper horns of candy and walnuts wrapped with gold and silver paper, tiny figures of angels Mary sewed together from scraps of white silk, and figures of old-fashioned girls she made from lovely fragments found in a trunk. The latter had elegant underwear made from lace taken from a grandmother's corset cover. We were not quite certain that it was proper to have the angel looking across at the froth of fancy slip peeking out from under the skirts, but always put them back on the tree in the slippery belief that sin was not in so shy an action, and that if it was anywhere, it would be in the mind of the beholder.

There was the exotic year when Mary found a box of scallop shells gathered on eastern Long Island along Gardiners Bay the summer before. She took crayons and drew many miniature pictures of shore birds, beach plants, gulls and sandpipers, cranberries found

The joyous family reunion pictured on this page took place in December 1945. World War II had just ended, and this was the first time in three years that the whole clan—parents, seven children, two sons-in-law, and four grandchildren—had been able to get together for the holiday. On a sad note, the husband of the oldest daughter had been reported missing over Japan the previous spring.

Left: The reunion gets off to a good start with the arrival of the Christmas tree, a cedar cut in a nearby field.
Below: In the sitting room of their parents' Kansas home, the three oldest daughters feed their infants and catch up on the news.

Right: Three generations join in the excitement of exchanging gifts and unwrapping bright packages. The youngest family members, oblivious to onlookers, have eyes only for the toys that Santa has left under the tree.

red and shiny in the dunes. These were put inside the shells, holes punched with an ice pick through shell and picture, all then tied together with gaily colored yarn to make actual books. Some she gave to us and others she hung on the tree, so that, among the midwestern decorations we had made, and the handsome ornaments my family had brought from the Black Forest three generations before (how did they stand the rough journey to a seaport, the stormy passage in a frail sailing vessel, the trip by train and oxcart out to frontier Iowa? but how did the mother of Christ stand the jolting trip by donkey to Bethlehem?), we had these cheerful reminders of the sea. The gravest danger to ornament, doll figure and shell book was, of course, the childish fingers handling them, and yet not one was broken. Such is the true spirit of Christmas—it can give sense and caution to the most exuberant fingers.

My most selfish Christmas arrived with a heavy, square box under the tree. Opening it, I found a new portable typewriter, which I terribly needed. My wife had earned it by designing and making and selling thousands of original Christmas cards. It was a gift which came out of strained eyes and hands knicked on the sharp edges of cut paper. I wrote six books on it.

My most embarrassing Christmas came when I bought my wife one of those elaborate dress forms which could be cunningly adjusted to reproduce any woman's figure. It was stored with a friend a few houses away, fully expanded in all its majestic lines. I carried it back in my arms in deep snow on Christmas Eve. Surely this is the most awkwardly shaped article any man could pick up in his arms. I stumbled through ruts and slipped on ice, clutching what must have seemed to my admiring neighbors some strange blonde I was trying to sneak into the house. You can't disguise a dress form; it just looks like itself, when seen close up, so my gift was identified the instant I entered the house, in spite of the sheet I had thrown over it and the red ribbon tied on its majestic bosom.

We always used Christmas, as my family had used it before, as a way of giving the children necessary clothing which we had let go until then. This resulted in some of the gifts being anticipated, although there was always some uncertainty about their exact characteristics. Mary, opening a box with a new sweater: "Oh mother, I thought you'd give me that blue one we looked at in the window. But this is the color I *really* wanted." Sara, taking out of vast wrappings a honey-colored pigskin saddle for her young horse: "That's just the size my mare needs, and I can always darken that icky color with neat's foot oil." And then she hugged it to her, the stirrup leathers hanging around her neck, as if it had been a longed-for doll.

Because Christmas had been this close family matter, it was natural, when we were talking about the possibility of getting a second car, somewhat as a holiday present to the whole family, Sara should say, "I think a one-ton truck would be nice. Then I could use it to haul my horses. Think of the kids I could drive to school." It is my guess that, if there is a car in one of our stockings hanging from the mantel some year soon, it will be a one-ton truck. 🐦

The photographs on these two pages tell the story of Christmas as celebrated by one family—a story filled with special traditions belonging to that family alone, but familiar to Americans everywhere.

Above left: The middle son sets out to string an outdoor tree with cheerful colored lights as the sun sets over his family's Long Island farm.

Above: In the warmth of the kitchen Mother, Grandmother, and a visiting cousin from Germany engage in a marathon pie-making session. All the fruit was grown in the family's 100-acre orchard.

Left: The sweet sounds of Christmas bring joy to a house-bound neighbor recuperating from an illness. The boys had practiced their program of carols for weeks and performed without a flaw.

Above: The old family pickup truck, wearing a fresh coat of red paint, makes a handy sleigh for Santa Claus to carry and deliver presents. A family friend, dressed as Santa, paid a surprise visit at 5:30 on Christmas morning.

Left: Decorating the tree progresses smoothly with so many helping hands. The radiator is an ideal perch for the oldest son to secure the ornament at the very top. While Mother drapes a tinsel garland across the bookshelves, another son straightens the tree skirt, and a third hangs the stockings on the mantel. Dad, meanwhile, acts as photographer for the event.

Below: Santa ceremoniously distributes gifts to everyone gathered in the living room. His tattered costume betrays the wear and tear of yearly Christmas visits around the neighborhood.

THE CHRISTMAS SPIRIT IN ACTION

The angels who announced the birth of Jesus on the first Christmas Eve brought a message of hope and comfort for all people. "Peace on earth, good will toward men," they declared, and their words became the motto of the holiday.

Even though peace remains an elusive goal on our planet, Christmas is still marked by an outpouring of good will on the part of millions of people. It is a time of sharing, of generosity, of selfless reaching out. The tradition of Christmas gift giving is, of course, a reflection of this spirit, but the angels' proclamation is most profoundly remembered through acts of charity toward those who are less fortunate. Compassion for the poor, the sick, the aged, and the orphaned is at the heart of the Yuletide tradition. Helping others is a means of putting the Christmas ideal of good will into practice—a satisfying way of fusing the social and religious aspects of the holiday. Benevolence and generosity form the underlying theme of the Nativity story and are still in many ways the essence of Christmas.

Tales of kindness offered and bounty shared recur throughout Christmas legend and lore. The story of the three wise men furnished the earliest model for charitable treatment of the poor by the privileged at Christmas time. Those illustrious visitors to the infant Jesus were not humble scholars, but kings accustomed to wealth and splendor who presented precious gifts to a family that had been reduced to taking refuge in a stable. Their example was followed by that of another regal figure who embodied the spirit of Christmas generosity—"Good King Wenceslas," a Bohemian ruler of the fourteenth century whose concern for his subjects is celebrated in the carol that bears his name.

But perhaps the best-known benefactor of the needy at Christmas was the fourth-century Bishop of Myra, better known as St. Nicholas. Born into a wealthy family, the legendary figure who has come down to us as "Santa Claus" was the patron saint of children and is said to have given his money secretly to the poor. The gifts that Santa brings to children each year are a reminder of the anonymous generosity of St. Nicholas.

The idea of giving comfort to the poor and unfortunate at Christmas found its most persuasive spokesman not in a king or a saint, however, but in a popular Victorian novelist. Charles Dickens was a young writer still struggling for recognition when he published *A Christmas Carol* in 1843. This vivid account of Ebenezer Scrooge's conversion from cold-hearted miser to compassionate keeper of the Christmas spirit is at once a plea for care of the poor and a hymn to human brotherhood. The reading public received *A Christmas Carol* with joyful enthusiasm. The great success of the work helped to foster a "carol philosophy" of compassion and good deeds on behalf of

the needy at Christmas. Nor was its impact limited to Dickens' native England. The story was embraced with equal enthusiasm in the United States, and audiences of as many as thirty-five thousand people flocked to hear the author recite it when he toured this country in 1867 and 1868. Today *A Christmas Carol* is as popular as ever. Thousands read the tale or see it enacted on the stage each year, while millions more know it through the television dramatizations that have become a regular part of our national Christmas celebration. Its influence in promoting Christmas charity over the years is incalculable.

But Americans did not wait for instruction from Mr. Dickens to honor the holiday with acts of kindness and good will. Although the early Puritans in New England did not exchange Christmas gifts with family or friends, they were expected to extend help to their less fortunate neighbors all year round. The harsh lives of the pioneers afforded little bounty, but they shared what they could at Christmas. In some prairie communities, horse-drawn sleds were used to distribute packages of food and clothing to impoverished families. Generosity was extended even to farm animals, who received extra portions of feed on Christmas Day. Swedish settlers in Minnesota brought from their homeland the practice of laying out sheaves of unthreshed wheat so that even the birds might feast on Jesus' birthday.

During the past century, as America grew and developed a more complex urban society, various charitable organizations emerged in response to social needs. Some of these groups are particularly active at Christmas. Perhaps best known is the Salvation Army. Although the organization was founded in Great Britain, its brass bands and bell-ringing fund raisers are a familiar sight in most American cities. Those "Christmas kettles" that hang ready to receive donations first appeared in 1891, when a Salvation Army worker in San Francisco enlisted a kitchen pot to dramatize the need for donations of food. The group provides meals, clothing, shelter, and other forms of care to millions of people annually.

Complementing the activities of the Salvation Army are those of the Volunteers of America, whose workers wear Santa Claus suits when soliciting contributions during the holiday season. Santa, in fact, has frequently been employed on behalf of worthy causes, but he has benefited from charitable activity also. In 1914, a group of New York City philanthropists founded the Santa Claus Association, whose goal was "to preserve children's faith in Santa Claus." The organization received letters addressed to Santa from needy children and, whenever possible, filled their requests. While these presents may not have proved Santa's existence, they certainly kept his spirit alive.

Christmas Seals, the annual campaign of the American Lung Association, began in 1907 in Delaware, where Emily Bissell, a resourceful social worker, needed to raise money to keep a small tuberculosis sanitorium from closing its doors. Inspired by news from Denmark of a special Christmas stamp sold to benefit ill and needy children, she designed one of her own showing a holly wreath and the legend "Merry Christmas." She sold the stamps in packets bearing this inscription:

Put this stamp with message bright
On every Christmas letter;
Help the tuberculosis fight,
And make the New Year better.

Proceeds from the stamps raised ten times the amount needed to save the hospital, and the Christmas seal tradition was born.

Not all Christmas charities are the work of purely charitable organizations. In 1912, the *New York Times* used its pages to publicize the "Hundred Neediest Cases," appealing for donations to relieve their plight. Revived each year during the holiday season, this campaign has been widely copied throughout the country.

Large institutional charities have collected billions of dollars in aid for the poor during Christmas over the years and have brightened the holidays of millions. But beyond the work of these agencies, and in all likelihood exceeding them in scope, are the countless acts of small-scale and private giving that occur throughout America each Christmas. In this form, generosity assumes a more personal character, one more satisfying for most Americans. In city after city

and town after town, the seasonal gestures of kindness and good will are repeated. Children march to school in the early morning half-light, their mittened hands clutching cans of soup, meat, or vegetables for the "grocery basket" their class is assembling for the local food bank. Police officers and firemen collect toys to distribute among children who otherwise would have no Christmas. In church basements, clothing brought by parishioners is sorted and wrapped for presentation to those in need. Holiday shoppers fumble with their packages to drop coins into the hands of the blind, lame, or homeless on the street, while businessmen spend their lunch hours serving meals to low-income senior citizens in community dining halls. Children in hospitals receive toys provided by anonymous donors and visits from volunteer Santas. Across the nation cookies are sold, rummage sales held, and collections taken for the benefit of unfortunate individuals and families.

These expressions of compassion and good will, these endless variations on the theme of charity, are a vital part of our celebration of Christmas. They stand in answer to charges that commercial exploitation has overwhelmed the original spirit of the holiday. For some people, preserving the character of Christmas is an important motive for charity as the year draws to a close. But most Americans, if asked their reasons for giving to those less fortunate during the holiday, would offer a simpler and more immediate explanation: that gladness and generosity naturally go hand in hand, and that joy shared is joy increased. ✄

Of the many charitable organizations active during the Christmas season, none is more conspicuous or more closely associated with the holiday than the Salvation Army. The group serves millions of Americans each year, providing food, shelter, and other goods and services. It also offers a way for more fortunate citizens to help their fellows by collecting and channeling donations.

Left: A Salvation Army volunteer solicits contributions in New York's Rockefeller Center. The "soup kettle" hung to receive donations has been a tradition of the organization since 1891.

Below: The Salvation Army's collection points receive donations from Americans of all ages and backgrounds. These children already understand the spirit of Christmas sharing.

Opposite page: The ideals of good will and benevolence are realized in many ways during the holiday season. Sharing bounty and good fortune brings joy to giver and receiver alike. But the Christmas spirit shines brightest when "those who have remember those who have not," a notion poignantly expressed in this 1876 engraving.

Right: Baseball great Babe Ruth goes to bat in 1921 for Christmas Seals, the annual fund-raising campaign of the American Lung Association.

Below: Santas working on behalf of the Volunteers of America enjoy a hearty breakfast before taking to the streets to open that organization's yearly funding drive.

Below right: It may not be a white Christmas, but this Volunteer of America Santa is not daunted by the weather.

While institutional charities like the Salvation Army and Volunteers of America furnish millions of dollars' worth of assistance to needy Americans each Christmas, an even greater total is provided by community efforts and individuals.

Left: Police and fire departments in many areas collect toys to distribute to children who otherwise would receive none at Christmas. Here the chief of a Maine fire department puts the finishing touches of paint on a toy car that will make some youngster very happy.

Below: An elderly woman receives a food basket from a pair of teenage volunteers.

CHRISTMAS FARE

Each year from Thanksgiving to New Year's Day, Americans feast on an array of tempting holiday foods. Plump turkey with crisp bronze skin, salty-sweet ham, nutmeg-flecked eggnog, sticky dark mincemeat, and fruitcakes dense with a mosaic of glacé fruit—these dishes are as much a part of the Christmas season as gift giving, caroling, and trimming the tree. They satisfy that yearning for familiar flavors that, no matter how sensible our diet may be the rest of the year, we always seem to feel as Christmas approaches.

Our holiday food customs originated in Europe and are as diverse as the different peoples who immigrated to this country many years ago. Although the stern Puritans outlawed Christmas—a protest against the rowdy, unreligious festivities in England—settlers from Holland, Sweden, Germany, and other lands continued to celebrate it with their native customs and foods. As the Puritans gradually relaxed their bans, English practices took hold as well.

By the mid-1700s, although Christmas was still primarily a religious holiday, a large festive meal had become part of the celebration. George Washington's Christmas menu in 1795 gives us an idea of what the new nation was eating for the holidays: roast duck, veal, ham, beef, suckling pig, and of course the native turkey. How the table must have creaked under the weight of it all! Martha Washington, we are told, liked to roast her pig with a generous seasoning of thyme and serve it with a breadcrumb sauce. "Jellies"—gelatin desserts—were the other prominent item on the menu. Vegetables weren't considered important enough even to mention, but oranges, apples, figs, and raisins were holiday favorites, cherished because of their scarcity the rest of the year.

A traditional Southern breakfast on Christmas morning begins with buttermilk waffles (use your favorite recipe) topped with pecans and a cherry. Celebrants will also enjoy Orange-Spiced Ham (recipe on page 42); hot chocolate steeped with cinnamon sticks and crowned with rich whipped cream; and for dessert, Honey-Poached Pears (recipe on page 50).

Christmas in nineteenth-century America was a time of joyous celebration, much as it is today. Tables were heaped with an abundance of all manner of foods, and especially sweets: whole cakes crowned silver platters, molded desserts shimmered in their delicate jellies, and fresh fruit was offered as a great luxury.

The American Christmas meal has always combined old-world traditions and new-world ingredients. The custom of pairing turkey with ham is a fine example: it recalls the choice of those early Europeans who celebrated their Christmases with roast peacock and boar. Turkey was an obvious American substitute for peacock, but whole roast pigs were favored to accompany it. Ham didn't begin to replace suckling pig as the holiday meat until the late 1800s.

Vegetable dishes, too, reflect both European and American origins. Cabbage, brussels sprouts, beets, onions, and chestnuts are among the old-world foods that we still enjoy, while pumpkin, corn, sweet potatoes, cranberries, squash, and yams are decidedly native. Corn shows up in many guises throughout the nation, from cornmeal stuffing to spoonbread, from tamales to hominy. Although stuffing is definitely an English import, preparing it with cornbread adds a distinctly American touch.

After all these other courses, we somehow still have room for dessert—and not the prim bowl of pudding or lone slice of cake that suffices at other meals! Americans adore holiday sweets, the more lavish the better. Clearly, dietary good sense flees when such sugary indulgences as mince pie, Yule logs, and spicy fruitcake appear. Candies abound, too, from chocolate fudge to popcorn balls to the minty candy canes first introduced by the Scandinavians. Plum pudding, once banned by the Puritans, is another hard-to-resist dessert. Interestingly, it began in medieval England as a soup made of mutton broth and plums.

The spirit of the season demands a taste of everything. In earlier periods, when the country was less prosperous and restraint was the dominant social attitude, Christmas treats were probably one of the few generous, even luxurious, pleasures allowed. A recipe for Christmas pudding from the 1800s illustrates the point: "Layer a goodly amount of strawberry jam," it instructs, "not too thin, for remember, it is Christmas!" With the same enthusiasm, the recipe urges the reader to enjoy the dish and to remember all the while, "It is Christmas!"

Cookies are perhaps the most evocative Christmas sweet. Just to smell them baking conjures up images of Christmases past. Crisp with glistening crystals of sugar, molasses-rich and chewy with nuts and candied fruits, or shaped and frosted to look like little people or trees, cookies are everywhere at Christmas time. America's wealth of cookie recipes has been handed down mainly from the German, Dutch, and

Scandinavian settlers. In the Midwest, for instance, which was colonized primarily by Scandinavians, the beginning of the holidays is heralded by the heady aroma of cardamom, cinnamon, and other spices baked into Christmas cookies. To children, cookies may be the most important holiday treat—next to gifts, of course. Children all over America still leave cookies out for Santa Claus—a kind of welcome and thank you in one.

Sweet flavors also permeate the special drinks of the season. Mulled wine or cider, warm and scented with spice, is inviting on a blustery winter's evening. Creamy eggnog is another holiday favorite, as are fruit punch and elegant champagne. As the drinks

A bountiful table in Williamsburg, Virginia, displays some of the countless foods that go into traditional American Christmas dinners. On the opposite page, some menus that can be made up from the recipes in this section.

are enjoyed, glasses may be lifted in celebration, to wish good health and good fortune to all. Toasting, as the well-wishing came to be known, originated in eighteenth-century England with the holiday punch called the wassail bowl, a concoction of spirits with bits of toasted bread floating on top. Merrymakers gathered around the bowl and passed the rich mixture from person to person, each guest drinking directly from the bowl and wishing the others good health. The toasted bread was eaten as a great delicacy. Now both the toast and the shared bowl have disappeared, but we still clink glasses together in exclamation of good cheer.

Of all the holiday beverages, eggnog is the one most associated with Christmas. It is descended from the two egg-milk-spirits mixtures called *syllabub* and *sack posset*. In the fifteenth and sixteenth centuries this rich brew was popular in English pubs, where it was ladled into small carved cups called noggins—hence the shortened name, "eggnog."

These traditional foods and drinks can be found on Christmas tables all across the nation. At the same time, menus and dishes vary from region to region, reflecting the culture and cuisine of the original settlers. Most groups have special ethnic foods that they prepare only at Christmas.

In the Midwest, many traditions bear the distinctive touch of the Scandinavians who made the region their home. The cold winters encourage baking in warm kitchens, and from the many sweets-making sessions come a vast array of cookies as well as the yeasty, sweet-and-spicy loaf called *julekake*. Another midwestern Christmas food is *lutefisk*, a salted fish potent in aroma, and not to everyone's taste. Swedish families follow the ritual of *doppa y grytan*: they begin the meal by dipping bread into the juices of the holiday ham.

Northeastern Christmas fare reflects its primarily English, Dutch, and German heritage. Chestnut-stuffed turkey, meat pies, and oyster stew are the substantial main dishes, with roasted chestnuts a favored snack. The popular and equally substantial sweets include fruitcakes, mincemeat pies, and plum puddings. A marvelous Italian contribution is *panetone*, a raisin-studded sweet bread.

In the Southeast, the Christmas feast might begin with a seafood stew or bisque, simply prepared but rich in sea flavors. A large fat turkey follows, accompanied by the intensely flavored hams of the South: Kentucky, Virginia, or Smithfield. Farther south, the character of the Christmas meal changes radically, most notably in the Creole feasts of Louisiana. Here, the cuisine is a colorful blend of Choctaw and Chickasaw Indian, French, Spanish, and Black influences, liberally splashed with fiery hot Louisiana red pepper sauce. In an area where any and every meal is reason for culinary celebration, the Christmas dinner tends to be an extravaganza.

Southerners also enjoy such holiday desserts as caramel cakes and fluffy coconut cakes. Another favorite is ambrosia, a heady concoction of oranges and coconut moistened with a good jolt of sherry.

Moving west, Christmas food takes on a Mexican flair. In New Mexico and Arizona, the special regional dishes prepared during the season include savory and sweet tamales and *posole*, the traditional Christmas Eve supper. *Posole* is a hearty stew of plump corn kernels called hominy, simmered along with green chile and chunks of pork. It is spooned up as a warming meal after Midnight Mass on December 24. On Christmas day, cooks outdo themselves in the preparation of all manner of local specialties, but above it all the aroma of stewing chile perfumes the air. The assortment of sweets has a distinctly regional flavor: anise-spiced cookies, pinenut pralines, and cinnamon-sugared fried pastries called *buñuelos*. *Capirotada*, a rich bread pudding, is also a Christmas favorite of Hispanics throughout the Southwest.

In Texas, holiday foods are a mix of Mexican, German, and southeastern influences, and there we find such eclectic combinations as ham glazed with fiery-sweet chile jelly accompanied by black-eyed peas in *jalapeño* vinaigrette. For Hispanic Texans, the food that most typifies Christmas is *champurrado*, a drink of Mexican-Indian origin. It is made from *masa harina*, or cornmeal, cooked with cinnamon, chocolate, and vanilla into a thin gruel and served warm in mugs. Texas sweets are apt to be German or English, with a local twist—pecans added to butter cookies, pinenuts to toffee, even cranberries to a trifle.

Californians are fortunate to have an abundance of fresh produce to round out the holiday menu. Christmas dinner generally includes not only the standard favorites—turkey, ham, stuffing, potatoes, yams—but also a few choice vegetables. With so many different ethnic groups the state also has a wealth of unusual holiday dishes; most recently, Vietnamese and other Southeast Asian immigrants have added their specialties to the Christmas pot.

In the lush Northwest, holiday fare includes the excellent smoked salmon of the region as well as homemade goodies preserved from the summer's bounty—flavorful jams of blackberry and blueberry, tiny tartly pickled onions, spiced seckel pears. The marvelous local apples are just right for pressing into cider and mulling with a few cloves and a stick of cinnamon into a warming holiday drink.

These Christmas foods are simply irresistible, especially when shared in the company of family and friends. Beyond this, the tastes and smells of traditional dishes link one holiday to the next, one generation to another, even new cultures to old, making the holiday table a welcome constant in a world of change. Good food shared in good company—few things contribute more to creating the atmosphere of cheer and good will that exemplifies the Christmas spirit.

On the following pages you will find a number of recipes for holiday favorites old and new. Some, like Plum Pudding, are historical favorites; others, like Orange-Sweet Potato Cups, became part of America's Christmas cuisine in modern times. These recipes can be combined into sumptuous menus, such as the breakfast and dinner suggestions shown at right, in which side dishes have been selected to complement the main feature of turkey, goose, or ham. Gifts of food are included here also. Food, after all, is made to be shared, and colorfully wrapped and beribboned cookies, candies, and fruit cakes are among the most welcome of Christmas gifts. ⚬

In an 1894 Harper and Brothers magazine, F. S. Church elevated the plum pudding cook to a lofty position.

 # ENTREES

ROAST GOOSE

TO SERVE 8

    An 8- to 10-pound goose
½ **teaspoon salt**
½ **teaspoon freshly ground black pepper**
3 **slices lean bacon, cut into ½-inch pieces**
6 **cloves garlic, minced or pressed**
1 **medium-sized onion, quartered**
1 **stalk celery, quartered**
2 **large apples, unpeeled and cut into wedges**
2 **cups beef broth**
2 **cups chopped onion**
1 **cup chopped celery**
1 **cup sliced mushrooms**
½ **cup chopped green bell pepper**
1 **cup dry red wine**
    Curly endive (optional)
    Grapes (optional)
    Kumquats (optional)

Remove the giblets from the goose. Pull off the lumps of fat from inside the body cavity. Rinse the goose thoroughly with cold water; pat dry.

Preheat the oven to 350°. Combine the salt and pepper and sprinkle ¼ teaspoon over the surface of and in the cavity of the goose. Cut pockets under the meaty part of the breast; stuff with the remaining salt and pepper, bacon, and garlic. Stuff the quartered onion, celery, and apples into the cavity of the goose, and close the cavity with skewers. Tie the ends of the legs to the tail with cotton string; lift the wing tips up and over the back so they are tucked under the bird securely. Place the goose in a roasting pan with a cover, breast side up. Insert a meat thermometer in the breast or the meaty part of the thigh, making sure it does not touch the bone.

Combine the broth, chopped onion and celery, mushrooms, bell pepper, and wine; pour into the roasting pan. Cover and bake for 1 hour. Draw off the fat with a bulb baster or large heavy spoon. Continue to bake, uncovered, 2 to 2½ hours longer, or until the thermometer registers 185°; baste the goose frequently with the pan liquid. Continue to draw off the fat as it accumulates.

Transfer the goose to a serving platter. Let it stand 15 minutes before serving. Garnish the platter with endive, grapes, and kumquats, if desired.

Opposite page: A variety of tempting side dishes complement classic Roast Turkey: Sausage-Cracker Stuffing (recipe on page 44); Festive Cranberry Salad (recipe on page 45); Orange-Sweet Potato Cups (recipe on page 46); Pickled Carrots, English Pea Casserole, and Giblet Gravy (recipes on page 47); and Easy Buttermilk Rolls (recipe on page 48).

ROAST TURKEY

TO SERVE 12 TO 16

    A 12- to 14- pound turkey
    Salt
    Melted butter or vegetable oil
    Fresh parsley sprigs
    Purple grapes
    Orange wedges

Preheat the oven to 325°. Remove the giblets and rinse the turkey thoroughly with cold water; pat dry. Sprinkle the cavity with salt. Tie the ends of the legs to the tail with cotton string. Lift the wing tips up and over the back so they are tucked under the bird securely.

Place the bird on a roasting rack, breast side up. Insert a meat thermometer in the breast or the meaty part of the thigh, making sure it does not touch the bone. Brush the entire bird with melted butter. Bake for 4½ to 5 hours, or until the meat thermometer registers 185°. Baste with pan drippings every 15 minutes during the last hour of cooking time. If the turkey starts to brown too much, cover it loosely with aluminum foil.

When the turkey is two-thirds done, cut the string holding the legs to the tail; this will ensure that the insides of the thighs are cooked. The turkey is done when the drumsticks can be moved up and down easily. Let it stand 15 minutes before carving. Garnish with parsley, grapes, and orange wedges.

Note: If you plan to stuff the turkey (see pages 44 and 45 for recipes), allow ¾ cup stuffing for each pound of turkey. Never stuff a turkey the night before cooking. Immediately before roasting, pack the stuffing loosely into the cavity of the turkey and close the cavity with skewers. Then tie the ends of the legs as directed above.

Stuffed turkeys require about 5 minutes more cooking per pound. Be sure to remove the stuffing before storing the leftover turkey in the refrigerator.

ORANGE-SPICED HAM

TO SERVE 10 TO 12

2 **one-inch-thick slices cooked ham (about 1½ pounds each)**
2 **cups ginger ale**
2 **cups fresh orange juice**
1 **cup firmly packed brown sugar**
¼ **cup plus 2 tablespoons vegetable oil**
2 **tablespoons white wine vinegar**
1 **tablespoon plus 1 teaspoon dry mustard**
1½ **teaspoons ground ginger**
1 **teaspoon ground cloves**
    Fresh spinach or other greens (optional)

Score the fat edges of the ham and place the ham in a shallow non-reactive baking pan. Combine the ginger ale, orange juice, brown sugar, oil, wine vinegar, and seasonings; pour over the ham slices. Cover and let stand at room temperature 1 hour or refrigerate overnight, spooning the marinade over the ham occasionally.

Preheat the broiler. Remove the ham from the marinade and drain briefly, reserving the marinade. Place the ham on a rack in a broiler pan. Broil 6 inches below the heat for 10 minutes on each side, brushing the ham several times with the marinade. Heat the remaining marinade and serve it with the ham. Serve the ham on a bed of spinach, if desired.

🦚 SIDE DISHES

PECAN-RICE STUFFING

TO MAKE ABOUT 12 CUPS

        A 12-ounce jar of fresh oysters
   4 tablespoons butter
   1 bunch green onions, chopped
   1 cup chopped celery
   1 cup chopped onion
   ½ cup chopped green bell pepper
   5 cloves garlic, minced or pressed
   1 pound lean ground pork
   ½ pound lean ground beef
   1¼ pounds chicken livers, chopped
   1½ cups uncooked long-grain rice
   3⅓ cups chicken broth
   ½ teaspoon salt
   ½ teaspoon freshly ground black pepper
   ½ cup chopped pecans, toasted
        Fresh parsley sprigs (optional)
   1 cherry tomato (optional)

Drain the oysters, reserving the liquid; set aside. Melt the butter in a 5-quart Dutch oven. Add the green onions, celery, onion, bell pepper, and garlic; sauté over medium heat, stirring occasionally, until the onion is soft but not browned. Remove from the pan and set aside.

Add the pork and beef to the pan; cook 5 minutes, stirring to crumble. Add the livers; cook 5 minutes or until the liver is no longer pink when slashed. Spoon out and discard the fat.

Return the sautéed vegetables to the pan. Add the rice, chicken broth, oyster liquid, salt, and pepper. Cover and bring to a boil; reduce heat and simmer 25 minutes. Add the oysters; cook for 5 minutes, or until the rice is tender and all the liquid is absorbed. Remove from heat; stir in the pecans.

If made ahead, cover and refrigerate for up to a day; let stand at room remperature for 30 minutes before stuffing poultry. To serve as a side dish, spread in a serving dish and garnish with parsley, and the cherry tomato cut like a daisy.

An early Jell-O advertisement suggests light desserts after the big meal.

ORANGE STUFFING

TO MAKE ABOUT 8 CUPS

   8 cups fresh bread cubes
   ½ cup chopped onion
   ½ cup chopped celery
   2 tablespoons butter
   2 tablespoons coarsely shredded orange peel
   1 cup chopped fresh parsley
   ½ teaspoon dried thyme
   ½ teaspoon ground sage
   2 teaspoons salt
        Freshly ground black pepper
   1 cup fresh orange juice

Spread the bread cubes in a large pan. Let them dry at room temperature for 1 hour. In a skillet, sauté the onion and celery in the butter until the vegetables are tender. In a large bowl, combine the bread cubes, sautéed vegetables, orange peel, parsley, thyme, sage, salt, and pepper. Sprinkle the orange juice over the bread mixture; toss until the bread cubes are lightly moistened.

If made ahead, cover and refrigerate for up to a day; let stand at room temperature for 30 minutes before stuffing poultry.

SAUSAGE-CRACKER STUFFING

TO MAKE ABOUT 14 CUPS

        About 1½ pounds turkey or chicken giblets
   4 cups water
   1 pound mild bulk pork sausage
   ½ cup (1 stick) butter
   4 large celery stalks, diced
   1 large onion, diced
   10 cups coarsely broken saltine crackers
   1 to 1¼ cups milk
   ¾ teaspoon dried rosemary
   ½ teaspoon freshly ground black pepper
   3 eggs, beaten
        Celery leaves (optional)
        Tomato rose (optional)

Place the giblets in a 3-quart pan with the water and bring to a boil. Cover, reduce heat, and simmer 1½ hours, or until the giblets are tender. Drain, reserving 1¾ cups broth. Chop the giblets.

Brown the sausage in a large skillet, stirring to crumble; remove the sausage with a slotted spoon. Add the butter to the drippings in the skillet; cook over low heat until the butter melts. Stir in the celery and onion; sauté until the vegetables are tender.

In a large bowl, combine the sautéed vegetables, chopped giblets, reserved giblet broth, crackers, milk, rosemary, pepper, and eggs. Stir well.

If made ahead, cover and refrigerate up to 4 hours before stuffing poultry. To serve as a side dish, preheat the oven to 350°. Place the dressing in a greased 9-by-13-inch baking dish. Bake, covered, for 25 minutes. Uncover and bake 20 minutes longer, or until heated through. Garnish with celery leaves and a tomato rose, if desired.

OLD-FASHIONED CORN BREAD STUFFING

TO MAKE ABOUT 7 CUPS

    4 cups crumbled corn bread
    1 cup saltine cracker crumbs
    1 cup crumbled day-old white bread
    1 teaspoon poultry seasoning
    ½ teaspoon salt
    ½ teaspoon ground sage
    ½ teaspoon freshly ground black pepper
    ½ teaspoon celery salt
    ½ cup chopped onion
    3 hard-cooked eggs, chopped
    2 to 2½ cups chicken or turkey broth

In a large bowl, combine the corn bread, cracker crumbs, white bread, poultry seasoning, salt, sage, pepper, celery salt, onion, and eggs. Mix evenly. Sprinkle over the chicken broth; toss until the bread crumbs are lightly moistened.

If made ahead, cover and refrigerate for up to a day; let stand at room temperature for 30 minutes before stuffing poultry. To serve as a side dish, preheat the oven to 350°. Place the dressing in a greased 3-quart casserole. Bake, covered, for 30 minutes, or until heated through. For a crunchy texture, bake uncovered.

FESTIVE CRANBERRY SALAD

TO SERVE 8 TO 12

    4 cups cranberries, washed and picked over
    1 large orange, washed and well scrubbed
    1 cup sugar
    1 envelope unflavored gelatin
    ⅓ cup cold water
    ⅔ cup boiling water
    1 three-ounce package lemon-flavored gelatin
    1 fifteen-ounce can crushed pineapple, undrained
    1 cup chopped walnuts
    ½ cup diced celery
      Lettuce leaves
      Mayonnaise

Set aside a few cranberries for garnish. Grind the remaining cranberries in a food grinder, blender, or food processor; remove and set aside. Cut the unpeeled orange in quarters; remove the seeds. Grind the orange. In a bowl, combine the ground cranberries, orange, and sugar; cover and chill 1 hour.

In a large bowl, soften the unflavored gelatin in the cold water; let it stand 1 minute. Stir in the boiling water and lemon-flavored gelatin; stir until the gelatin dissolves. Gently stir in the cranberry mixture, pineapple, walnuts, and celery. Spoon the mixture into a 6-cup mold; chill until firm. Unmold on a lettuce-lined serving plate. Line the center ring with lettuce; spoon mayonnaise in the center. Top with the reserved cranberries.

SPICED ACORN SQUASH

TO SERVE 8

    4 medium-sized acorn squash
    ½ cup packed dark-brown sugar
    1 teaspoon ground cinnamon
    ½ teaspoon grated nutmeg
    ¼ teaspoon ground cloves
    ½ teaspoon salt
    ½ cup (1 stick) butter, melted
    ½ cup maple syrup
      Eight ½-inch pieces of lean bacon
      About 2 cups boiling water

Preheat the oven to 350°. Cut each squash in half and with a teaspoon scrape out the seeds and fibers. In a small bowl, combine the brown sugar, cinnamon, nutmeg, cloves, salt, and melted butter, and stir them together thoroughly.

Arrange the squash in a shallow ovenproof baking dish just large enough to hold them comfortably. Spoon an equal amount of the spiced butter mixture into the hollow of each squash, and over that pour a teaspoon or so of maple syrup. Top with a piece of bacon. Add boiling water to the baking dish to a depth of about 1 inch. Bake for 30 minutes, or until the squash can be easily pierced.

BRAISED BRUSSELS SPROUTS

TO SERVE 6

    2 to 2½ pounds Brussels sprouts
    ½ cup (1 stick) butter, cut into small pieces
    1 teaspoon salt
    ½ teaspoon freshly ground black pepper
    ¼ cup fresh lemon juice

Preheat the oven to 350°. Trim off and discard the sprout stem ends and discolored leaves. Rinse the sprouts well and place them in a heavy casserole with a tight-fitting lid. Scatter the butter pieces on top and sprinkle with the salt, pepper, and lemon juice. Bake, covered, for 25 to 35 minutes, or until barely tender.

Sausage-Cracker Stuffing,
Festive Cranberry Salad.

RED CABBAGE WITH APPLES

TO SERVE 4 TO 6

    A 2- to 2½-pound red cabbage
⅔ cup red wine vinegar
2 tablespoons sugar
2 teaspoons salt
2 tablespoons lard or bacon fat
2 medium-sized cooking apples, peeled, cored and cut into ⅛-inch-thick wedges
½ cup finely chopped onion
1 whole onion, peeled and pierced with 2 whole cloves
1 small bay leaf
1 cup boiling water
3 tablespoons red wine
3 tablespoons red currant jelly (optional)

Wash the cabbage under cold running water, remove the tough outer leaves, and cut the cabbage into quarters. Cut out the core and slice the quarters crosswise into ⅛-inch-wide strips.

Drop the sliced cabbage into a large mixing bowl, sprinkle it with the vinegar, sugar, and salt, then toss to coat them evenly.

In a heavy 4- to 5-quart casserole, melt the lard or bacon fat over moderate heat. Add the apples and chopped onion and cook, stirring frequently, for 5 minutes, or until the apples are lightly browned. Add the cabbage, whole onion with cloves, and bay leaf; stir thoroughly and pour in the boiling water. Bring to a boil over high heat, stirring occasionally, and reduce the heat to its lowest possible point.

Cover and simmer for 1½ to 2 hours, or until the cabbage is tender. Check from time to time to make sure that the cabbage is moist. If it seems dry, add a tablespoon of boiling water. When the cabbage is done, there should be almost no liquid left in the casserole.

Just before serving, remove the clove-studded onion and the bay leaf, then stir in the wine, and the currant jelly if desired. Taste for seasoning, transfer to a heated platter or bowl, and serve.

BRANDIED SWEET POTATOES

TO SERVE 8 TO 10

6 large sweet potatoes
½ cup sugar
1 tablespoon cornstarch
½ teaspoon salt
½ teaspoon grated nutmeg
1 cup water
⅓ cup brandy
1 tablespoon fresh lemon juice
½ cup chopped pecans
1 to 1½ cups miniature marshmallows (optional)

In a large pan, cook the sweet potatoes in boiling salted water 25 to 35 minutes, or until tender when pierced. Drain. Let cool to the touch; peel and cut crosswise into ½-inch slices. Arrange the potatoes in a lightly greased 9-by-13-inch baking dish. Set aside.

Combine the sugar, cornstarch, salt, and nutmeg in a saucepan; stir to blend. Gradually add the water; cook over medium heat, stirring constantly, until the mixture comes to a boil. Boil 1 minute, stirring constantly. Add the brandy and lemon juice; pour over the sweet potatoes. Sprinkle with the pecans. Bake at 375° for 25 minutes; sprinkle with the marshmallows, if desired, and bake an additional 5 minutes.

ORANGE–SWEET POTATO CUPS

TO SERVE 8

8 large oranges
4 large sweet potatoes
1 cup sugar
2 eggs
1 teaspoon vanilla extract
⅓ cup milk
½ cup (1 stick) butter, softened
½ cup packed brown sugar
2½ tablespoons all-purpose flour
½ cup finely chopped walnuts
2 tablespoons butter, softened
    Fresh parsley sprigs (optional)

Cut a thin slice from the bottom of each orange so it will not roll. Cut a ¾-inch slice from the top of each orange. Using a curved grapefruit knife, gently remove the pulp, leaving the shells intact (reserve the pulp for other uses). Set aside.

In a large saucepan, cook the sweet potatoes in boiling water to cover for 25 to 35 minutes, or until tender when pierced. Drain. Let cool to the touch; peel and mash.

Preheat the oven to 350°. In a large bowl, combine the sweet potatoes, sugar, eggs, vanilla, milk, and ½ cup butter; beat until smooth. Spoon into the orange cups. Place the orange cups in a baking pan.

In a small bowl, combine the brown sugar, flour, walnuts, and 2 tablespoons butter; sprinkle the mixture over the orange cups. Bake for 10 to 15 minutes, or until heated through. Arrange on a platter and garnish with parsley, if desired.

In 1919 Red Star stoves promised to bring the efficiency of city cooking to the country.

PICKLED CARROTS

TO SERVE 8 TO 10

- 2 **pounds carrots, peeled and cut into 3-by-¼-inch strips**
- 1½ **cups sugar**
- 1½ **cups distilled white vinegar**
- 1½ **cups water**
- ¼ **cup whole mustard seeds**
- 3 **half-inch pieces of cinnamon sticks**
- 3 **whole cloves**

In a large saucepan, cook the carrots, covered, in a small amount of boiling water for 14 minutes, or until tender when pierced. Drain the carrots and place in a non-reactive container.

In a medium-sized saucepan, combine the sugar, vinegar, water, mustard seeds, cinnamon, and cloves. Bring to a boil; simmer for 20 minutes. Pour over the carrots; stir gently to evenly distribute the spices. Let the pickling broth cool. Cover tightly; then refrigerate overnight.

Note: The carrots may be stored in the refrigerator for 2 weeks. The liquid may be reused; cook additional carrots as directed.

ENGLISH PEA CASSEROLE

TO SERVE 8 TO 10

- 2 **ten-ounce packages frozen peas**
- 2 **tablespoons butter**
- 2 **tablespoons all-purpose flour**
- 1 **cup milk**
  Salt and pepper to taste
- 1 **two-ounce jar of diced pimientos, drained**
- 4 **hard-cooked eggs, chopped**
  Fried onion rings (optional)
- 1½ **cups (6 ounces) shredded Cheddar cheese**
  Parsley sprigs

Preheat the oven to 350°. Cook the frozen peas according to package directions; drain. Melt the butter in a 2-quart saucepan over medium heat. Add the flour and cook, stirring, until bubbly. Stirring constantly, pour in the milk. Cook, stirring, until the sauce boils and thickens. Remove from heat. Add salt and pepper to taste, peas, pimientos, chopped eggs, and half of the onion rings, if desired. Mix well.

Spoon half of the pea mixture into a greased 2-quart casserole. Top with half of the cheese. Spoon the remaining pea mixture over the cheese. Top with the remaining cheese. Sprinkle the remaining onion rings over the top. Bake, uncovered, for 20 to 30 minutes, or until heated through. Garnish with parsley sprigs.

Note: This recipe can be made ahead. It tastes even better after an hour or so.

GIBLET GRAVY

TO MAKE ABOUT 2 CUPS

- **Giblets from 1 turkey**
- **Turkey neck**
- 2 **cups chicken broth**
- 1 **medium-sized onion, chopped**
- 1 **cup chopped celery**
- ½ **teaspoon poultry seasoning**
- ½ **cup corn bread stuffing (see page 45)**
  Salt and freshly ground pepper, to taste
- 2 **hard-cooked eggs, sliced (optional)**

Place the giblets and turkey neck in a 2-quart saucepan with the chicken broth. Bring to a boil over high heat. Cover, reduce heat, and simmer 1½ hours, or until tender. Remove the giblets and the neck from the broth; cool. Remove the meat from the neck and discard the bones; chop the giblets and return all the meat to the broth; cool.

Add the onion, celery, poultry seasoning, and stuffing to the broth mixture; cook until the vegetables are tender. Stir in the salt, pepper, and egg slices, if desired.

Note: All-purpose flour may be used instead of stuffing to thicken the gravy. Dissolve 2 tablespoons flour in a small amount of water and stir it into the broth.

Giblet Gravy and Orange-Sweet Potato Cups are tasty companions for all-American turkey.

EASY BUTTERMILK ROLLS

TO MAKE 2 DOZEN

- 4 to 4½ cups all-purpose flour
- 2 tablespoons active dry yeast (2 envelopes)
- 3 tablespoons sugar
- 1 teaspoon salt
- ½ teaspoon baking soda
- 1¼ cups buttermilk
- ½ cup water
- ½ cup shortening

In a large bowl, combine 1½ cups flour, yeast, sugar, salt, and baking soda; mix well. In a small saucepan, combine the buttermilk, water, and shortening; place over low heat until hot (120° to 130°). Gradually add the milk mixture to the dry ingredients, stirring to combine; then beat well until very smooth. Stir in the remaining flour until the mixture comes away from the sides of the bowl.

Turn the dough out onto a lightly floured surface and knead until smooth and elastic (about 5 minutes).

Place the dough in a greased bowl; turn to grease the top. Cover and let rise in a warm place, free from drafts, for 35 minutes or until doubled.

Punch the dough down, turn out on a lightly floured surface, roll out, and divide into 24 pieces. Shape each piece into a 1½-inch ball. Place the balls on a greased jelly roll pan. Cover loosely with plastic wrap and let rise in a warm place for 35 minutes, or until doubled. Preheat the oven to 400°. Bake for 18 to 20 minutes, or until golden.

German immigrants introduced many of our Christmas treats. Here a boy baker shows off a cookie dressed up for the season.

DRESDNER STOLLEN

Two recipes give you a choice between a traditional stollen and a quicker, lighter version. Either one is excellent to have on hand for the holidays. You can serve this sweet German yeast bread for breakfast, as a tea bread, or as dessert. If you are making stollen as a gift, choose the Dresdner Stollen—its higher butter content will help keep it moist longer.

TO MAKE TWO 13-INCH LOAVES

- ½ cup seedless raisins
- ½ cup dried currants
- 1 cup mixed candied citrus peel
- ¼ cup candied angelica, cut into ¼-inch dice
- ½ cup candied cherries, cut in half
- ½ cup rum
- ¼ cup warm water (105° to 115°)
- 2 packages active dry yeast
- ¾ cup plus a pinch of sugar
- 5½ cups plus 2 tablespoons all-purpose flour
- 1 cup milk
- ½ teaspoon salt
- ½ teaspoon almond extract
- ½ teaspoon finely grated fresh lemon peel
- 2 eggs, at room temperature
- ¾ cup unsalted butter, cut into ¼-inch bits and softened
- ½ cup (1 stick) unsalted butter, melted
- 1 cup blanched slivered almonds
- ¼ cup confectioners' sugar, sifted

Combine the raisins, currants, candied citrus peel, angelica, and cherries in a bowl. Pour the rum over them, tossing the fruit about to coat the pieces evenly. Soak for at least 1 hour.

Pour the warm water into a small bowl and sprinkle it with the yeast and a pinch of sugar. Let the mixture stand for 2 or 3 minutes, then stir to dissolve the yeast completely. Set the bowl in a warm, draft-free place (such as a turned-off oven) for about 5 minutes, or until the mixture almost doubles in volume.

Meanwhile, drain the fruit, reserving the rum, and carefully pat the pieces completely dry with paper towels. Place the fruit in a bowl, sprinkle it with 2 tablespoons of the flour, and stir until the flour is completely absorbed. Set aside.

In a heavy 1½- to 2-quart saucepan, combine the milk, ½ cup of the sugar, and the salt. Heat to warm (105° to 115°), stirring constantly until the sugar dissolves. Turn off the heat, stir in the reserved rum, the almond extract and fresh lemon peel, and finally the yeast mixture.

Place 5 cups of the flour in a large bowl and with a fork stir in the yeast mixture, a cup or so at a time. Beat the eggs until frothy and stir them into the dough, then beat in the bits of softened butter. Gather the dough into a ball and place it on a board sprinkled with the remaining ½ cup of flour. Knead the dough for about 15 minutes, or until all the flour is incorporated and the dough is smooth and elastic. Flour your hands lightly from time to time.

Now press the fruit and almonds into the dough, ⅓ cup or so at a time, but do not knead or handle it too much or the dough will discolor. Coat a deep bowl with 1 teaspoon of melted butter and drop in the dough. Brush the top of the dough with another 2 teaspoons of melted butter, drape a towel over the bowl, and set it in a warm, draft-free place for 2 hours, or until the dough doubles in bulk.

Punch the dough down and divide it into two equal pieces. Let them rest for 10 minutes, then roll the pieces out into strips about 12 inches long, 8 inches wide and ½ inch thick. Brush each strip with 2 tablespoons of the remaining butter and sprinkle each with 2 tablespoons of the remaining sugar. Fold each strip lengthwise in the following fashion: bring one long side over to the center of the strip and press the edge down lightly. Then fold the other long side across it, overlapping the seam down the center by about 1 inch. Press the edge gently to keep it in place. With lightly floured hands, taper the ends of the loaf slightly and pat the sides gently together to mound it in the center. The finished loaf should be about 3½ to 4 inches wide and 13 inches long.

With a pastry brush and 1 tablespoon of melted butter, coat the bottom of an 11-by-17-inch jelly-roll pan. Place the loaves on the pan and brush them with the remaining 2 tablespoons of melted butter. Set the loaves aside in a warm draft-free place for about 1 hour, or until doubled in bulk. Preheat the oven to 375°. Then bake the bread for 45 minutes, or until golden brown and crusty. Transfer the loaves to wire racks to cool completely. Just before serving, sprinkle the loaves with the sifted confectioners' sugar.

Traditional Dresdner Stollen, a fruit-filled sweet bread baked specially for the holiday, is among the many contributions German immigrants have made to America's Christmas.

STOLLEN

TO MAKE 2 LOAVES

- 1 package active dry yeast
- ¼ cup warm water (105° to 115°)
- ¼ cup sugar
- ½ cup (1 stick) butter, softened
- 1 teaspoon salt
- 2 eggs
- 1 cup milk, scalded and cooled to 105° to 115°
- 4½ cups all-purpose flour
- ½ cup chopped almonds
- ½ cup coarsely chopped candied red and green cherries
- ½ cup raisins
- 1 cup sifted confectioners' sugar (optional)
- 2 tablespoons hot water (optional)
  Sliced almonds (optional)
  Red and green candied cherry halves (optional)

Sprinkle the yeast over the warm water in a small bowl; add a pinch of the sugar, stir to dissolve, and let stand 5 minutes.

Cream the butter, sugar, and salt in a large bowl until light and fluffy. Add the eggs, one at a time, beating well after each addition. Stir in the milk and yeast mixture. Add the flour, 1 cup at a time, stirring well, until a soft dough is formed. Cover tightly and let rise in a warm, draft-free place for 1½ hours, or until doubled.

Punch the dough down. On a lightly floured surface, knead in the almonds, candied cherries, and raisins. Divide the dough in half. Roll each half to a 10-inch circle; fold in half and place on a greased baking sheet. Cover loosely with plastic wrap and let the loaves rise in a warm place for 30 minutes, or until doubled.

Preheat the oven to 375°. Bake the loaves for 25 to 30 minutes, or until golden brown; the loaves will sound hollow when tapped on the bottom. Cool on wire racks for 2 to 3 minutes.

If a glaze is desired, combine confectioners' sugar and hot water; spread over each loaf. Garnish with sliced almonds and candied cherries, if desired. Store in an airtight container for up to 2 days.

HONEY-POACHED PEARS

❙ Honey-Poached Pears.

TO SERVE 10

10	**firm pears**
	Fresh lemon juice for brushing
6	**cups water**
2	**cups honey**
¼	**cup fresh lemon juice**
4	**three-inch pieces of cinnamon sticks**
	Chilled heavy cream
	Orange rind strips (optional)

Peel the pears, leaving the stems intact. Trim the bottom of each pear to form a flat base. As each pear is peeled, brush it with lemon juice to prevent discoloration.

In a 5-quart kettle, combine the water, honey, lemon juice, and cinnamon sticks; bring to a boil. Stand the pears, stem up, in the kettle. Cover, reduce heat, and simmer 15 to 25 minutes or until the pears are tender when pierced. Remove from the pan with a slotted spoon and cool at room temperature.

Just before serving, beat the cream in a chilled bowl just until thickened (but not stiff); pour into a shallow serving dish. Stand the pears upright in the cream; garnish with strips of orange peel, if desired.

CHRISTMAS DINNER AT THE CRATCHITS

When Charles Dickens wrote A Christmas Carol, *he helped to popularize the celebration of Christmas in Victorian England. The story of Ebenezer Scrooge, Bob Cratchit, and Tiny Tim has become a part of the American Christmas. You can re-create the famous dinner in the passage quoted here with the Roast Goose on page 42 and the Plum Pudding on page 51.*

His active little crutch was heard upon the floor, and back came Tiny Tim, escorted by his brother and sister to his stool beside the fire; and while Bob, turning up his cuffs, compounded some hot mixture with gin and lemons in a jug and put it on the hob to simmer, Master Peter and the two young Cratchits went to fetch the goose, with which they soon returned in high procession.

Such a bustle ensued that you might have thought a goose the rarest of all birds; and, in truth, it was something very like it in that house. Mrs. Cratchit made the gravy hissing hot; Master Peter mashed the potatoes with incredible vigor; Miss Belinda sweetened up the applesauce; Martha dusted the hot plates; Bob took Tiny Tim beside him in a tiny corner at the table; the two young Cratchits set chairs for everybody, and crammed spoons into their mouths, lest they should shriek for goose before their turn came to be helped. At last the dishes were set on, and grace was said. It was succeeded by a breathless pause, as Mrs. Cratchit, looking slowly all along the carving knife, prepared to plunge it in the breast; but when she did, and when the long-expected gush of stuffing issued forth, one murmur of delight arose all round the board, and even Tiny Tim beat on the table with the handle of his knife and feebly cried Hurrah!

There never was such a goose. Bob said he didn't believe there ever was such a goose cooked. Its tenderness and flavor, size and cheapness, were the themes of universal admiration. Eked out by applesauce and mashed potatoes, it was a sufficient dinner for the whole family; indeed, as Mrs. Cratchit said with great delight (surveying one small atom of a bone upon the dish), they hadn't ate it all at last! Yet everyone had had enough, and the youngest Cratchits were steeped in sage and onion to the eyebrows!

Now Mrs. Cratchit left the room alone—too nervous to bear witnesses—to take the pudding up, and bring it in. Suppose it should not be done enough! Suppose it should break in turning out! Suppose somebody should have stolen it, while they were merry with goose—a supposition at which the two young Cratchits became livid!

Hallo! A great deal of steam! The pudding was out of the copper. In half a minute Mrs. Cratchit entered—flushed, but smiling proudly—with the pudding, like a speckled cannonball, blazing in ignited brandy, with Christmas holly stuck into the top.

Oh, a wonderful pudding! Bob Cratchit said that he regarded it as the greatest success achieved by Mrs. Cratchit since their marriage. Mrs. Cratchit said that, now the weight was off her mind, she would confess she had her doubts about the quantity of flour. Everybody had something to say about it, but nobody said or thought it was at all a small pudding for so large a family. Any Cratchit would have blushed to hint at such a thing.

At last the dinner was done, the cloth cleared, the hearth swept, and the fire made up. The compound in the jug being tasted, and considered perfect, apples and oranges were put upon the table, and a shovelful of chestnuts on the fire. Then all the Cratchit family drew round the hearth in a half circle; and at Bob Cratchit's elbow stood the family display of glass: two tumblers and a custard cup without a handle. These held the hot stuff from the jug, however, as well as golden goblets would have done; and Bob served it out with beaming looks, while the chestnuts on the fire crackled noisily. Then Bob proposed:

"A merry Christmas to us all, my dears. God bless us!"
Which all the family re-echoed.

"God bless us every one," said Tiny Tim, the last of all.

PLUM PUDDING

TO MAKE FOUR 1-POUND PUDDINGS

- 1½ cups dried currants
- 2 cups seedless raisins
- 2 cups golden raisins
- ¾ cup finely chopped candied mixed fruit peel
- ¾ cup finely chopped candied cherries
- 1 cup blanched slivered almonds
- 1 medium-sized tart cooking apple, peeled, quartered, cored, and coarsely chopped
- 1 small carrot, scraped and coarsely chopped
- 2 tablespoons finely grated orange peel
- 2 teaspoons finely grated lemon peel
- ½ pound finely chopped beef suet
- 2 cups all-purpose flour
- 4 cups fresh soft bread crumbs
- 1 cup packed dark-brown sugar
- 1 teaspoon ground allspice
- 1 teaspoon salt
- 6 eggs
- 1 cup brandy
- ⅓ cup fresh orange juice
- ¼ cup fresh lemon juice
  Brandy Butter, following (optional)
- ½ cup brandy, for flaming (optional)

In a large bowl, combine the currants, raisins, candied fruit peel, cherries, almonds, apple, carrot, orange and lemon peel, and beef suet, tossing them until well mixed. Stir in the flour, bread crumbs, brown sugar, allspice, and salt.

In a separate bowl, beat the eggs until frothy. Stir in the 1 cup brandy and the orange and lemon juice, and pour this mixture over the fruit mixture. Knead vigorously, then beat until all the ingredients are blended. Cover and refrigerate for at least 12 hours.

Spoon the mixture into four 1-quart pudding basins, deep stoneware bowls, or plain molds, filling them to within 2 inches of their tops. Cover each mold with a strip of buttered aluminum foil, turning the edges down and pressing the foil tightly around the sides to secure it. Drape a dampened kitchen towel over each mold and tie it in place around the sides with a long piece of kitchen cord. Bring two opposite corners of the towel up to the top and knot them in the center of the mold; then bring up the remaining two corners and knot them similarly.

Place the molds in a large pot and pour in enough boiling water to come about three-fourths of the way up their sides. Bring the water to a boil over high heat, cover the pot tightly, reduce the heat to its lowest point, and steam the puddings for 8 hours. As the water in the steamer boils away, replenish it with additional boiling water.

When the puddings are done, remove them from the water and let them cool to room remperature. Then remove the towels and foil and re-cover the molds tightly with fresh foil. Refrigerate the puddings for at least 3 weeks before serving. Plum puddings may be kept up to a year in the refrigerator or other cool place.

To serve, place the mold in a pot and pour in enough boiling water to come about three-fourths of the way up the sides of the mold. Bring to a boil over high heat, cover the pot, reduce the heat to low and steam for 2 hours. Run a knife around the inside edges of the mold and place an inverted serving plate over it. Grasping the mold and plate firmly together, turn them over. The pudding should slide out easily. Serve with Brandy Butter, if desired.

To flame the pudding, warm the ½ cup of brandy in a small saucepan over low heat, ignite it with a match, and pour it over the pudding.

❙ Flaming Plum Pudding.

BRANDY BUTTER

TO MAKE ABOUT ¾ CUP

- 4 tablespoons unsalted butter, softened
- ½ cup superfine sugar
- 3 tablespoons brandy
- ½ teaspoon vanilla extract

Cream the butter until it is light and fluffy. Beat in the sugar, a few tablespoons at a time, and continue beating until the mixture is very white and frothy. Beat in the brandy and vanilla. Refrigerate at least 4 hours, or until firm.

COCONUT CAKE WITH LEMON FILLING

TO MAKE ONE 9-INCH 4-LAYER CAKE

Cake

- 2 tablespoons butter, softened
- 2 tablespoons plus 2 cups all-purpose flour, sifted before measuring
- 1 teaspoon baking powder
- ⅛ teaspoon salt
- 8 egg yolks
- 2 cups sugar
- ¼ cup fresh lemon juice
- 2 teaspoons finely grated fresh lemon peel
- 8 egg whites

Filling

- 1½ cups sugar
- ¼ cup cornstarch
- ⅛ teaspoon salt
- 2 eggs, lightly beaten
- 2 tablespoons butter, cut into ¼-inch bits
- 2 tablespoons finely grated fresh lemon peel
- ⅔ cup fresh lemon juice
- 1 cup water

Icing

- 4 egg whites
- ½ cup confectioners' sugar
- 1 teaspoon vanilla extract
- 1½ cups white corn syrup
- 2 cups freshly grated peeled coconut meat or packaged shredded coconut

Preheat the oven to 350°. Spread the 2 tablespoons of softened butter over the bottom and sides of two 9-inch round cake pans. Add 1 tablespoon of flour to each pan and, one at a time, tip the pans from side to side to distribute the flour evenly. Then invert each pan and rap it sharply to remove the excess flour.

Combine the remaining flour, baking powder, and salt and sift them together. Set aside.

In a deep bowl, beat the egg yolks and sugar for 4 to 5 minutes, or until the mixture forms a slowly dissolving ribbon when the beater is lifted from the bowl. Beat in the lemon juice and lemon peel. Then add the flour mixture, about ½ cup at a time, beating well after each addition.

Beat the egg whites in another bowl until they form stiff peaks. Fold the egg whites gently but thoroughly into the batter.

Pour the batter into the prepared pans, dividing it equally between them and smoothing the tops. Bake for about 20 minutes, or until a toothpick inserted in the center comes out clean. Let the cakes cool in the pans for about 5 minutes, then turn them out on wire racks to cool to room temperature.

Meanwhile, prepare the filling: Combine the sugar, cornstarch, salt, and beaten eggs in a heavy 1½- to 2-quart saucepan and mix well. Stir in the butter, lemon peel, lemon juice, and water; blend well.

Set the pan over high heat, and bring to a boil, stirring constantly. Immediately reduce the heat to low and continue to stir until the filling is smooth and thick enough to coat the spoon heavily. Scrape the filling into a bowl and let it cool to room temperature.

When the cake and filling are cool, prepare the icing: In a small saucepan, bring the corn syrup to a boil over high heat and cook briskly until it reaches a temperature of 239° on a candy thermometer, or until a drop spooned into ice water immediately forms a soft ball.

Meanwhile, beat the egg whites until they form soft peaks. Sprinkle them with the confectioners' sugar and vanilla and continue to beat until stiff and glossy. Beating constantly, pour in the corn syrup in a slow, thin stream and continue to beat until the icing is smooth, thick, and cool.

To assemble, cut each cake in half horizontally to make four thin layers. Place one layer, cut side up, on an inverted cake or pie tin and spread about one-third of the lemon filling over it. Put another cake layer on top, spread with filling, and cover it with the third layer. Spread this layer with the remaining filling, and place the fourth layer on top.

Smooth the icing over the top and sides of the cake. Then sprinkle the coconut generously on the top and pat it onto the sides of the cake. Carefully transfer the coconut cake to a serving plate and serve at once. If the cake must wait, drape wax paper around the top and sides to keep the icing moist.

WHITE FRUIT CAKE

TO MAKE ONE 6-POUND CAKE

- ¾ cup (1½ sticks) plus 2 tablespoons butter, softened
- 3 cups all-purpose flour
- 2 teaspoons baking powder
- ½ teaspoon grated nutmeg
- ¾ teaspoon salt
- 2 cups golden raisins
- ¾ cup finely slivered candied lemon peel
- ¾ cup finely slivered candied orange peel
- ¾ cup finely slivered candied pineapple
- ¾ cup finely slivered candied citron
- 1 cup sugar
- 1¼ cups bourbon
- 1½ cups slivered blanched almonds
- 8 egg whites

Preheat the oven to 250°. Spread 1 tablespoon of the softened butter over the bottom and sides of a 9-by-3-inch springform tube cake pan. Coat two strips of wax paper with another tablespoon of the butter and fit the strips around the tube and the sides of the pan, with the greased surfaces facing out. Set aside.

Combine the flour, baking powder, nutmeg, and salt and sift them together into a large bowl. Add the raisins, lemon peel, orange peel, pineapple, and citron, and toss the fruit until the pieces are evenly coated.

In another large bowl, cream the remaining ¾ cup butter and the sugar until light and fluffy. Stir in the flour-and-fruit mixture a cup or so at a time. Then add ¾ cup of the bourbon and, when it is completely incorporated, stir in the slivered almonds.

Beat the egg whites until they form stiff peaks. Fold the egg whites into the batter. Pour the batter into the paper-lined pan, filling it about three quarters full, and smooth the top. Bake in the middle of the oven for 2½ to 3 hours, or until a toothpick inserted in the center comes out clean.

Let the cake cool overnight before removing the sides of the springform pan. Then slip the cake off the bottom of the pan and carefully peel away the paper. Place the cake on a serving plate and sprinkle it evenly with the remaining ½ cup of bourbon. Wrap in cheesecloth and set the cake aside at room temperature for at least 24 hours before serving. Securely wrapped in foil or plastic, it can be kept for several months, and its flavor will improve with age.

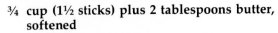

A trade card for the Christmas season features Gail Borden's Eagle Brand condensed milk.

Christmas in the South means an array of mouth-watering desserts. Clockwise from top left: Coconut Cake with Lemon Filling; White Fruit Cake; Divinity Candies (recipe on page 61); Bourbon Balls (recipe on page 56); and Traditional Eggnog (recipe on page 63).

JEWELLED CROQUEMBOUCHE

TO SERVE 20

Cream Puffs

 1 cup milk

 ½ cup (1 stick) butter

 1 cup all-purpose flour

 4 eggs

Cream Filling

 1 cup sugar

 ½ cup cornstarch

 4 eggs

 4 cups milk, scalded

 2 tablespoons chopped candied ginger

Caramel

 1½ cups sugar

 ½ cup water

 1 tablespoon fresh lemon juice

 Candied fruit and cherries

To make the cream puffs, bring the milk and butter to boil in a heavy saucepan. Beat in the flour quickly until the dough pulls away from the sides of the pan. Remove from heat. Beat in the eggs, one at a time, until smooth. Preheat the oven to 425°. Pipe the batter from a pastry bag or drop by teaspoonfuls onto a greased baking sheet (the shapes will be more rounded if piped). Bake 15 to 20 minutes, or until the puffs are dry to the touch and golden brown. Remove the puffs from the oven and pierce the bottom of each with a knife; set aside to cool on racks.

To make the filling, combine the sugar and cornstarch in a heavy saucepan. Beat in the eggs, one at a time, until creamy. Whisk the hot milk into the egg mixture. Stirring, cook over medium heat until thick and bubbly. Add the ginger; cool and refrigerate. Spoon the filling into a pastry bag fitted with a star tip. To fill the puffs, insert the tip of the pastry bag into the pierced bottom of each puff.

Just before assembling, make the caramel: Place the sugar, water, and lemon juice in a heavy saucepan. Heat over medium heat, without stirring, until it comes to a boil. Reduce heat and cook until clear and light gold. Watch carefully, to prevent the caramel from burning.

Make a circle of puffs on a serving platter. Dip the bottom of one of the remaining puffs into the caramel. Quickly place on top of circle. Repeat with all the remaining puffs, gradually tapering toward the top to form a pointed tower.

When the tower is formed, decorate it with fruit and cherries. Drizzle the remaining caramel glaze over the puffs. Serve the same day as made.

Opposite page: Studded with glazed fruit, Jewelled Croquembouche is as pleasing to the eye as to the palate.
Right: Heirloom Fruit Cake makes a fine gift for the entire family.

HEIRLOOM FRUIT CAKE

TO MAKE 1 FRUIT CAKE

 1½ cups seedless raisins

 1½ cups golden raisins

 1 cup mixed candied fruits

 1 cup whole candied fruits

 1 cup whole candied cherries

 1 cup candied pineapple chunks

 1 teaspoon ground cinnamon

 ½ teaspoon grated nutmeg

 ½ teaspoon ground ginger

 ½ teaspoon ground allspice

 ½ cup brandy or fruit juice

 1 cup walnut pieces

 ½ cup (1 stick) butter, softened

 1½ cups packed brown sugar

 2 eggs

 2 cups all-purpose flour

 1 teaspoon baking soda

 1 teaspoon salt

 Brandy for aging

In a large bowl, combine the fruits, spices, and brandy. Mix well. Cover and let stand several hours or overnight.

Preheat the oven to 325°. Add the walnuts to the fruit mixture. Grease a 9-by-5-inch loaf pan, then line it with greased heavy brown paper. In a large bowl, cream the butter and brown sugar until light and fluffy; stir in the eggs, one at a time, until well mixed. Sift together the flour, baking soda, and salt; stir into the creamed mixture. Mix in the fruit-nut mixture until well distributed. Turn the batter into the prepared loaf pan.

Bake for about 2 hours or until a wooden toothpick inserted in the center comes out clean. Let stand in the pan for ½ hour. Remove from the pan; gently peel off paper. Brush with brandy. Soak a large piece of cheesecloth in brandy; wrap the fruit cake in the soaked cloth, then in plastic wrap. Store in a cool place to age for 2 weeks to 3 months.

COOKIES AND CANDIES

PFEFFERNÜSSE

TO MAKE ABOUT 30 COOKIES

> **Soft butter**
> 4 **cups all-purpose flour**
> 1 **teaspoon baking powder**
> 1 **teaspoon ground cloves**
> ½ **teaspoon ground allspice**
> ½ **teaspoon ground cinnamon**
> ¾ **cup honey**
> 1 **cup dark corn syrup**
> ¾ **cup sugar**
> 2 **tablespoons butter**
> 1 **tablespoon shortening or lard**

Preheat the oven to 400°. Coat two large baking sheets lightly with butter. Combine the flour, baking powder, cloves, allspice, and cinnamon in a bowl, and set aside. In a large heavy saucepan, bring the honey, corn syrup, and sugar to a boil over moderate heat, stirring until the sugar dissolves. Reduce the heat to low, and simmer, uncovered, for 5 minutes. Remove the pan from the heat, add the butter and shortening, and stir until melted. Beat in the flour mixture a cup or so at a time. When the batter is smooth, drop it by teaspoonfuls onto the baking sheets, leaving an inch or so between the cookies.

Bake for about 15 minutes, or until the cookies are firm to the touch and light brown. Transfer them to a cake rack to cool, and proceed with the remaining batches, coating the baking sheets with a little butter each time. Pfeffernüsse can be stored for 6 to 8 weeks in tightly sealed jars or tins.

MILLER'S MOCHA MORSELS

TO MAKE ABOUT 2½ DOZEN COOKIES

> ¼ **cup boiling water**
> 2 **one-ounce squares unsweetened chocolate, coarsely chopped**
> 2 **teaspoons instant coffee powder**
> 6 **tablespoons unsalted butter, softened**
> 1 **cup sugar**
> 2 **eggs**
> ½ **teaspoon vanilla extract**
> 1 **cup all-purpose flour**
> ¼ **teaspoon salt**
> 1½ **cups chopped walnuts**
> 1 **cup raisins**
> 1 **cup chocolate chips**
> **Confectioners' sugar (optional)**

Preheat the oven to 350°. In a saucepan, combine the water, unsweetened chocolate, and coffee powder. Warm over low heat to melt the chocolate, stirring occasionally; set aside. In a large bowl, cream the butter and sugar until light and fluffy. Stir in the chocolate-coffee mixture, eggs, and vanilla. Stir the flour and salt into the creamed mixture. Mix in the walnuts, raisins, and chocolate chips. Drop teaspoonfuls onto lightly greased baking sheets.

Bake 13 to 15 minutes, or until the edges are crisp but the centers are still soft (do not overbake). Remove to racks to cool. Dust with confectioners' sugar, if desired.

BOURBON BALLS

TO MAKE ABOUT 60 ONE-INCH CANDIES

> 8 **one-ounce squares semisweet chocolate, coarsely chopped**
> 60 **vanilla wafers, ground in a blender or finely crushed with a rolling pin (about 3 cups)**
> 1 **cup finely chopped pecans**
> 1⅔ **cups sugar**
> ½ **cup bourbon**
> ¼ **cup light corn syrup**

In a small heavy skillet, melt the chocolate over low heat, stirring constantly to prevent the bottom from scorching. Remove the pan from the heat and let the chocolate cool to lukewarm.

Combine the vanilla wafer crumbs, pecans, and ⅔ cup of the sugar in a large bowl. Pour in the chocolate, bourbon, and corn syrup and stir until the ingredients are well combined.

To shape each bourbon ball, scoop up about a tablespoon of the mixture and pat it into a ball about 1 inch in diameter. Roll the balls in the remaining cup of sugar and, when they are lightly coated on all sides, place them in a container with a securely fitting lid. Cut two rounds from a double thickness of paper towels to fit inside the lid. Moisten the paper rounds with a little additional bourbon and press them tightly into the lid.

Seal the container with the paper-lined lid and set the bourbon balls aside at room temperature for 3 or 4 days before serving. Tightly covered, the bourbon balls will keep for 3 to 4 weeks.

MORAVIAN ANIMAL COOKIES

TO MAKE ABOUT 8 DOZEN COOKIES

    3 cups unsifted all-purpose flour
    1 teaspoon ground ginger
    ½ teaspoon salt
    ½ cup (1 stick) butter, softened
    4 tablespoons shortening or lard, softened
    ½ cup sugar
    1 cup dark molasses
    1 tablespoon rum

Combine the flour, ginger, and salt, and sift them together. Set aside. In a large bowl, cream 4 tablespoons of the softened butter, the shortening, and sugar until light and fluffy. Beat in about 1 cup of the flour mixture and, when it is well mixed, add about ⅓ cup of the molasses. Repeat two more times, alternating 1 cup of the flour mixture with ⅓ cup of molasses and beating well after each addition. Stir in the rum, cover the bowl with plastic wrap, and refrigerate the dough for at least 8 hours, or overnight.

Preheat the oven to 350°. Spread 1 tablespoon of the remaining softened butter evenly over the two large baking sheets.

Cut off about one quarter of the dough and shape it into a ball. (Return the rest to the refrigerator.) On a lightly floured surface, roll the ball of dough out into a rough circle about ⅛ inch thick.

Cut the dough into animal shapes with animal cookie cutters. Gather the scraps together into a ball and roll out as before. Then cut as many more animal cookies as you can.

With a wide metal spatula, arrange the animal cookies about 1 inch apart on the baking sheets. Bake for 5 to 8 minutes, or until the tops feel firm. With the spatula, transfer the cookies to wire racks to cool.

Let the baking sheets cool completely, then repeat the entire procedure three more times, using 1 tablespoon of the softened butter to grease the pans for each batch of animal cookies and rolling and baking one quarter of the dough at a time.

The cookies will keep for 2 to 3 weeks if tightly covered.

Opposite page: Thin molasses-flavored Moravian Animal Cookies are traditionally made in huge quantities, both to eat and to use as decorations.
Right: Gingerbread Cookies and Miller's Mocha Morsels.

GINGERBREAD COOKIES

TO MAKE ABOUT 2 DOZEN COOKIES

    ½ cup (1 stick) butter, softened
    ½ cup sugar
    ½ cup molasses
    1 egg
    3 cups all-purpose flour
    1 teaspoon baking powder
    ½ teaspoon baking soda
  1½ teaspoons ground cinnamon
    1 teaspoon ground ginger
    ½ teaspoon ground cloves
    ½ teaspoon grated nutmeg
    1 cup raisins, coarsely chopped

In a large bowl, cream the butter, sugar, and molasses; beat in the egg. Sift the flour, baking powder, baking soda, and spices together; gradually mix into the creamed mixture. Stir in the raisins. Chill the dough at least 1 hour.

Preheat the oven to 350°. Roll the dough to a ⅛-inch thickness on a floured board; cut into desired shapes with sharp-edged cookie cutters. Bake on greased baking sheets for 10 to 12 minutes, or until set and lightly browned on the bottom. Remove to racks to cool. Decorate as desired.

Painted Christmas
Cookies add to the
colorful, festive spirit
of the holiday. Take a
decorating hint from the
ones pictured here, or let
your imagination go.

PAINTED CHRISTMAS COOKIES

TO MAKE ABOUT 2½ DOZEN COOKIES

Cookies

- ½ cup (1 stick) butter, softened
- ½ cup shortening
- 1 cup sifted confectioners' sugar
- 1 egg
- 1 teaspoon vanilla extract
- 2½ cups all-purpose flour
- 1 teaspoon salt

Egg Yolk Paint

- 1 egg yolk
- ¼ teaspoon water
- Assorted colors of paste food coloring*

In a bowl, cream the butter and shortening; gradually add the sugar, beating well. Add the egg and vanilla; beat well.

Combine the flour and salt; stir into the creamed mixture. Divide the dough in half; wrap in plastic wrap and chill at least 1 hour.

To make the Egg Yolk Paint, combine the egg yolk and water; mix well. Divide the mixture into several custard cups; tint as desired with paste food coloring. Keep the paint covered until ready to use. If the paint thickens, add a few drops of water and mix well.

Preheat the oven to 375°. Roll half of the dough to a ⅛-inch thickness on a lightly floured baking sheet; keep the remaining dough chilled. Cut the dough into desired shapes; remove the excess dough. Using a small paint brush, paint assorted designs on the cookies with Egg Yolk Paint.

Bake for 9 to 10 minutes or until the cookies are lightly browned. Remove from the baking sheet and let cool completely on a wire rack. Repeat with the remaining dough.

*Paste food coloring may be found in specialty food stores or cookware shops.

CHOCOLATE BROWNIES

TO MAKE 16 BROWNIES

- 2 one-ounce squares unsweetened chocolate
- ½ cup (1 stick) butter
- 1 cup sugar
- 2 eggs
- ½ cup all-purpose flour
- ½ teaspoon baking powder
- ½ teaspoon salt
- 1 teaspoon vanilla extract
- 1 cup coarsely chopped walnuts

Preheat the oven to 350°. Melt the chocolate in a small heavy saucepan over low heat, stirring constantly. Set aside to cool slightly. In a large bowl, cream the butter and sugar until light and fluffy. Beat in the eggs, one at a time, and then the cooled chocolate. Sift the flour, baking powder, and salt together into the mixture and beat for 10 to 15 seconds, or until the ingredients are well combined. Stir in the vanilla and walnuts.

Lightly butter an 8-inch-square baking pan. Pour in the batter and bake the brownies for 30 to 35 minutes, or until a small knife inserted in the center comes out clean. Cool for about 10 minutes, then cut into 2-inch squares.

MINT-CHOCOLATE SNAPS

TO MAKE ABOUT 7 DOZEN COOKIES

- 1 six-ounce package chocolate chips
- ½ cup (1 stick) plus 1½ tablespoons butter
- ¾ cup sugar
- 1 egg
- ¼ cup light corn syrup
- 1 teaspoon peppermint extract
- 1 teaspoon vanilla extract
- 2 cups all-purpose flour
- 1 teaspoon baking soda
- ¼ teaspoon salt
- ¼ cup crushed peppermint candy
- About ⅓ cup sugar for coating

Preheat the oven to 350°. In a small heavy pan on the lowest possible heat, stir the chocolate chips just until melted; set aside.

In a large bowl, cream the butter; gradually add ¾ cup sugar, beating until light and fluffy. Beat in the melted chocolate. Add the egg, corn syrup, and peppermint and vanilla extracts; beat well. Combine the flour, baking soda, and salt; stir into the chocolate mixture. Stir in the peppermint candy.

Shape the dough into 1-inch balls and roll in ⅓ cup sugar. Place the balls 2 inches apart on ungreased cookie sheets; bake for 12 to 15 minutes, or until the edges are browned. Cool on cookie sheets 5 minutes; transfer to wire racks and cool completely.

SWISS ALMOND TEA WAFERS

TO MAKE ABOUT 5½ DOZEN COOKIES

- 1½ cups sliced almonds, lightly toasted
- ½ cup plus 2 tablespoons sugar
- 2 teaspoons grated orange peel
- ½ cup (1 stick) butter, softened
- 1 egg
- 3 egg yolks
- 2 tablespoons Amaretto liqueur
- 2¼ cups all-purpose flour
- ¼ teaspoon salt
- 1 tablespoon water
- Silver candy decorations

Combine the almonds, ½ cup of the sugar, and orange peel in the container of a food processor or electric blender; process until finely ground.

In a large bowl, cream the butter; add the almond mixture, beating well. Add the egg, 2 of the egg yolks, and Amaretto; beat well. Combine the flour and salt; add to the creamed mixture and blend well. Shape the dough into a ball; wrap in plastic wrap and chill until firm.

Preheat the oven to 350°. Roll the dough to a ¼-inch thickness between two sheets of wax paper. (Turn the dough over and loosen the paper frequently while rolling to allow the dough to spread.) Cut the dough using a 2-inch cutter, rerolling scraps of dough.

Place the cookies ½ inch apart on greased and floured baking sheets. Combine the remaining egg yolk and the water; brush over the cookies. Sprinkle cookies lightly with the remaining sugar, and decorate as desired with candy decorations. Bake for 15 to 18 minutes, or until the cookies are browned around the edges and golden in the center. Cool on racks; store in airtight containers for up to 1 week.

COOKIE GIFT BOXES

MAKES 4 COOKIE GIFT BOXES

Cookies

- 1 cup molasses
- 3 tablespoons butter, melted
- 1 egg, beaten
- ½ teaspoon baking soda
- 1 teaspoon ground allspice
- ¼ teaspoon grated nutmeg
- 3½ to 4 cups all-purpose flour

Melted Sugar

- ½ cup granulated sugar

Royal Icing

- 3 egg whites, at room temperature
- ½ teaspoon cream of tartar
- 1 sixteen-ounce package confectioners' sugar
- Paste food coloring*

Cut the following shapes from cardboard to make patterns for boxes: one 3¾-by-2½-inch rectangle for the bottom; two 3¾-by-1½-inch rectangles and two 2¾-by-1½-inch rectangles for the sides; and one 4-by-3-inch rectangle for the lid. Set aside. Grease and flour two baking sheets.

To prepare the cookie dough, combine the molasses, butter, egg, baking soda, and spices in a large bowl; mix well. Gradually add 2½ cups flour to the molasses mixture, stirring well. Knead in enough remaining flour to make a stiff dough. Gather the dough into a ball.

Preheat the oven to 325°. Divide the cookie dough into 2 equal portions. Roll each portion of dough to cover a prepared baking sheet, rolling the dough to a ¼-inch thickness. Arrange the cardboard patterns on one dough-filled baking sheet, spacing the patterns ½ inch apart; cut around the patterns using the tip of a sharp knife. Remove the excess dough, reserving it for rerolling. Remove the patterns and arrange them on the second dough-filled sheet; repeat the trimming procedure.

Bake the cookies for 20 to 25 minutes, or until firm and golden brown (reverse the baking sheets on the oven racks after 15 minutes for more even browning). Remove them from the baking sheets and cool completely on wire racks. Reroll scraps of dough onto two greased and floured baking sheets; repeat the tracing and trimming procedures to make the parts for two additional cookie boxes. Bake and cool as directed.

Place the bottom cookie rectangle, top side up, on a board covered with greased wax paper. Have the other cookie rectangles close by.

Prepare the melted sugar: place the granulated sugar in a small heavy saucepan; cook over medium heat, stirring constantly, until syrupy and caramel-colored. Reduce the heat to very low, and keep the melted sugar warm (be careful not to let it burn; you may want to place the saucepan in a pan of hot water over very low heat). Working very quickly, dip one long edge and two side edges of a cookie rectangle side into the melted sugar; press onto the long edge of the box bottom, and hold in place until set (about 2 seconds). (Be careful not to touch the sugar; it is very hot.) Repeat with the three other cookie rectangle sides, dipping the edges into the melted sugar and holding them in place on the corresponding edges of the box bottom. Repeat the procedure with the remaining cookie pieces and melted sugar to make three additional boxes.

Cookie Gift Boxes make attractive, edible containers for candy and other holiday treats.

To make the icing, combine the egg whites and cream of tartar in a large mixing bowl. Beat on high speed with an electric mixer until frothy. Add one-half of the confectioners' sugar, mixing well. Add the remaining sugar and beat 5 to 7 minutes at high speed. (*Note:* Royal Icing dries very quickly; keep it covered at all times with a damp cloth. Do not double this recipe. If additional icing is needed, prepare another batch.)

Place small amounts of Royal Icing into separate bowls for each color desired; color with paste food coloring. Pipe desired trim on boxes using a No. 16 fluted tip for borders, a No. 67 leaf tip for leaves, and a No. 2 or 3 round tip for berries. Let dry overnight. Fill the cookie gift boxes with cookies or candy; top each with a lid, and tie together with ribbon, if desired. Store in airtight containers up to 1 month.

*Paste food coloring may be found in specialty food stores or cookware shops.

CAJUN PRALINES

TO MAKE 3½ DOZEN

  2 cups granulated sugar
  1 cup packed brown sugar
  1 cup milk
  ½ cup (1 stick) butter
  2 tablespoons corn syrup
  4 cups pecan halves

In a large heavy saucepan, combine the sugars, milk, butter, and corn syrup; bring to a boil. Cook, stirring constantly, until the mixture reaches 225° on a candy thermometer. Add the pecans and continue cooking, stirring constantly, until the mixture reaches soft ball stage (236°). Remove from heat and beat vigorously until the mixture just begins to thicken. Working rapidly, drop by tablespoonfuls onto greased wax paper. Let stand until firm. Store in an airtight container.

GRANOLA SNACK MIX

TO MAKE 5½ CUPS

  1½ cups rolled oats
  1 cup coarsely chopped walnuts
  1 cup flaked coconut
  1 cup shelled sunflower seeds
  ½ teaspoon apple or pumpkin pie spice
  ½ cup butter-flavored syrup
  1 cup carob-coated raisins
  1 cup banana chips (optional)

Preheat the oven to 300°. In a large bowl, combine the rolled oats, walnuts, coconut, sunflower seeds, and pie spice; mix well. Pour the syrup over the oat mixture, stirring well. Spread the mixture in a single layer on a lightly greased jelly roll pan. Bake for 1 hour, stirring every 15 minutes. Then cool completely.

Add the carob-coated raisins and banana chips to the cooled mixture; store in airtight containers up to 2 weeks.

DIVINITY CANDIES

TO MAKE ABOUT 2 DOZEN CANDIES

  2 cups sugar
  ½ cup water
  ⅓ cup light corn syrup
  2 egg whites
  ½ teaspoon vanilla extract
  1½ cups coarsely chopped pecans

Combine the sugar, water, and corn syrup in a heavy 1½- to 2-quart saucepan and bring to a boil over high heat, stirring until the sugar dissolves. Then cook briskly, uncovered and undisturbed, for 10 to 15 minutes, until the syrup reaches a temperature of 255° on a candy thermometer, or until a drop spooned into ice water immediately forms a compact and almost brittle ball.

Meanwhile, in a large bowl, beat the egg whites until they form stiff peaks. As soon as the syrup reaches the proper temperature, remove the pan from the heat. Whipping the egg whites constantly with the whisk or beater, pour in the syrup in a very slow, thin stream. (Do not scrape the saucepan; the syrup that clings to it is likely to be too sugary.) Add the vanilla and continue to beat for about 10 minutes longer, or until the candy begins to lose its gloss and is thick enough to hold its shape almost solidly in a spoon. Stir in the pecans at once.

Immediately drop the divinity by tablespoonfuls onto wax paper, letting each spoonful mound slightly in the center. Let stand undisturbed until firm.

CHRISTMAS ALMOND BRITTLE

TO MAKE ABOUT 1½ POUNDS

  ¼ cup sugar
  ½ cup honey
  ½ cup (1 stick) plus 2 tablespoons butter
  1 pound almonds or walnuts, chopped (about 4 cups)

In a heavy skillet, heat the sugar over low heat until it has melted and is delicately browned; watch carefully to see that it doesn't burn. Add the honey and butter; simmer for 20 minutes. Stir in the nuts and cook for 10 minutes. Line a platter or pan with wax paper and drop tablespoonfuls of the brittle onto the paper. Let the brittle harden.

BUTTERSCOTCH POPCORN BARK

TO MAKE ¾ POUND

  2 cups popped corn
  1 cup whole blanched almonds, toasted
  3 six-ounce packages butterscotch morsels
  ½ teaspoon ground cinnamon
  1 six-ounce package chocolate chips

In a large bowl, combine the popped corn and almonds. In a heavy saucepan over the lowest possible heat, stir the butterscotch morsels just until melted. Add the cinnamon; stir until smooth. Pour over the popped corn and nuts, stirring to coat well. Spread the mixture evenly in an 8-by-12-inch oiled baking pan; refrigerate for 30 minutes, or until firm. Place the chocolate chips in a small heavy saucepan. Melt over the lowest possible heat, stirring until smooth. Pipe or drizzle in a lacy pattern over the candy. Refrigerate 15 minutes, or until set.

ALMOND CREME LIQUEUR

TO MAKE 4⅓ CUPS

    1 fourteen-ounce can sweetened condensed milk
1¾ cups Amaretto liqueur
    1 cup heavy cream
    4 eggs
    1 teaspoon instant coffee powder
    2 teaspoons almond extract
    2 teaspoons vanilla extract

Combine all the ingredients in the container of an electric blender; process until blended. Store in a tightly closed jar in the refrigerator for up to 1 month. Serve chilled; stir before serving.

HOT CRANBERRY TEA

TO MAKE 3½ QUARTS

    3 cups cranberries
3½ quarts water
  12 whole cloves
    4 cinnamon sticks
       Juice of 2 lemons
       Juice of 2 oranges
    2 cups sugar

In a large enamel or stainless steel kettle, combine the cranberries, water, cloves, and cinnamon; bring to a boil. Cover, reduce heat, and simmer 12 minutes. Strain through several thicknesses of cheesecloth, squeezing gently. Return to the kettle. Add the lemon juice, orange juice, and sugar; stir until the sugar dissolves. Serve hot.

These holiday desserts present a picture of Christmas bounty. Almond Creme Liqueur waits in attractive bottles. Cookie Gift Boxes (recipe on page 60) overflow with goodies—Butterscotch Popcorn Bark and Granola Snack Mix (recipes on page 61). Front and right, a bowl of star-shaped Swiss Almond Tea Wafers (recipe on page 59). In the background, a modern version of the classic German Stollen (recipe on page 49).

FIRESIDE GLÖGG

TO MAKE ABOUT 1 QUART

Peel from ½ large orange, cut in a spiral strip
1 **teaspoon whole cloves**
¾ **cup raisins**
⅓ **cup whole blanched almonds**
12 **small sugar cubes**
2 **cinnamon sticks, halved**
½ **teaspoon ground cardamom**
1 **bottle dry red wine**
¾ **cup aquavit or vodka**

Stud the orange peel with the cloves; set aside. In a small bowl, combine the raisins, almonds, sugar cubes, cinnamon sticks, and cardamom. Toss gently to coat the raisins with the cardamom. Add the orange peel. In a 3-quart enamel or stainless steel saucepan, combine the raisin mixture with the wine. Bring to simmering over low heat; simmer 5 minutes. Add the aquavit; simmer 2 minutes. Ladle into heatproof punch cups or mugs, including some of the raisins and almonds in each serving. Serve with spoons.

To give glögg mix as a gift: Place the studded orange peel in spiral form on a rack in a 250° oven. Bake until dry, about 45 minutes. Cool; add to raisin-spice mixture. Seal in a plastic bag; tie with ribbon. Include instructions for making glögg. Give with a bottle of wine, if desired.

Nothing is more warming on a cold winter night than a mug of steaming mulled cider, wine, or Fireside Glögg.

TRADITIONAL EGGNOG

TO SERVE 12

12 **egg yolks**
½ **cup superfine sugar**
1 **fifth (about 26 ounces) blended whiskey or bourbon**
1½ **cups dark Jamaica rum**
2 **cups milk**
1 **quart heavy cream, chilled**
12 **egg whites**
1 **tablespoon grated nutmeg**

In a large bowl, beat the egg yolks and sugar together until the mixture makes a slowly dissolving ribbon when the beater is lifted from the bowl. Then beat in the whiskey, rum, and milk. Cover the bowl with plastic wrap and refrigerate for at least 2 hours or, even better, overnight.

Just before serving, whip the cream in a large chilled bowl until it is stiff. Beat the egg whites in a separate large bowl with a clean beater. When they form firm peaks, fold the whipped cream gently but thoroughly into the whites.

Pour the egg-yolk mixture into a large chilled punch bowl, add the egg-white mixture, and fold together until no trace of white remains. Sprinkle with nutmeg and serve at once from chilled punch cups.

ORNAMENTS AND DECORATIONS

Glass beads and birds, cookies and brightly wrapped candies, snowflakes and shiny tinsel, popcorn and painted wooden toys—anything at all may adorn a Christmas tree. The choice is rich, and no wonder: for centuries busy imaginations have been at work, in this country and in Europe, to make the decorated tree the centerpiece of the Christmas season.

When German immigrants brought the custom of dressing the evergreen to these shores in the mid-1700s, they brought prized ornaments along, and a wealth of decorating ideas as well. Their candle-lit trees wore bright paper roses, stars and snowflakes of lead and primitive glass, gilded nuts and apples, cookies, honey cakes and gingerbread, and an assortment of colorfully wrapped candies. A wax angel—symbol of the Christ Child—presided at the top.

Food was central to the decorating. So every December, German families baked huge batches of cakes and cookies, candies and sugared fruits. Some of these goodies were meant to be enjoyed during the holidays, but most were for the tree and would not be eaten until after it came down. Thrifty cooks planned ingredients with care. They used their finest flour for edible pastries and substituted cornmeal, salt, and even glue for those intended just for show.

Not all the homemade decorations were from the kitchen; some came from the fields and woods. Straw was soaked in water until pliable and bent into stars, angels, and bells. Seed pods became containers for tiny dried flowers and grasses. Prickly teasel heads were fashioned into animal shapes. And, as today, popcorn and cranberries were strung into colorful ropes. The scrap box was another source of inspiration. Squares of paper could be twisted into cornucopias to hold candies and nuts, bits of fabric could dress a clothespin doll, and ribbon ends were just right for making into tiny flags.

Many more Germans came to this country from the 1820s on, and by the 1850s their luggage contained Christmas ornaments made of tin, lead, wax, and glass. Their trees fascinated America. But the custom was slow to catch on because Americans had no manufactured ornaments to choose from. Around 1870, imported decorations began to be sold in German communities. Next they turned up in a few variety and toy stores, and in catalogs. Then, in 1880, F. W. Woolworth reluctantly agreed to display a few glass ornaments in his store. To his amazement, they sold out within a couple of days. By 1890 Woolworth was traveling to Germany to select his wares, and soon virtually every American household boasted a few imported decorations.

The first glass ornaments on the scene were solid, heavy pieces shaped as balls and fruits and plainly colored. Within a few years, though, all sorts of more delicate items were available. There were tiny trumpets made from twisted straws of glass, hand-blown and painted vases and birds, fancy globes silvered on the inside or lacquered outside. There were multicolored molded figures of acorns and elephants, ornate churches, and dignified St. Nicks. Silver foil icicles and crinkly wire tinsel added shine, as did chains of tiny beads imported from Czechoslovakia. By far the largest number of ornaments came from Germany, especially the town of Lauscha, near Nuremberg. There, entire families worked year-round to craft Christmas decorations.

Tree trimmers of the time took great pleasure in cardboard ornaments, unusual as that may sound today. These little decorations from Dresden, Germany, were often miniature works of art. They came in many shapes, from alligators and banjos to locomotives and trolley cars. Cut from embossed cardboard faced with gold or silver, most had two sides and were fairly simple. The more elaborate designs were three-dimensional and had hand-painted details. One four-inch steamship came complete with portholes, propeller, and cotton smoke; a two-inch lady's shoe contained a tiny silk drawstring bag—a perfect place in which to hide a piece of candy. Unbreakable, imaginative, and fun, it's no wonder they were such popular items.

The ornaments called "scraps" were pieces of paper printed by color lithography that could be used in a number of creative ways. Some people pressed them against cookie dough or pasted them on cardboard candy boxes to be hung on the tree. Or they attached scrap faces and other details to cotton batting ornaments. Popular scrap themes included Nativity scenes, cherubs, and angels, and the most popular of all was the European-style Santa Claus, a tall gaunt fellow dressed in long dark robes.

By the turn of the century, the choice of Christmas ornaments was staggering. Trees were so laden with glass, tin, paper, and sweets that barely any room was left for candles. But candles there had to be, to give the tree its special glow. The risk of fire was great, so German families tapered their candles to make them more stable and shaped them in spirals to reduce dripping. When they could, they used beeswax or bayberry wax instead of the more flammable tallow. Safer candle holders were developed, too—counterweighted or equipped with a spring clip, or with dishes to catch drippings. Special clip-on glass lanterns shaped like flowers, faces, or fruits held candles but isolated the flame from the tree. Sometimes glass-sided lanterns or metal lanterns with celluloid panels, called Christmas lights, replaced candles. They had tiny oil-burning wicks that floated on water, and they hung from the branches like ornaments.

The electric light bulb was invented in 1879 and quickly adapted for the Christmas tree. It was one of America's unique contributions to the Christmas scene. The first tree lit up in New York City in 1882, with eighty lights of red, white, and blue flashing on and off as the tree revolved.

Early Christmas tree bulbs were simply night lights put to another use. They went from pear-shaped to round, then to a corrugated cone, and finally to the smooth cone so common today. Americans have had some fancy bulbs to choose from as well. The Viennese gave us delicate painted birds, flowers, fruits, Santa Clauses—all hand-blown just for the Christmas tree. The Japanese supplied bulbs in the 1920s and 1930s that looked like popular American cartoon figures. Imagine Little Orphan Annie, Dick Tracy, and Popeye aloft in the tree!

In the mid-1940s and 1950s, the country went wild over the bubble light, a made-in-America bulb with a liquid-filled tube on top and a colored plastic casing. When the bulb heated up, the liquid in the tube reacted in a way that looked like bubbles. Bubble lights are again being produced today, but the colors are not as intense.

The tree may be the most spectacular decoration in the American home, now as then, but it's by no means the only one. The house is filled with the fragrant greenery of wreaths and garlands, and the candles long banished from the tree now light the mantel or glow invitingly in windows.

Decking the halls is as old a tradition as honoring the tree. It stems from the same ancient belief that won the tree its special place—the idea that evergreens must have magical powers to thrive all year round. To the ancients, this quality recalled the renewal of life. Romans would welcome the approach of the new year by nailing laurel to their doorposts and bringing branches inside to hasten blossoming. In northern Europe, people thought that fir boughs harbored friendly spirits. They would twist the boughs into circles and place them on the door or in the house to ward off witches.

All evergreens were held in high regard, but those with berries were especially honored as symbols of fertility. This led to at least one mistaken belief. The white-berried mistletoe, actually a parasite, was thought to preserve the oak tree's life during the winter. Couples stood or kissed beneath its cluster, hoping for fertility and a long life.

The popularity of the red-berried holly has both pagan and Christian roots. It was said to have many powers, not all good. But because of its festive appearance, it has always been a favorite Christmas green. Holly grew wild in colonial America, and once the Puritan ban on celebrating Christmas was lifted, it made its way into countless homes.

In America, the traditional wreath on the front door has become a gesture of friendship and welcome. Most often, a simple round of fresh evergreens topped by a big red bow greets visitors. A wreath often decorates the interior as well. It may be made entirely of pine cones, as in some Scandinavian and Italian families, or fashioned from dozens of dried flowers and herbs, a choice that was popular in England in the Middle Ages. Others of European descent may suspend an Advent wreath from the ceiling, a circle of fir decorated with four candles to be lit one

by one on the four Sundays before Christmas. A purely American custom, begun in the Williamsburg, Virginia, settlement, was to interweave garlands of fruits and vegetables with evergreens.

Where evergreens grow in abundance they often find their way inside in great quantity. Branches of fir and pine spiral up the staircase, drape the mantel, or frame windows, doors, and even pictures. Where conifers are scarce, decorators have had to improvise. During the 1800s, it was a custom on the plains to braid wreaths from strips of padded fabric. Farm families used straw or grapevines, or even dried fruits from the pantry. In the South, boxwood, ivy, and privet supplied the greenery for wreaths.

But greenery has never been the only choice for decking the halls. Apple pyramids were a common sight in eighteenth-century Williamsburg homes. They were made of the finest red apples and small pine cones, garnished with greenery, and sometimes encircled by candles. In homes of French heritage and among the German Moravians who settled in Pennsylvania, little Nativity scenes decorated table tops and mantels. In the Italian *ceppo*, a manger scene, greens, candles, and fresh fruits were arranged in a three-tiered wooden pyramid. The miniature figures in these displays were crafted from wood or plaster and finished in fabric and paint. They were both beautiful to look at and reminders of the deeper meaning of the holiday. Years ago, Portuguese families living on the New England coast placed a candle in each window to welcome visitors to their homes. Modern New Englanders of many backgrounds do the same, but with electric candles.

Wherever you turn at Christmas, there is color.

Opposite page: Garlands of greenery and fruit deck the entrance of a building in Old Town Alexandria, Virginia. The custom of interweaving fruits, and sometimes vegetables, with pine cones and evergreens originated in the Williamsburg settlement two centuries ago.

Right: Delicate silvery hand-crafted glass ornaments from Germany, slender icicles, and paper American flags compete for space on this tree, which is pictured in full on page 145. This grandly decorated tree—as well as the one bearing blown-glass fruits and the feather tree seen on pages 142 and 143—displays ornaments belonging to Christmas collector James Morrison of Georgetown, Maryland. Morrison's collection includes an amazing variety of nineteenth-century Christmas decorations, from antique glass figurals and rare cardboard ornaments to homemade tinsel-trimmed Victorian "scrap."

Color cheers us up in the cold and gray of winter; it makes us feel more festive where winters are mild and the landscape less bleak. Traditional red and green, the colors of the berry and the evergreen, are freely mixed with gold and silver and even blue. A favorite Christmas decoration is the poinsettia, used singly in the home and in clusters and rows in public places. During the winter months, its flowerlike upper leaves turn a brilliant red or, less commonly, a pink or striking white. The plant is native to Mexico, where it has been connected with Christmas for centuries. It was introduced into this country in 1828 by Joel Poinsett, the first American ambassador to Mexico.

Christmas outdoors is as cheerful as Christmas indoors. In many families, children—and parents—eagerly await the annual nighttime trip to the local neighborhood known for its splendid decorations.

Americans pioneered the use of outdoor Christmas lights and sprinkle them abundantly about their yards. But there's more to marvel at in these "Christmas tree lanes" than lights edging rooflines and sparkling in trees and shrubbery. The lawn can be the stage for a life-size Nativity scene, illuminated by spotlights. Or Frosty the Snowman may greet you, even in areas where there's no snow—he might even have a tumbleweed body. A mechanical Santa may be working in a toy-filled workshop, aided by elves. Or, up on the rooftop, an illuminated plastic Santa may have started his climb down the chimney, leaving his eight tiny reindeer waiting patiently nearby.

Indoors or out, on the tree or on the mantel, decorations help set the Christmas mood. On pages 75 to 91 you will find instructions for creating some special holiday ornaments of your own. 🎄

Above: Paper candy holders commonly decorated Victorian Christmas trees. This red and gold cornucopia, 8 inches tall, was manufactured in 1877 by Cornell & Shelton, Birmingham, Connecticut, with color lithography by L. Prang & Co. of Boston. The tapered candy box, circa 1880, was probably given to drugstore customers to carry their Christmas candies home.

Right: This handsome red and white Santa Claus stands 19½ inches tall. The home-assembled figure has an upper body of chromolithographed die-cut scrap. The lower part is fashioned from white cotton batting decorated with foil stars and a crepe-paper border. The cornucopias and Santa are from the collection of John L. Grossman.

The ornaments on this page once graced Victorian-era Christmas trees.

Top left: Tinsel ornaments, more durable and less expensive than glass ones, were sold by mail-order firms like Sears, Roebuck & Co.

Top right: Wax figures were popular from the 1870s well into the twentieth century.

Middle left: These lacquered canines are examples of molded glass figurals hand-painted in Lauscha, Germany.

Middle right: Paper sails, tiny American flags, and crinkled wire tinsel embellish these fanciful glass ornaments made in Germany.

Bottom left: Victorian families often made decorations from paper "scrap" such as this colorful page printed in Germany.

Bottom right: Pressed cotton ornaments were made by folding and glueing the material over a cardboard or wire frame and then sculpting it into the desired shape.

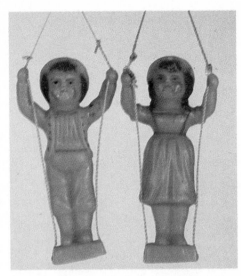

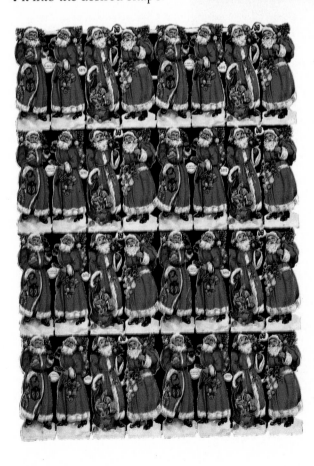

Left: Christmas enthusiast Bruce Catts, of New York City, designs and constructs replicas of Victorian decorations. This tree, lavishly trimmed with his creations, is shown in full on page 145.

Above: Even though they created a fire hazard, candles added a special glow to nineteenth-century trees that electric bulbs can't duplicate.

Left: Crafted in a folk-art style, this hooked rug depicts the hustle and bustle of Christmas morning in a large American family. Grandmother rocks the baby by the fire; mother reaches for a stocking hung in a tree trimmed with mostly edible ornaments; and father attempts to quiet the group of excited youngsters trying out their new toys. Probably hung as a wall decoration, this colorful rug was made around 1930.

Left: American folk art decorates the 1975 Blue Room tree at the White House. In keeping with the theme of an old-fashioned Christmas, First Lady Betty Ford requested that ornaments preserve a traditional feeling by employing materials typically used in the nineteenth century. Many of the three thousand ornaments were crafted by volunteers of the Colonial Williamsburg Foundation, including paper chains made from white cedar wood shavings, hand-carved miniature weathervanes, tiny baskets fashioned from milliners' supplies, and hundreds of hand-sewn creations.

Below: Blown-glass fruits and vegetables, crafted in Germany in the mid-to-late 1800s, transform this spruce into a garden of delights. The apples, oranges, and nuts traditionally associated with holiday trees are joined by an unexpected crop of vegetables, including cucumbers, carrots, and tomatoes. The complete tree appears on page 142.

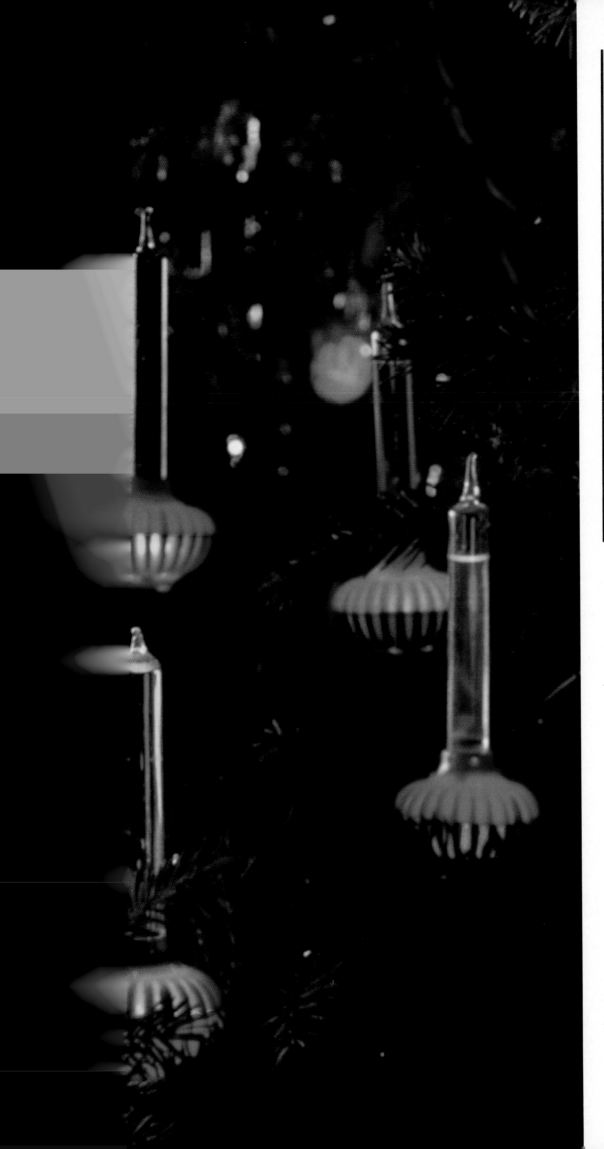

And then there were bubble lights. . . . From the mid-1940s through the 1950s, nearly every American Christmas tree wore at least one strand of these jukebox-like lights across its branches. Bubble lights were first marketed in 1945 by the NOMA Electric Company of New York. They were so successful that within a few years more than thirty styles and brands were on the market. Most bubble lights have three basic parts: a light bulb at the base; a sealed glass vial, partially filled with a liquid chemical (usually methylene chloride), that sits over the bulb; and an unbreakable plastic base that houses the bulb. The heat from the bulb boils the liquid to create the bubbling action. Bubble lights are manufactured today, but few match the color and design of the originals.

DECORATIVE ORNAMENTS TO MAKE

There's something about the approach of Christmas that inspires young and old alike to recapture some of the traditional aspects of the celebration. Store-bought ornaments have their place, of course, but there's nothing like home-crafted items to transform the Christmas evergreen into a family treasure. The following pages offer some ideas and instructions for making traditional decorations and ornaments for the tree and the home.

Below: This charming pine cone rendition of Father Christmas was crafted recently by a Christmas enthusiast, following directions printed in the December 1868 issue of *Godey's Lady's Book*, a popular women's magazine. The instructions are reproduced here, as they appeared in 1868.

Old Father Christmas

Many of our subscribers will be happy to copy the well-known figure on our illustration for their young darlings, and thus make Merry Christmas still merrier. This doll is principally composed of five fir-cones. Two of them form the arms, two the legs, one the body. The boots, which are cut out of wood, are fastened upon a board, and are pointed off at the top. These points, two inches long, are inserted into the fir-cones which form the legs, after holes have been bored into the latter. The arms and legs are fastened on the body with gum and wire. The hands are made of papier-mâché, and are gummed on the arms. The head is also of papier-mâché, the hair and beard of flax. The doll has a waistband of moss to hide the wire. The neck and shoulders are covered with a black crochet comforter, the head with a fur cap. The doll has, moreover, a basket of blue cardboard on the back, filled with confectionery and small toys; on the other shoulder a net filled with nuts and apples; in one hand a miniature Christmas tree; in the other a nutcracker and birch-rod.

Every December Eleutherian Mills, the home of Eleuthère Irénée du Pont de Nemours, near Wilmington, Delaware, opens its doors to offer holiday visitors a glimpse of Christmas as it might have been celebrated by the du Pont family during the nineteenth century.

Above: This simple but elegant tree ornament was fashioned from a peacock feather and a sprig of money plant.

Left: A pyramid-shaped cranberry tree ringed with ivy leaves, here silhouetted against a Victorian-style Christmas tree, makes a festive table decoration. Directions to assemble the 16-inch tree below.

HOW TO MAKE A CRANBERRY TREE

Materials Needed
☐ One rectangle of hardware cloth, measuring 16 by 32 inches (coarse ¼-inch mesh material, available at hardware stores)
☐ Tin snips
☐ Wire for fastening
☐ Sphagnum moss (available at florist suppliers)
☐ Three boxes of toothpicks
☐ Two pounds of fresh cranberries, picked over (Buy an additional package if you want all berries to be dark red.)
☐ Large ivy leaves
☐ Sprig of holly
☐ Low cake plate or stand

Method
1. Trim the hardware cloth into a semicircle with tin snips, keeping the diameter at 32 inches (the radius will be 16 inches). Bend it into a cone. Fasten the overlapping edge with wire at 2-inch intervals. (The greater the overlap, the smaller the circumference and the narrower the cone.) Trim the bottom, if necessary, to level the cone.

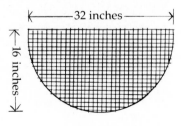

2. Soak sphagnum moss in water to soften, and stuff it into the cone. Let moss drip dry if necessary.

3. Insert a toothpick into each cranberry.
4. Push berry-topped toothpicks into the moss, covering the frame completely.
5. Place the cone on the cake plate and add the finishing touches: a sprig of holly at the top and ivy leaves tucked around the base.

HOW TO MAKE A WREATH

Evergreen wreaths can be easily assembled at home and need little more than a festive bow and a few holly sprigs to dress them up for the holidays. A coat hanger bent into a circular shape makes a handy frame with a built-in hook. Branches trimmed from the base of the Christmas tree may provide enough greenery for the wreath. Otherwise, most Christmas tree lots and plant nurseries sell bundles of evergreens fairly cheaply.

Materials Needed for a Basic Wreath
- ☐ Coat hanger or wire wreath frame
- ☐ 24 to 36 evergreen branches, 6 to 10 inches long
- ☐ Colored florist's wire
- ☐ Florist's tape
- ☐ Wire cutters and scissors
- ☐ Ribbons and other decorative items

Bend the coat hanger into a nearly circular shape, leaving the hook in place. Cover with florist's tape.

Begin winding florist's wire around the frame; then attach the first branch opposite the hook.

Continue wrapping wire around the frame, to prevent slipping. Overlap branches to cover the last attachment and to produce a fuller wreath.

Attach fruit, pine cones, or other decorations, pushing wire through as shown on the apple or wrapping wire around as shown on the pine cone.

While the traditional evergreen wreath is both beautiful and fragrant, many people prefer wreaths that last longer. An alternative is to make an everlasting wreath, one that will give pleasure for years to come.

Left: This wreath, already ten years old, is as lovely as ever. Its natural materials include cones of various shapes and sizes, some cut into rosettes; lotus pods; teasel heads; and dried leaves.

Below left: A weather-beaten red door in Pennsylvania makes a picturesque backdrop for a dried herbal wreath that's as fragrant as it is attractive. Silver foliage intermixes with lavender, tiny red rosebuds, and statice in a delicate-appearing decoration that will last for years if stored carefully.

Below: The same herb wreath rests on a work table, as a Christmas artist begins assembling another. The dried materials—selected for color, texture, and perfume—are first tied into small bunches; then the bunches are layered around a wire wreath frame.

ORNAMENTS FROM NATURAL MATERIALS

Miniature wreaths crafted from dried natural materials make delightful little ornaments. Natural materials are available in fields and woods all across the country; nearly all the materials on this page were gathered in the countryside in eastern Pennsylvania. Florists and craft shops are also a good source. The 2-inch wreaths shown on this page were fashioned from thin, pliable wild grapevines, wrapped with another piece of vine and decorated with wild berries and the tips of strawflowers, clover, wheat, and tiny pine cones. The little heart wreath, also 2 inches in size, was built on a cardboard base with Spanish moss glued on both sides and bits of red statice added for color. Corn-husk flowers and bows can be bent or tied into shape. Soak the dried corn husks in lukewarm water until pliable and keep them moist while working with them by wrapping them in a damp terry-cloth towel.

Ever since the Brandywine River Museum in Chadds Ford, Pennsylvania began decking its halls for holidays in 1973, its Christmas trees have displayed distinctive natural ornaments fashioned by volunteers from plant materials found in nearby gardens, fields, and forests. In 1984, when the museum was invited to decorate the White House Blue Room tree, volunteers spent six months creating three thousand ornaments.

Left: At the museum, two evergreen trees display an eye-catching collection of imaginative ornaments made from dried natural materials.

Bottom right: This wise little owl has a teasel-head body and acorn cup eyes. His spectacles and beak are fashioned from the curved ends at the base of the teasel head, his hat and book from sycamore bark.

Bottom left: A childlike angel wears a patterned robe that's really a large piece of tree fungus. Pheasant feathers form the wings, silky milk-weed hair covers a nut head, and a necklace of strawflowers decorates the robe.

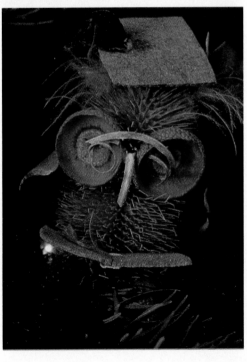

HOW TO MAKE A DRIED-LEAF ANGEL

Materials Needed
☐ White tissue paper
☐ Thin white fabric
☐ Small rubber bands
☐ Stiff white, gold, or silver paper for robe
☐ Dried leaves painted gold or white. Or make paper wings using the pattern below. (Winterthur uses the leaves of the ginkgo, or maidenhair, tree because the leaf's fan shape, veining, and leathery texture are well suited for an angel's wing.)
☐ Yarn, cord, or thin ribbon
☐ White craft glue

Method
1. Roll a small bit of tissue paper into a ball about ¾ inch in diameter.
2. Cut a circle of fabric with a diameter of 5 inches.
3. To form the angel's head, place the ball of tissue on the fabric circle. Bring the fabric together and secure it with a rubber band.
4. Cut a circle of paper with a diameter of 8 inches. Cut the circle in half.
5. To make the angel's robe, roll the paper semicircle into a cone shape around the base of the angel's head, with the ball sticking out of the tip of the cone and the excess fabric inside. Secure the edges with glue. Trim the bottom edge of the robe to make it even.
6. To make wings, attach a dried or paper leaf to the robe with glue. If the angel's robe is made from white paper, gilded wings are attractive; with gold or silver paper, try white.

At Christmas time, the rooms of the Henry Francis du Pont Winterthur Museum in Winterthur, Delaware, are decorated in a traditional manner. The tree shown on this page is trimmed with hand-made paper ornaments—candy-filled cornucopias crafted from gold paper, and a host of little angels with wings fashioned from dried ginkgo leaves. Gilded walnuts and electric candles, a safe substitute for the tallow tapers of earlier days, also adorn the tree. The dried-leaf angel is easy to make at home. On the drawing below, each square equals ½ inch.

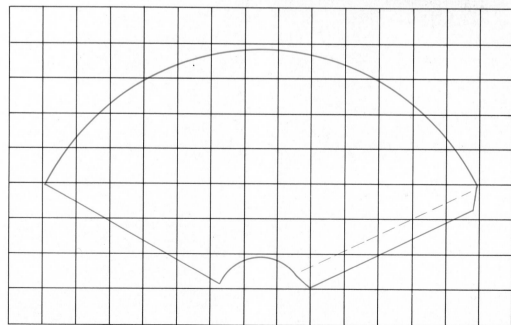

EDIBLE ORNAMENTS

The earliest trees were trimmed almost entirely with edible ornaments: apples and nuts, honey cakes and spice cookies, chocolates and sugarplums. In many families, mothers and daughters worked side by side for weeks to produce Christmas cakes, pretzels, gingerbread figures, and all kinds of cookies. Some were set aside to be offered with coffee when friends stopped by, while others—like the gingerbread house described here—decorated the mantel or table. Families today enjoy the same tradition of creating edible decorations, as pretty to look at as they are delicious to eat.

HOW TO MAKE A GINGERBREAD HOUSE

Baked in broad slabs, gingerbread can be cut into house elements that fit together when shaped with the aid of the cardboard templates described below. The scale can be varied; the plan below provides the correct proportions.

The slabs must be cut while they are warm and soft; they harden when they cool. The house should be built on a board that you can turn as you work. Thick Royal Icing, which dries quickly, cements the pieces together. The same icing can be spread over the roof to simulate snow, and piped onto the walls to outline windows.

Half the fun of creating a gingerbread house is decorating it. Nuts, grated coconut, candied fruits, and small candies such as gumdrops, held in place with icing, are among the traditional ornaments. The recipe at right will make enough gingerbread for your house. Double the icing recipe if you want more elaborate decorations. The following two pages give step-by-step instructions for creating a gingerbread house.

GINGERBREAD

2⅔ cups firmly packed brown sugar
1⅓ cups molasses
4 teaspoons ground cinnamon
4 teaspoons ground ginger
½ teaspoon ground cloves
¾ pound (3 sticks) butter
2 tablespoons baking powder
16 cups all-purpose flour
Pinch of salt
4 eggs, lightly beaten
Thick Royal Icing, following

In a heavy-based pan over low heat, dissolve the sugar with the molasses, spices, and butter. Slowly and carefully bring the mixture to a boil, cool it to room temperature, and mix in the baking powder. Place the flour in a bowl with a pinch of salt and make a well in the center. Pour in the cooled syrup mixture and the eggs, and stir from the center to incorporate the flour. Turn the dough out onto a floured surface and knead; then wrap it in wax paper and refrigerate it for about 30 minutes.

THICK ROYAL ICING

4 cups confectioners' sugar
2 egg whites
1½ teaspoons strained fresh lemon juice

Using a wooden spoon, stir about half of the sugar into the egg whites. Add the lemon juice and beat the mixture with the wooden spoon until it is thoroughly blended; then add the remaining sugar a little at a time, beating well after each addition. Continue to beat the mixture for 15 minutes, or until it is smooth and creamy. The icing can be used immediately or kept for about 30 minutes if covered with a damp cloth. If kept longer, the icing will begin to set.

Making Templates
Using a pencil and ruler, draw the shapes shown here on stiff cardboard. Work to scale—each square on the grid represents 1 inch. With a sharp knife and the ruler, cut out templates for the base, two roof pieces, front wall, back wall, two end walls, four wall supports, and three chimney sections.

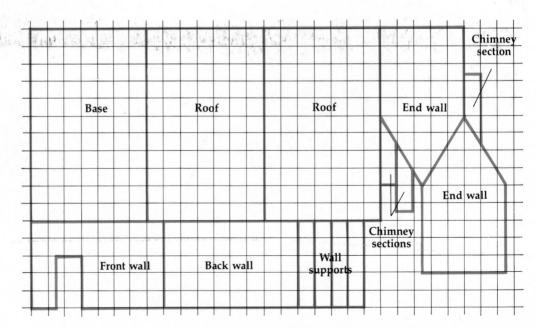

1. Cutting the gingerbread. Make templates according to the instructions on the previous page. Roll gingerbread dough ½ inch thick. Bake it in slabs in a preheated 350° oven for 25 minutes. Lay the templates on the warm gingerbread and cut around them with a knife. The rectangle cut from the front wall will be the door.

2. Beginning the house. Prepare Thick Royal Icing. Set the base of the house on a board or tray. Lay one end wall on the work surface. With a metal spatula, spread a wall support with icing. Lay the support face down parallel to one side of the wall and ½ inch from the edge. Affix a second support to the other side.

5. Erecting the chimney. Join the three chimney sections together with icing, making sure that their tops and bottoms are parallel. Ice the slanting bottom of the assembled chimney and press it into place on the roof on the front of the house so that it rests in a perpendicular position.

6. Icing the roof. Apply icing to one small section of the roof at a time, swirling icing with the tip of the spatula to create a rough finish. Then ice the chimney, leaving the inner side of the chimney plain if you like.

3. Joining the walls. Ice two adjoining edges of both the back wall and the prepared end wall. Join the two walls to form a corner, pressing the side edge of the back wall to the wall support. Set the joined walls in place on the base. Prepare the second end wall in the same fashion as the first, cement it to the front wall, and set the two on the base.

4. Adding the door and roof. Ice one long edge of the door. Working from the inside, secure the door—opening inward and slightly ajar—at the top in the front wall. Spread the top edges of the walls with icing. Gently press one roof piece into position, holding it until it does not slip. Affix the second roof piece. Ice the ridge.

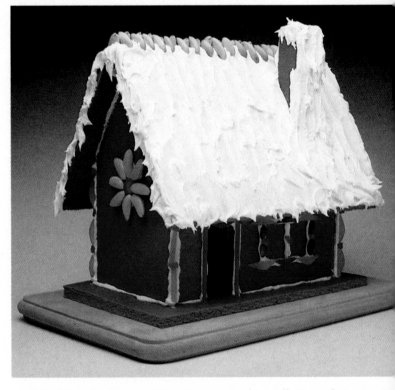

7. Decorating. Make decorations—here, whole blanched almonds, strips of angelica, and candied fruits cut into various shapes. Before the icing hardens, stick almonds onto the roof ridge.

8. Finishing the house. Pipe icing onto the walls to make windows. Use dabs of icing to stick the other decorations onto the walls.

Of all the Christmas traditions enjoyed by families year after year, baking cookies is one of the most eagerly awaited. Experienced cooks mix an extra-large batch of dough, knowing that kitchen helpers will nibble scraps as they roll and cut wreaths and stars, and that freshly baked cookies will magically disappear from the cooling rack. Decorating cookies can be as much fun as making them, especially when they're destined to hang on the tree: Santas suited in red and white frosting, green trees sprinkled with tiny candies, lacy snowflakes dusted with powdered sugar, or sturdy rounds iced to look like glass ornaments. The colorful cookies on these pages offer several imaginative examples of edible ornaments made from one dough recipe. Recipe and directions appear on the opposite page. (See the recipe for Moravian Animal Cookies on page 57 for additional edible ornament possibilities.)

Above: Festive cookies in rainbow colors make terrific, tempting tree ornaments.

Opposite page: The same holiday shapes that fill the centers of the ornaments above may be baked separately (far right) in pairs, then sandwiched together with icing and a popsicle stick to make a doubly delicious Christmas treat (right).

RAINBOW CHRISTMAS COOKIES

TO MAKE ABOUT 2 DOZEN LARGE COOKIES

- 1 **cup (2 sticks) butter, softened**
- 1½ **cups granulated sugar**
- 3 **eggs**
- 1 **teaspoon vanilla extract**
- 1 **teaspoon baking powder**
- ½ **teaspoon salt**
- 4 **cups all-purpose flour**
- **Red and green food coloring**

Cream butter and sugar until fluffy. Beat in the eggs until they are well incorporated. Stir in the vanilla, baking powder, and salt. Mix in the flour one cup at a time. Chill at least 1 hour.

Preheat the oven to 375°. Divide the dough into three equal parts. Color one part green, one part red, and leave one part plain. Roll out dough to a thickness of about ⅛ inch. Cut Christmas shapes, such as stars or bells, out of one color and cut larger circles out of another color. Place the circles on a greased baking sheet. Out of the circles, cut Christmas shapes. Remove the shapes and replace them with different-colored ones. Bake 6 to 10 minutes, or until cookies are firm to the touch. Cool on racks. Decorate the cookies with candies and icing. If desired, form a hole at the top of each cookie before baking so that cookies may be hung on the tree.

COOKIE ICING

TO ICE ABOUT 2 DOZEN LARGE COOKIES

- 3 **egg whites**
- 1 **pound sifted confectioners' sugar**

To make the icing, beat the egg whites until they form soft peaks. Gradually add the confectioners' sugar while continuing to beat the mixture. Beat until the icing is stiff.

CHRISTMAS COOKIES ON A STICK

Cut matching shapes out of cookie dough. Place half of the shapes right side up on lightly greased baking sheets; place the remaining shapes upside down on the baking sheets. Bake in a preheated 375° oven for 5 to 6 minutes, or until firm to the touch. Sandwich cookie pairs together with icing, placing a 6-inch stick between them (use a popsicle stick, a wooden coffee stirrer, or a cocktail pick). Allow the icing to dry; then decorate the cookies with more icing and candies.

 A FAMILY CHRISTMAS CLAYBAKE

In the San Francisco home of artist and sculptor Ruth Asawa, her children—and now grandchildren as well—and their friends have been gathering for years for an annual tradition they call the "Christmas Claybake." Working at the big kitchen table, participants fashion colorful tree ornaments from baker's clay, actually just a stiff dough made from flour, salt, and water that may be colored or not. After they are shaped into angels or Santas or whatever strikes the artists' fancy, the ornaments are baked in a low-temperature oven for above two hours, cooled, and coated with varnish to make them more durable.

Ruth Asawa began making dough figures with her children when they were young. "No one feels he or she has to be an artist to work in dough with kitchen utensils," she observes. To launch your own Christmas claybake, you'll need to stock up on plenty of flour and salt, a few jars of nontoxic powered tempera paint (available at hobby shops and art supply stores), a can of clear-finish varnish, a small paint brush, and a spool of 18- or 20-gauge copper wire. You'll also need some kitchen utensils, wooden skewers and toothpicks, a chopstick or pencil, a rolling pin, and paper towels. Two hints for working with the dough; use the tiniest bit of water when joining the pieces, and wash hands when changing colors.

BAKER'S CLAY

- **4 cups unsifted all-purpose flour**
- **2 heaping tablespoons nontoxic powdered tempera paint**
- **1 cup salt**
- **1½ cups water, approximately**

1. Mix the flour, salt, and tempera thoroughly. If you wish your ornaments to have several colors, make a different batch of dough for each.

2. Add the water gradually, mixing thoroughly with both hands to make a stiff but not sticky dough. If the dough feels too stiff to work, add a bit more water.

3. Turn the dough out onto the table and knead it for 3 to 5 minutes. If the dough seems too soft, sprinkle a little flour on the table and knead it in. Knead colored dough on a nonstaining surface, and make ornaments on paper towels.

4. Let participants make whatever ornaments they wish. Ruth Asawa's daughter, Aiko, demonstrates steps and general techniques for an angel ornament on pages 88 and 89. The dough does not store well, and is best used within 4 hours.

5. To bake, place ornaments on nonstick or foil-lined baking sheets. Bake colored items at 275° to 300°, plain ones at 300° to 325°, for approximately 2 to 2½ hours. Oven temperatures vary, so check frequently during the last half hour to be sure the ornaments don't get too brown.

6. Remove ornaments from baking sheets while still hot to prevent sticking. Cool completely on a rack.

7. Spray the surface with clear-finish varnish, or paint varnish on with a 1-inch brush, filling all cracks and grooves and covering both sides. Allow to dry completely.

Above: Winter berries and holly share the circle of Ruth Asawa's whimsical wreath with a pastel dragonfly, a bee, and an odd-looking beetle.

Above right: This Nativity scene is the joint effort of several members of the Asawa family.

Left and below: In the kitchen, Ruth Asawa (in purple), a neighbor, and a gathering of grand-children and friends are absorbed in the creative disarray of a "Christmas Claybake." Knives, forks, and skewers are pressed into service to fashion ornaments for the tree. Children work on paper towels to keep dough from sticking to the big butcherblock table.

Bottom left: An imaginative assortment of ornaments from the day's claybake.

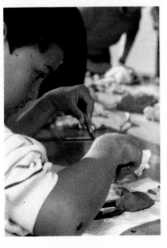

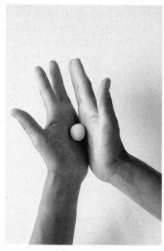

1. You will need 5 colors to make this 4″ angel. Start with the wings. Roll a little white dough into a 1″ ball between your palms.

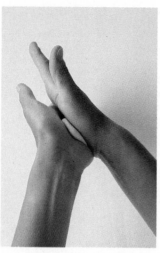

2. Flatten the ball to about ³⁄₁₆″ thick. Shape it with your fingers into a wing. Make two wings.

3. Place the wings on a sheet of paper towel. Use a fork to score the feathers of each wing.

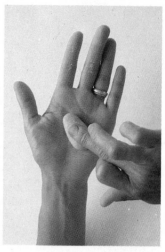

4. Roll some pink dough between your palms into a 2″ ball. With your fingers, make it into an oblong shape.

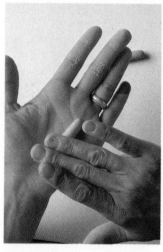

9. Make arms with two 1″ balls of pink dough. Roll each ball into a fat pencil about 2″ long.

10. Press one end of each arm to flatten into a hand. Cut away a little wedge between thumb and hand.

11. Put one arm just underneath one side of the body, the other against the body and over the wings. Leave arms outstretched.

12. Make legs from two 1¼″ balls of red dough, rolling each into a fat pencil. Press against body.

17. Cut the last green piece in two, for sleeves. Make buttons with red dough, pressing in place with a skewer.

18. To make a dove, roll some white dough into a ½″ ball. Roll ball between palms into an oval.

19. Use your fingers to pinch ends up and shape the oval into a bird.

20. Use a knife to score feathers. Make an eye with a toothpick and press on a tiny red beak.

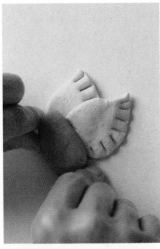

5. Overlap the wings and press gently together. Place body on wings and press again. With a toothpick, dab water sparingly where the pieces join.

6. Form a 1″ pink ball for head. Roll little balls of green for eyes and pink for nose. Press in place with a pencil top or skewer. Make pupils with toothpick.

7. Roll a little ball of red dough for the mouth and press in place. Use a knife to make lips.

8. With your thumb, press the very top of the body to make a cradle for the head and ease head into place.

13. Make angel's dress from a 1½″ ball of green dough rolled into cigar shape. Flatten with rolling pin into a 1″ × 7″ strip.

14. Cut a 1″ × 4″ piece from the strip. Gather the piece along one edge with your fingers to make a skirt.

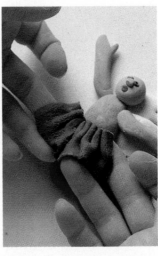

15. Pinch the gathered top to fit the body. Lay in place and press gently. Shape lower edge of skirt with fingers.

16. Make the blouse from the remaining strip of green. Cut the strip in two and press one piece in place on upper body.

21. Place dove on angel's chest and bring arms together underneath. Make hair from a ¾″ ball of black dough rolled into a 5″ rope.

22. Drape black dough over head and press gently in place. Hair may be any color you wish.

23. Make a hanger. Bend a 1½″ length of copper wire around a pencil to form a loop and twist ends. Place hanger in wing.

24. Now the finished angel is ready to bake. Remove from paper towel and bake according to directions on page 86.

These delightful tree ornaments represent just a few of the favorites crafted by three generations of Ruth Asawa's family during their yearly claybakes.

To keep your family's claybake treasures safe for Christmases to come, wrap each ornament in a paper towel, place each one in a small tightly sealed plastic bag, and store the collection in a closet that's room temperature and dry—not in the attic or basement.

THE MUSIC OF CHRISTMAS

On the first Christmas Eve, nearly two thousand years ago, the hills around Bethlehem echoed with song. Sleepy shepherds learned of Jesus' birth from angels singing praises to God and journeyed, amazed, to visit the infant in the manger. As they walked back to their flocks the shepherds, too, sang songs of rejoicing.

People the world over still sing at Christmas time, raising their voices to proclaim the glad tidings of the season. In music we find our most natural expression of joy and wonder, the heart of the Christmas spirit. The Yuletide would be as bleak without music as it would be without Christmas trees, stockings, or mistletoe.

Some of history's greatest composers have contributed to the rich musical tradition of Christmas. Johann Sebastian Bach's *Christmas Oratorio* and Hector Berlioz' dramatic cantata *The Childhood of Christ* are among the masterpieces inspired by the Nativity story. The oratorio *Messiah*, by George Frideric Handel, is sung each year by choruses in communities across the country, and the music to the delightful Christmas ballet *The Nutcracker*, by the Russian composer Peter Ilyich Tchaikovsky, never fails to enchant children and grown-ups alike.

Amahl and the Night Visitors, an imaginative children's opera, tells the story of a lame shepherd boy miraculously cured during a visit by the three kings on their journey to bring gifts to the infant Jesus. The Italian-American composer Gian-Carlo Menotti wrote *Amahl* in 1951 for the National Broadcasting Company, and today it is one of the best-loved works of its kind. Millions of people, laughing and crying with the stubborn shepherd boy and his worried mother, watch Menotti's opera on television every Christmas.

For all the magnificence of these compositions, the most familiar and characteristic form of Christmas music is the carol. Carols are popular songs in the truest and best sense of the term. Their verses convey the Christmas message with simplicity and directness, and their melodies and harmonies are universally appealing. Certainly carols provide the most accessible musical expression of Christmas feeling. Not everyone can negotiate the difficult passages of "For unto Us a Child Is Born" from *Messiah*, but no musical training is needed to join in a chorus of "Silent Night" or "Away in a Manger."

In America, holidays often mean great public spectacles, but we still tend to celebrate Christmas in personal ways. The modest scale and intimate tone of most carols reflect that special aspect of the holiday. Christmas is a time of family visits and cozy gatherings of friends and neighbors around tree or hearth. Grand productions of the great Christmas oratorios may produce matchless musical splendor, but to find the family spirit of the season you must look in the choir loft of a small church during the carol ceremony on Christmas Eve, or out to the street, where a band of strolling singers offers the timeless tunes simply for the joy of singing them—and for the enjoyment of those listening at windows and in doorways. If the carolers linger long enough they may be treated to mugs of steaming cider or chocolate, the traditional reward for sweetening the night with song. Then it's off to neighboring houses, bringing their serenade to other families, their voices drifting away down streets and lanes, fading at last into the Christmas night.

Like Americans themselves, the carols we sing today came to these shores from many lands. From England came "God Rest Ye Merry, Gentlemen," with its "tidings of comfort and joy," and "Good King Wenceslas," which tells of a master who warmed the

Let holly deck the rafters and mistletoe beside,
For token of the holy time, for joy of Christmas-tide.

Opposite page: These angelic singers won third prize in Louis Prang's 1882 Christmas card competition.
Left: A starry night is sweetened by the harmony of a Late Renaissance quintet. This card, by artist Harry Arnuld, was published around 1880.

snow with his footprints so his servant could endure "the rude wind's wild lament and the bitter weather." From France came "O Holy Night," foretelling a "new and glorious morn." German immigrants gave us the popular "O Christmas Tree" and "Silent Night," the restful lullaby of heavenly peace.

And what of America itself? Some of our favorite Christmas songs originated right here. A clergyman from Philadelphia, Phillips Brooks, wrote "O Little Town of Bethlehem" in 1868 to express his feelings about a pilgrimage he had made to the site of Jesus' birth. We owe the enduring one-horse sleigh of "Jingle Bells" to James Pierpont, a Southerner who also wrote songs to rally Confederate partisans during the Civil War. "Away in a Manger," the sweet prayer for little children, was long attributed to the sixteenth-century religious leader Martin Luther, but was actually created in a small country church in Pennsylvania. And some of the most beautiful songs of Christmas grew from the spiritual and gospel-singing traditions of Black Americans. In "Go Tell It on the Mountain," the singer jubilantly sends the story of Jesus' birth "over the hills and everywhere." "Mary Had a Baby" tells of the naming of the holy child.

The music to which carol verses are sung similarly comes from a variety of sources. Many carols are true folk songs, their tunes composed by forgotten minstrels and passed from village to village, and from generation to generation, simply in the singing of them. People knew and sang some carols and hymns for centuries before anyone ever wrote them down. "O Come, O Come, Emmanuel," the earliest carol still widely sung today, dates from the Middle Ages. This and other old carol tunes were probably embellished over the years before assuming the forms familiar to us today. But not all the composers are unknown. In the Alpine village of Oberndorf, the choir master, Franz Gruber, composed "Silent Night" on his guitar because the church organ was too broken down to play. George Frideric Handel, who gave us *Messiah*, also composed the music for "Joy to the World." The verses of "Hark, the Herald Angels Sing" are set to a chorus by Felix Mendelssohn.

Many carols and hymns set the first Christmas to music, memorializing all the familiar details—the manger, the star shining brightly overhead, the three kings, the shepherds, the kindly animals who shared the stable. Some recall the first Christmas musicians themselves, the angels who sang to the shepherds: "Angels we have heard on high, sweetly singing o'er the plain." But there is a secular side to Christmas, too, and many carols simply celebrate the gaiety of the holiday season. Singers rollick through "Deck the Halls" with its cheerful fa-la-las and draw smiles with their demands for figgy pudding in "We Wish You a Merry Christmas." Indeed, many old carols were created for dancing around great fires in open fields on Christmas Day. That custom has all but vanished, but the songs survive—partly because of their pleasing melodies and mostly, perhaps, because of the relish singers take in perpetuating them.

The songs of Christmas also celebrate family and ethnic tradition. There are carols for such traditional Christmas pastimes as sleigh riding and building a snowman, carols for offering food and wine and

gifts, and "counting carols" like "The Twelve Days of Christmas," with its list of outrageous gifts from the singer's true love. Some carols are woven into colorful ceremonies in our country's various ethnic communities. Many Americans of Scandinavian descent begin the holiday season on December 13 by celebrating the feast of Santa Lucia. A young girl wearing a lovely white gown and a crown of evergreen branches and glowing candles represents the saint. She presents the family a special sweet bread, and her entrance is accompanied by the beautiful Christmas song "Santa Lucia."

From the Hispanic settlements of the Southwest comes the custom of *Las Posadas*, a reenactment of Mary and Joseph's unsuccessful search through Bethlehem for room in an inn. (The word *posada* means "inn" in Spanish.) The whole community takes part. On Christmas Eve, a party representing Mary and Joseph walks through the pueblo, or village, stopping at selected homes where they sing carols and ask for shelter. By tradition, the group is turned away eight times. But at the ninth stop, usually a public hall or larger house, they are admitted, and the rest of the townspeople join them for a performance of a Nativity play, *Los Pastores*, which means "The Shepherds."

Christmas songs of recent years reflect both the changing styles of popular music and our more worldly Christmas customs. Santa Claus naturally is the subject of an increasing number of songs like "Here Comes Santa Claus" and "Santa Claus is Coming to Town." Sometimes Santa's helpers also appear in the lyrics—most famously, of course, in "Rudolph the Red-Nosed Reindeer."

Some of the most successful new Christmas songs have come to us from Broadway and from the movies. "Winter Wonderland," "It's Beginning to Look Like Christmas," and "Let it Snow! Let It Snow! Let It Snow!" are all creations of Tin Pan Alley tunesmiths. In 1942, the film *Holiday Inn* introduced a song entitled "White Christmas." Composed by Irving Berlin and sung by Bing Crosby, this ballad to sleigh bells in the snow went on to become the best-selling Christmas song of all time. And "I'll Be Home for Christmas" gave American soldiers of World War II a nostalgic hope for home and the holidays, "if only in [their] dreams."

Pop culture of recent years has produced its share of Christmas hits, among them "Jingle Bell Rock," "Please Come Home for Christmas," and "Blue Christmas." Occasionally a songwriter approaches Christmas in a humorous vein, as in "All I Want for Christmas Is My Two Front Teeth" and "Grandma Got Run Over by a Reindeer," which presents some unusual evidence of Santa's visit.

No one can say which of these recent Christmas songs will endure, nor can anyone say what changes may alter the standard Christmas repertory of carols and hymns. Surely the timeless carols, those that have warmed the hearts of generations, will stay with us. New songs will emerge as they always have, keeping the musical expression of Christmas vital and current. Beyond this, we can only be certain that, for as long as there is Christmas, someone will be remembering the angels and the shepherds—and someone will be singing.

Christmas carols celebrate both the sacred and the secular aspects of the holiday. Some urge us to "rest merry" and "deck the halls with boughs of holly," as the children at the left seem to be doing. Others, like "Silent Night" and "Away in a Manger" evoke the innocence and purity of spirit that shines in the faces of the carolers below.

THE CHRISTMAS CAROL SINGERS

Christmas is traditionally a time of community and family closeness, and music serves to strengthen these bonds.

Above: Townspeople gather to sing carols on the lawn of a church in the Connecticut seaport of Mystic.

Above right: The joy of Christmas is evident on the faces of young choristers as they raise their voices in the songs of the season.

Right: A family in the Midwest has extra reason to be thankful at Christmas, 1945. With their young men safely home from World War II, how can they keep from singing?

Left: A 55-foot Christmas tree in Boston's Prudential Center provides a colorful background for members of a children's choir as they sing "Silent Night" under the direction of Boston Pops conductor John Williams.

Below: In Van Nuys, California, the carolers *are* the Christmas tree.

SANTA CLAUS SOAP

BEST FOR THE LAUNDRY.

MADE ONLY BY

THE N.K. FAIRBANK COMPANY,

CHICAGO, ST LOUIS, NEW YORK.

(OVER)

CHRISTMAS ADVERTISING

It begins soon after Halloween with the first displays set against red and green backdrops in store windows. Before the first snowfall in many parts of the country, decorated trees, surrounded with beautifully wrapped boxes, have appeared in shopping malls from coast to coast. Soon Santa smiles down from billboards and makes personal appearances at department stores, setting children on his knee in a specially reserved area of the toy department. Christmas in America is both a sacred and a secular holiday, at once a solemn religious observance and the occasion for a great national shopping spree.

This was not always so, of course. The colonial settlers of our country (who would scarcely recognize our present-day Christmas if they could return to see it) did not celebrate the holiday with widespread exchanges of gifts. The ones they did give tended to be simple, homemade, and most often presented to children. As the pioneers pushed west, they brought with them a Christmas celebration that was equally modest, in keeping with their austere frontier surroundings. In these circumstances, even the most humble presents brought joy.

But as America began to change from a nation of farmers to an industrial giant, the celebration of Christmas changed also. By the early nineteenth century, factories made available a variety of mass-produced consumer goods—kitchen utensils, clothing, even toys—and manufacturers began to use public notices to sell their wares. Advertisements tailored specifically for Christmas first appeared in the 1820s in New York City newspapers. Two decades later they could be found in publications throughout New England.

Ads to promote Christmas buying did not become really common until after the Civil War, however, and they did not spread to the entire nation until the 1890s. An early and particularly attractive kind of promotional message to holiday shoppers was the trade card, a larger and more elaborate forerunner of today's business card. Many of these were ornamented with seasonal motifs and carefully printed on expensive paper. They were beautifully crafted—outstanding examples of what we now call "commercial art." Soon, however, merchants turned to more public displays—posters, calendars, and newspaper and magazine ads—where they showed their products side by side with such symbols of the season as wreaths and Christmas trees.

By the early part of this century, manufactured goods had largely replaced handmade ones in most American homes, and it had become common to buy rather than make Christmas gifts. Also, many periodicals had begun to circulate nationally, allowing manufacturers who advertised in them to reach potential buyers in every corner of the country. For the first time, the American public regularly saw standardized Christmas images—and it was Santa Claus who was most affected by the expanding publicity.

In 1931 the Coca Cola Company commissioned artist Haddon Sundblom to paint Santa enjoying a bottle of its beverage. Sundblom was able to draw on a number of images. Nineteenth-century illustrators, reflecting the wide range of popular notions about St. Nick, had created figures who were short and gnomelike, thin and elfish, tall and gaunt—even beardless! To Sundblom, however, Santa was a large cheerful sort who looked like somebody's grandfather. His paintings for Coca Cola, which he produced annually until 1968, appeared on posters and in magazines, where they were seen by millions of Americans. They were so popular that the "Sundblom Santa" soon became the accepted portrait of Santa Claus, one that the whole world has come to know. For the first time, the public shared a common idea about Santa's appearance.

While Haddon Sundblom established a new image for an ancient Christmas character in our collective imagination, other advertisers managed to create entirely new characters. The most famous of these appeared in 1939, when the Montgomery Ward Company printed a children's story, written by Robert L. May, for distribution as a Christmas giveaway. This tale concerned a forlorn but unexpectedly heroic member of Santa's reindeer team. It proved so popular that nearly two and one-half million copies were distributed in that first year alone, and the legend of "Rudolph the Red-Nosed Reindeer" was born.

The story of Rudolph became even more familiar in 1947 when the song describing his adventures began to be heard on radios across the country. But radio and television have brought more than Christmas songs and stories into the home; they have introduced a flood of commercial messages as well. In fact, complaints about the increasingly commercial tone of Christmas are nothing new. Long before radio and television appeared on the scene, in the days when our modern Christmas celebration was beginning to take form, clergymen and others worried about the materialism they saw as a threat to the most sacred day of the year. They feared that good will and brotherhood were being replaced by a preoccupation with gifts. Soon, they warned, the original spirit of the holiday would be forgotten. Over the years many religious groups have objected to the coupling of Christmas and commerce, some so strongly that they oppose the symbol of Santa Claus and discourage gift giving. A more broadly based expression of concern is the movement to "Keep Christ in Christmas," which emphasizes the holiday's spiritual values over its material ones.

For the most part, the advertising industry has been careful to avoid the sacred images of Christmas—the Nativity scene, the star, the angels—in designing holiday promotions. Instead, Santa Claus has become the season's "super salesman," called on to sell not only toys and cola but everything from cough

syrup, auto parts, and shoes to whiskey, soap, and chewing gum. Other popular symbols, such as decorated trees, reindeer, and snowmen, as well as Christmas music, are similarly used to promote sales.

There are some obvious benefits to the annual appearance of Christmas advertisements. Americans do enjoy giving and receiving gifts, and Christmas advertisements provide useful ideas and information to ease the burden of last-minute shopping. Holiday catalogs are planned months in advance, and many department stores provide "gift counselors" at year's end to advise shoppers on appropriate presents. Also, some promotional devices contribute to the festive atmosphere of the season. Lights and other decorations transform the plainest shopping districts, and the elaborate mechanical displays in the windows of many department stores are designed with imagination and taste. In New York, it has long been a tradition for families to take outings along Fifth Avenue, where the most spectacular of these can be found. This practice has now spread to many other cities, where animated scenes decorate storefronts and delight passersby. And we all enjoy the many holiday events advertisements make possible, particularly television programs with Christmas themes.

No matter how we view the influence of advertising on the national celebration of Christmas, it seems certain that this aspect of the holiday is here to stay. Both the sacred and material sides of the season are firmly established, and Christmas is big enough to accommodate both. Nativity scenes can coexist with images of Santa Claus and reindeer, and carols and commercials alike will continue to be heard across the land.

Merry Christmas

Happy New Year

No. 1652 Inside $2.00 per 100 Net.
No. 1653 Outside $1.00 per 100 Net.
No. 1654 Brand Top 75cts. per 100 Net.
Also Blank.
Special Price in 1000 Lots.

From SCHMIDT & CO.,
37 & 39 E. 21st. Street, New York.

COPYRIGHT 1911, SCHMIDT & CO NEW YORK

HOLIDAY GREETINGS

Commercial artists in years past used holiday motifs with simplicity and elegance. This cheerful cigar box label dates from 1911.

Opposite page: These three pages are from the original Rudolph the Red-Nosed Reindeer, published in 1939 by Montgomery Ward & Co.

WHERE most reindeers' noses are brownish and tiny,
Poor Rudolph's was red, very large, and quite shiny.

In daylight it dazzled. (The picture shows that!)
At night-time it glowed, like the eyes of a cat.

And putting dirt on it just made it look muddy.
(Oh boy was he mad when they nick-named him "Ruddy!")

Although he was lonesome, he always was good . . .
Obeying his parents, as good reindeer should!

That's why, on this day, Rudolph almost felt playful:—
He hoped that from Santa (soon driving his sleighful

Of presents and candy and dollies and toys
For good little animals, good girls and boys)

He'd get just as much . . . and this is what pleased him . . .
As the happier, handsomer reindeer who teased him.

So as night, and a fog,
    hid the world like a hood,

He went to bed hopeful;
    he knew he'd been good!

In 1939 Robert L. May, a copy writer for Montgomery Ward, was assigned to write a children's booklet as a Christmas promotional giveaway. In 1975, May wrote about the creation of Rudolph the Red-Nosed Reindeer, "And then I found myself wondering. Would this be just another gimmick to clutter a holiday landscape already crowded with jolly elves and sugarplum fairies? But what if this book did more than entertain? What if it carried a message of hope and encouragement? . . .

"I started puzzling over the plot. It should have a triumphant ending, tied to an unhappy beginning. And, of course, it must carry a lesson.

"But what could a little reindeer teach children?

"Suppose he were an underdog—a loser, yet triumphant in the end. But what kind of underdog? . . .

"Outside, the fog swirled in from Lake Michigan, dimming the street lights. Light. Something to help Santa find his way on a night like this. That was it! A reindeer with eyes like a cat. But then he would not be handicapped or an underdog. He'd be a superdeer.

"Suddenly I had it! A nose! A bright red nose that would shine through fog like a floodlight. Quickly I worked up a rough plot about a little reindeer burdened with such a nose, a nose that other reindeer laughed at, but a nose that would help Santa bring joy to others. . . .

"Today children all over the world read and hear about the little deer who started out in life as a loser, just as I did. But they learn that when he gave himself for others, his handicap became the very means through which he achieved happiness."

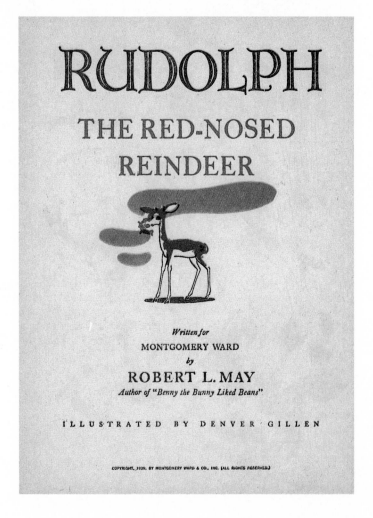

RUDOLPH

THE RED-NOSED
REINDEER

Written for
MONTGOMERY WARD
by
ROBERT L. MAY
Author of "Benny the Bunny Liked Beans"

ILLUSTRATED BY DENVER GILLEN

During the last quarter of the nineteenth century, trade cards were a common and attractive form of Christmas advertising. Designed by skilled artists and printed by an elaborate process of multicolor lithography onto high-quality stock, these forerunners of our modern business card often revealed a rare level of craftsmanship.

Their color and general attractiveness caught the eye of consumers of all ages, and today they are prized by collectors.

For the Little Friends of
LANSBURGH'S

A Merry Christmas and
A Happy New Year.

JOHN NEUN & CO.,
1205 & 1207 S. Broadway,   St. Louis, Mo.

TRY ATMORE'S MINCE MEAT and GENUINE ENGLISH PLUM PUDDING.

WOOLSON SPICE CO'S. Christmas Greeting

Trade cards usually measured about 4 by 6 or 7 inches, although a few were as long as 12 inches. Handed out in shops or tucked discreetly inside product packages, they showed various scenes and symbols associated with the Victorian Christmas. Santa Claus, the decorated evergreen tree, family gatherings, and children at play were favorite themes. The cards publicized a wide range of products. Grocers, milliners, toy makers, purveyors of household goods—virtually every commercial enterprise published trade cards each year at Christmas. Perhaps best-known were the cards of the Woolson Spice Company, which were dispensed with every pound of the firm's coffee. These exquisitely wrought cards, like the one on this page, set the standard by which all others were judged.

E. J. LARRABEE & Co's HOLIDAY BISCUITS.
ALBANY, N.Y.

"Santa Claus," "Kris Kringle," "Father Christmas"—by these and other names the gift-bearing elf has long been a symbol of prosperity and plenty at Christmas time. Artists who designed trade cards a century ago were as quick to call on his services as are advertisers today. St. Nick figures prominently in four cards on this page. Sometimes, though, a clever designer could invoke the holiday without displaying its familiar symbols. In the Frear ad on this page, the depiction of a child play-acting beside a table of toy soldiers suggests that these would make fine Christmas gifts. And the advertisement for Nabisco Sugar Wafers evokes the season by its liberal use of traditional holiday colors and by the cheerful "Greeting" that heads the message.

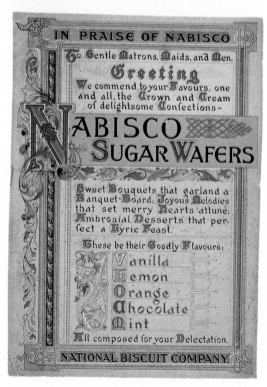

HAVE YOU EVER CONSIDERED the value of artificial light for decorations? What charm would the Christmas tree have without lights among its branches?

Heretofore the candle, with its lurking danger of fire, has limited the holiday lighting to a few anxious moments, and even if no accident occurred, soot and grease were among the unpleasant results. All this is now avoided through the use of a **Ready to Use** Electric Lighting Outfit, composed of strings of miniature Edison electric lamps in colors, which lend themselves to all manner of decorations and will neither scorch nor ignite the daintiest fabric.

With this outfit the most effective lighting effects can be secured by the simple turn of a switch. The little electric lamps burn without attention or possible danger as long as desired. Its possibilities are unlimited for all forms of decorations in homes, halls, churches or other places having electric service.

The outfit is well constructed, light and flexible, absolutely safe and will last for years, giving repeated service at no additional expense. It is neatly packed in an attractively decorated wooden box and forms a most useful and serviceable device, which should be in every electrically lighted home.

These outfits are supplied complete with lamps in the following sizes: 8, 16, 24 or 32 lights. They are so constructed that extra lights can be connected and thus the number of lamps increased or reduced as desired.

MANUFACTURED BY THE
GENERAL ELECTRIC CO.,
HARRISON, N. J.

By the turn of the century, trade cards began to be replaced by more potent and cost-effective forms of publicity, especially advertisements carried in nationally circulated periodicals. But although the medium was new, the use of Christmas as a theme in advertising remained unchanged. Magazine and newspaper ads helped greatly to hasten the public's awareness and acceptance of new products, such as electric Christmas lights (above) and the automobile (left).

Home for Christmas

Snapshots never meant so much as now

CHRISTMAS, 1941—you are sure, by now, that it will have special meaning. As the family comes together for this day of peace and plenty, every scene and episode will be more than ever important . . . precious things for snapshots to capture and keep, fresh as the day they happen.

The timeliest gift of all . . . A bright new Gift Package filled with Kodak Film for every camera owner on your Christmas list. An inexpensive gift yet bright and early Christmas morning it will go to work... And through the day, and all the holiday season, this generous reserve supply of film will be on hand to keep the snapshot record. Get your gift packages of Kodak Film at your Kodak dealer's. Eastman Kodak Co., Rochester, N. Y.

Give Kodak Film

In addition to drawing on such well-known holiday symbols as Santa Claus and reindeer, Christmas advertising frequently addresses other ideas that are closely associated with the season.

Above left: This ad for the Kodak Company evokes peace and family togetherness, two themes that are almost synonymous with Christmas. The image was particularly timely when it was published—exactly a week after the attack on Pearl Harbor plunged America into World War II.

Below left: Large advertising budgets and professional layouts aren't always necessary at Christmas. The display in this butcher shop window captures the spirit of the holiday in a humble, do-it-yourself manner.

Right: Although adults outgrow their childhood playthings, something of the child remains in each of us—so we are reminded in this advertisement for Lionel Trains, long a popular Christmas gift.

To the GRANDFATHERS *of America*

You may not be aware of this, but somewhere a boy is dreaming of owning a LIONEL electric train this Christmas. A score of other delightful gifts may present themselves to your mind, but we assure you, after dealing with boys for almost half a century, that no gift in the world so stirs his imagination as the gift of a swiftly moving LIONEL—with its realistic puffs of smoke, and its exciting whistle. No other gift so completely carries him off into the magic land of make-believe. It may be, too, that the boy in you will find you sprawling on the floor with him this Christmas Day—two fascinated LIONEL railroaders, both young in heart. (May we suggest that you send for the LIONEL catalog?)

LIONEL TRAINS

Send for Color Catalog

— and Book on Model
R. R. Scenery Building

Catalog illustrates and describes in detail all trains and accessories.

Santa Claus has been called the "super salesman" of the Christmas season and has been used to sell almost every product and service imaginable. In contemporary America the range of commercial activities is greater than ever, and Santa's roles have widened accordingly. Sometimes he finds himself in decidedly untraditional places and poses, such as a Hollywood car wash or a motorcycle display window.

Drink
Coca-Cola
elicious and Refreshing

"**M**Y HAT'S OFF to
the pause that refreshes"

Old Santa, busiest man in the world, takes time out for *the pause that refreshes* with ice-cold Coca-Cola. He even knows how to be good to himself. And so he always comes up smiling. So can you. Wherever you go shopping, you find a cheerful soda fountain with ice-cold Coca-Cola ready. You relax and enjoy that tingling, delicious taste and its wholesome, cool after-sense of refreshment. That rests you. Thus shopping does not tire you out. The Coca-Cola Co., Atlanta, Ga.

LISTEN IN
Grantland Rice–•–Famous
Sports Champions –•–
–•–Coca-Cola Orchestra.
Every Wed. 10:30 p. m.
Eastern Standard Time.
–•–Coast-to-Coast
NBC Network.

OVER NINE MILLION A DAY . . . IT HAD TO BE GOOD TO GET WHERE IT IS

We owe our popular image of Santa Claus as a portly, vivacious, and grandfatherly figure above all to artist Haddon Sundblom, who for more than thirty years painted ads for the Coca-Cola Company that featured St. Nick and its product. Before Sundblom began working, Santa had appeared to Americans in a variety of guises. Sundblom endowed him with a bright-red suit, large belt and buckle, ruddy complexion, and round belly. Coca-Cola's annual Christmas ads were so widely circulated—and Sundblom's conception so universally appealing—that everyone came to picture Santa in this way. The first "Sundblom Santa" appeared in 1931, in the ad reproduced at left. By the 1950s, when the ads shown below were painted, Sundblom's image was firmly established in the public's mind.

"...and a Merry Christmas to all"

The pause that refreshes

Drink
Coca-Cola

CHRISTMAS IN WASHINGTON, D.C.

"Christmas," said President Benjamin Harrison in 1891, "should be an occasion of general rejoicing throughout the land, from the humblest citizen to the highest official. . . . We intend to make it a happy day at the White House."

True to the spirit of President Harrison's words, when Christmas comes to Washington, D.C., the whole city lights up. At its heart, the towering National Community Christmas Tree glows with thousands of tiny electric bulbs. Smaller trees nearby, representing the individual states and U.S. territories, echo the big tree. The White House stands bathed in reflected light, and the Capitol dome, a mile away, brightens the skyline.

The nation's capital lights up with parties, too. In a merrymaking tradition that goes back to the early days of the Republic, the White House joins in with splendid festivities. Statesmen and socialites, diplomats and staff—everyone partakes of the holiday good will and good cheer. And the circle of celebration extends further: keeping alive the spirit of giving, as presidents over the years have done, the president and first lady host special parties for some of America's less fortunate citizens.

In the midst of all the public excitement, the famous house at 1600 Pennsylvania Avenue is still just "home" to the president and his family. There, in the privacy of the family circle, Christmas happens in much the same way as anywhere else in America. Stockings are hung from the mantel, friends and family come together to sing by the fire, and gifts accumulate under the decorated tree.

Although it's hard to imagine Christmas without it, the Christmas tree was not always a part of the holidays at the White House. It was unheard of back in George Washington's day. Christmas at his Mt. Vernon home was observed in typical southern style—with noisy firecrackers and horns, and feasting and dancing well into the evening—but there was no tree.

The first president to install one in the White House was probably Benjamin Harrison. The year was 1889 and the place was the Oval Room. The whole family joined in to trim the tree with real candles, and the president himself dressed up as Santa Claus to give out gifts.

The National Community Christmas Tree of 1984 sparkles with a dazzling display of red and white poinsettias. Twenty thousand people gathered to watch President Reagan light up the 30-foot Colorado spruce.

Even though the tradition was well established by Theodore Roosevelt's time, there was to be no tree in his White House. A dedicated conservationist, Roosevelt refused to allow a tree in the presidential mansion and hoped his example would discourage the frivolous cutting of the nation's precious and dwindling forests. But his young son Archie had other ideas. With the help of a brother, he smuggled an evergreen into the house and hid it in his closet, decorating its branches in secret and unveiling it on Christmas day. Dismayed at first, his father was reassured by conservation experts that the proper cutting of Christmas trees could be an asset in thinning overly dense timberlands. "Archie had a little Christmas tree of his own," Roosevelt wrote, apparently tickled in spite of himself, "and each of us got a present off of it."

Over the course of the twentieth century, the "White House tree" has come to include many trees in many places, indoors and out. Mamie Eisenhower so enjoyed decking the halls that one year she placed trees in twenty-six rooms, including the laundry. Generally the first family trims an evergreen of its own, especially when children and grandchildren take part in the festivities. But the elegant oval-shaped Blue Room is always the backdrop for a very special tree, whose colors and decorative theme vary from year to year. Lillian Parks, who worked as a maid at the White House for many years, writes of little Caroline Kennedy's "look of amazement" when she saw the Blue Room evergreen of 1961. What Caroline saw was a tree "decorated with all the toys and wonders of the Nutcracker Suite. There were toy soldiers, flutes and drums, flowers and musical instruments of every toy variety and lollipops and candles and little sugar plum fairies right out of a musical dream."

On the eve of the 1976 Bicentennial Celebration, when the Gerald Fords were living at the White House, the Blue Room displayed a Christmas tree that might have stepped out of America's past. The twenty-foot fir was trimmed top to bottom with traditional folk-art ornaments, hand-crafted from natural materials—dried fruits, corn husks, peanuts, seashells—and embellished further with bits of fabric and yarn. By contrast, the Reagans' elegant 1986 Blue Room tree was dressed in glittering gold, while across the hall in the East Room two spruces clothed in silver stood side by side.

Washington's most famous tree—and favorite ceremony—must surely be the National Community Christmas Tree and the Pageant of Peace. In 1923, President Calvin Coolidge placed a large spruce on the South Lawn and had it strung with lights. Designated as the National Community Tree, it was intended as a shining symbolic reminder to Americans of the spiritual meaning of Christmas. As a side effect, when the president pushed the button to light up the tree, he also promoted the novel idea of using electricity to decorate outdoors. Every Christmas since then, crowds have gathered on the Ellipse to watch the illumination of the great tree and to join the president in a prayer for peace.

By Franklin Delano Roosevelt's time, the lighting ceremony drew thousands of onlookers. Then suddenly, in December 1941, America found itself thrust into the Second World War. The celebration took on a more somber note. At the Christmas Eve lighting that year, with English Prime Minister Winston Churchill by his side, President Roosevelt said, "Against enemies who preach the principles of hate and practice them, we set our faith in human love and God's care for us and all men everywhere." For the next two years, the nation's tree wore no lights, but each of its ornaments carried the name of a serviceman caught up in the fighting overseas.

President Harry Truman had little affection for the city of Washington during the holidays and preferred to escape to his home in Independence, Missouri. He had no particular interest in the tree-lighting ceremony, either, and the public began to lose interest too. But in 1954 President Eisenhower boosted the image of the national tree and brought it prominently before the public eye once more. The tree that year was huge and elaborately trimmed. It was moved to its present location, the Ellipse, on the field between the White House and the National Monument, and the lighting ceremony was changed from Christmas Eve to December 17. That same year the ceremony was expanded into the Pageant of Peace, with participants from nearly every state and many foreign countries as well. At first the Pageant focused on themes of national and world peace, but gradually it expanded to include live reindeer, Santa in his sleigh, and a traditional Yule log that burns night and day.

The National Tree has weathered the storms of our times—the long and painful Vietnam era, for example, and the Iranian hostage crisis, during which President Carter chose not to light the tree. It has survived train derailments on the way to its site, downpours during the ceremony, and winds so fierce that they toppled it over. Now televised in color around the world, the lighting of the tree has become a universally enjoyed spectacle.

Before the Christmas tree had even taken root in Washington, holiday partying was already a firmly embedded tradition across the Potomac River in Virginia, where so many of the nation's early leaders lived. The tradition moved to Washington with John and Abigail Adams. In 1800 they hosted a children's Christmas party, and then a New Year's reception, in the still-unfinished cold and drafty President's House. When the widower Thomas Jefferson was president he asked Dolley Madison, wife of his Secretary of State, to help plan a party for his grandchildren and a New Year's "open house," to which nearly all of Washington was invited. With Dolley's charm and exuberance, the parties were an enormous success. When James Madison took over the presidency, and Dolley became first lady, she organized a series of truly gala Christmas parties: first a great banquet in the State Dining Room; then games, singing, and dancing; and to top it all off, firecrackers and gun salutes out on the lawn.

Because children and Christmas go hand in hand, it's not surprising that many White House parties have included the younger set, not only those of the presidential circle but also less privileged children from all over town. In 1835 Andrew Jackson, an orphan himself, hosted a terrific party for Washington youngsters. The president's French chef created fantastic-looking, delicious-tasting cakes and frozen desserts and concocted an imaginative centerpiece for the table that featured a pyramid of artificial snowballs.

Finding ways to share Christmas cheer with America's needy has been a continuing concern of presidents and their families over the years. One Christmas day Tad Lincoln, Abraham Lincoln's young son, showed up at the White House kitchen with a group of street children. Much to the dismay of the cook, President Lincoln invited them all in for a turkey dinner with all the fixings. In the Depression years of the 1930s Herbert Hoover's wife, Lou, made special efforts to bring a little Christmas joy to needy families. One year she and the Hoover grandchildren sponsored a kind of Santa Claus exchange. The invitation that went to the children's friends read in part, "This is not like the Christmas parties you usually go to, where you get lots of toys and presents to take home, and very many good things to eat. But it is a party where you bring toys and warm gay sweaters or candy, or things other children would like who otherwise would not have much."

In the executive mansion, first families have celebrated the season much the way other American families do—sending out Christmas cards, squeezing in last-minute shopping, enjoying reunions with children and close friends. The Lyndon Johnsons, who brought Texas-style warmth and informality to the White House, trimmed the Blue Room tree with gingerbread cookies, nuts, and popcorn. The Nixons put lighted wreaths in every window and outlined the boxwood hedge along the drive with strings of tiny lights.

To Franklin and Eleanor Roosevelt, Christmas was the most special time of the year. During his three terms in office, they made a particular effort to preserve a home atmosphere and a family spirit. Mrs. Roosevelt loved to shop personally for everyone, including each member of the White House staff. Every year she made stockings for her grandchildren and filled them on Christmas Eve with peppermint sticks, chocolates, little china animals—and always something practical, like a toothbrush or a fancy bar of soap.

In her memoirs, Mrs. Roosevelt writes of Christmas in the White House in words that might apply to countless family celebrations across the nation: "I would arrange piles of presents on chairs or even on the floor, always leaving some toys under the tree and handing these to Franklin to give to the children. . . . Christmas dinner always meant gathering together any of our family who lived in Washington. After dinner, we usually had a movie, and then everyone went home, with the feeling that Christmas had been well celebrated." ⁂

Above: Franklin Delano and Eleanor Roosevelt made Christmas at the White House a family affair. In this 1939 group portrait of four generations, FDR occupies center stage, while the first lady looks on from the end.

Right: In 1941 the Roosevelts extended holiday greetings to their staff with an autographed picture showing the presidential couple engaged in favorite pastimes: FDR was an avid reader, especially fond of mystery novels, and Eleanor enjoyed knitting so much that she made new Christmas stockings for their grandchildren every year.

Left: Harry Truman beams with Christmas cheer on the walkway of his home in Independence, Missouri.

Below: Emblazoned with the Presidential Seal, Dwight D. Eisenhower's official Christmas card of 1955 extends season's greetings on a patriotic note.

Bottom: Christmas Day, 1956, found President and Mrs. Eisenhower in the company of their grandchild on the threshold of the executive mansion.

Season's Greetings
1955

Top: For President and Mrs. John F. Kennedy, holiday celebrations meant a gathering of the large family clan, here including their children, Caroline and John, and a little visiting angel.

Above: On the Kennedys' greeting card for 1962, Caroline's pet pony, Macaroni, gives a sleigh ride across the White House lawn to Caroline and First Lady Jacqueline Kennedy.

Above: President and Mrs. Kennedy share a moment together in front of the tree in 1961.

Right: President and Mrs. Lyndon B. Johnson, their daughters Luci Baines and Lynda Bird, and grandchildren posed for a family portrait on Christmas Eve, 1968, in the Yellow Room of the White House. In her diary, Lady Bird wrote of the evening, "Fire-light danced on the Christmas-tree star—the same star that had been used by the Roosevelts when they lived in the White House."

Below: The presence of the "first family" dogs adds a homey touch to the Richard Nixons' celebration of Christmas, 1971. Daughters Julie and Tricia and their husbands encourage the president to play with King Timahoe, the Irish setter, while First Lady Pat Nixon turns her attention to Vicky, the miniature poodle, and Tasha, the Yorkshire terrier.

Above: First Lady Betty Ford and daughter Susan get some help from their puppy, Liberty, as they add the finishing touches to homemade tree decorations in the White House solarium.

Left: President Jimmy Carter, First Lady Rosalynn, and daughter Amy pose before the 1977 Blue Room tree.
Below: The Carter's 1978 greeting card.

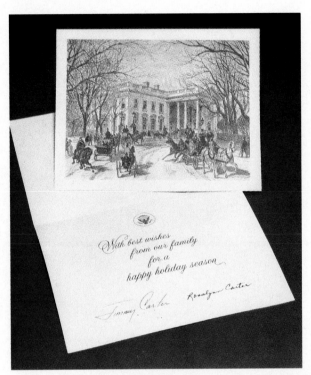

Right: One of Ronald and Nancy Reagan's White House trees for 1986 offers a splendid collection of traditional decorations.
Below: The Reagans' official Christmas card of 1981, by artist Jamie Wyeth.

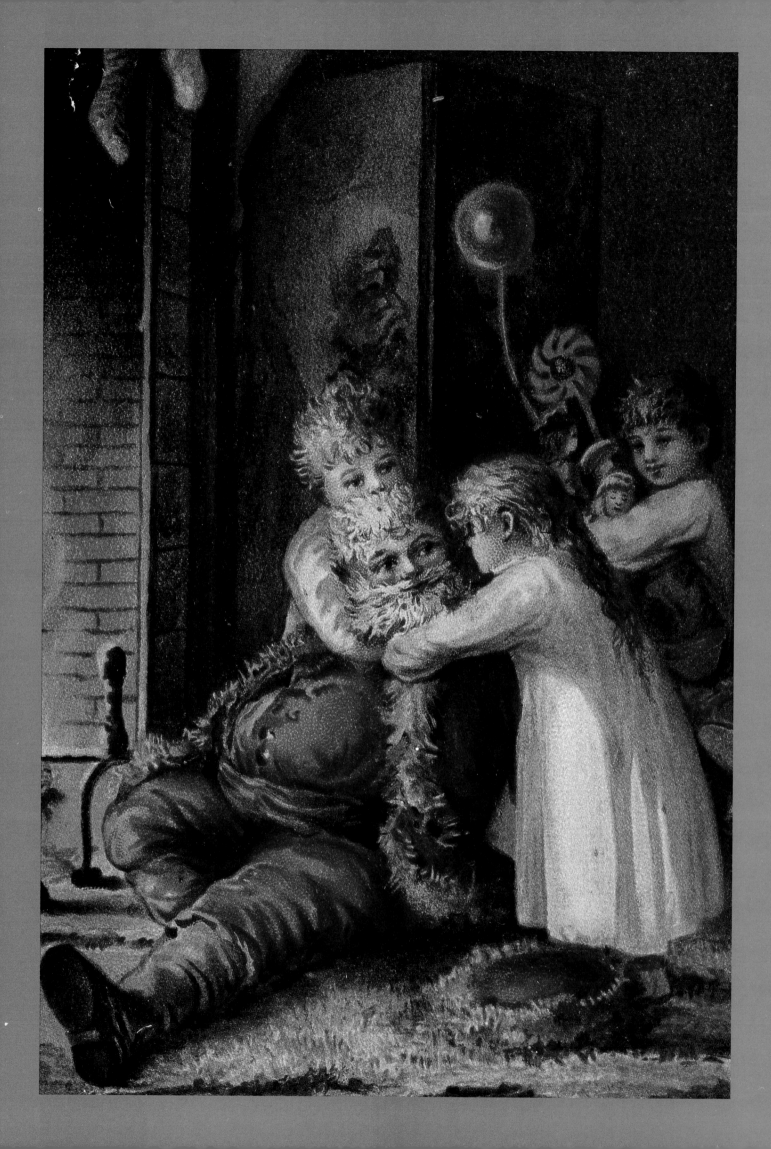

SANTA CLAUS

It's hard to imagine Christmas in this country without Santa Claus. That round, rosy-cheeked, white-whiskered fellow clad in a fur-trimmed red suit and cap is the very picture of the good cheer of the holiday season. Just about every American—man, woman, and child—knows Santa Claus. What's not so well known is that he's a rather modern figure, and an American contribution, at that!

Now it's true that a kind-hearted gentleman bearing gifts for good boys and girls has been associated with Christmas in Europe for centuries, in the form of St. Nicholas. But the Santa we know—the jovial man in red from the North Pole, who is whisked about by a team of reindeer, his sled brimming with toys—this Santa emerged only about one hundred twenty-five years ago. He grew out of the many legends and images brought to this land by European immigrants.

The story of Santa Claus in America begins with the Dutch settlements in New York. When the first Dutch families landed safely in what is now Manhattan on Christmas Day, 1624, they named St. Nicholas the patron of their new-found home. "Sinterklaas," as the good saint was called, had been honored in Holland as a protector of sailors, tradesmen, pawnbrokers, maidens, children—just about everyone. As a champion of children and a generous gift giver, he quite naturally came to be connected with Christmas.

St. Nicholas himself dates back to the fourth century in Asia Minor. There, as a bishop, he is said to have performed kind, even miraculous deeds. He also brought gifts to the needy. In one story, he saved three poverty-stricken sisters from unhappy marriages by tossing three bags of gold coins through the smoke-hole of their home. One sack fell in a stocking hung by the fireplace to dry, inspiring Dutch children to begin the tradition of hanging holiday stockings.

As word of St. Nicholas' good deeds spread northward through medieval Europe, his legend became mixed with local folk tales. He turned into an almost magical figure, embodying traits of the Norse god Odin and of elfin witchlike deities who rewarded good children and punished naughty ones. He also had elements of the pagan figure, Father Christmas, who was tied to midwinter celebrations.

By the time Europeans began to arrive in the New World, St. Nicholas meant Christmas in every Dutch household. Wearing a bishop's red robes, he traveled on a white horse. He was usually preceded by a sinister assistant named Black Pete, whose job it was to weed out naughty youngsters. St. Nicholas then rewarded the good boys and girls by leaving treats and small toys near the hearth. In anticipation, children left straw and carrots for the horse and an apple to appease Black Pete, and they hung their stockings by the chimney. When "Sinterklaas" accompanied Dutch children to New York, he brought along his red robes, white horse, and sack of gifts. But—and American children won't be sorry to hear this—he left Black Pete behind.

With the Pilgrims of New England, it was an altogether different story. They carried no such figure with them to their new homes. Because Christmas in England had lost much of its religious significance, the church fathers had banned its celebration as worldly and sinful. In the new country, families privately held quiet services and perhaps toasted the occasion, but there was no room in their sparse lives for a Santa Claus of any kind. Gradually, though, many Pilgrim families moved away from their original settlements and met up with Dutch Christmas customs. St. Nicholas slowly worked his way into the hearts of the English children and their parents. By the late 1600s he was known as "Sancte Clause," only a short step from Santa Claus, and his annual visit had leaped ahead from December 5—St. Nicholas' nameday—to Christmas Eve, December 24.

Not much appears in colonial literature concerning the whereabouts of Santa Claus during the 1700s. Of all the children's books published during that century, not one even mentions him. It took a long time for old ideas about Christmas to change, but starting in the early 1800s Santa gradually took on the personality that we know today. He was shaped by many hands. People from northern Europe, especially the Scandinavians, but also others of Russian heritage, contributed his fur-trimmed coat, sleigh (drawn by one reindeer or a pair of goats), Far North residence, and troupe of toy-making elves.

Then, as towns sprang up side by side throughout the East, all these people got to know each other's holiday traditions and customs. In the mid-Atlantic states, for example, groups of German descent shared two Christmas figures—the "Christkindl," an angelic child messenger of the new-born Jesus, who often carried the gift of a tree, and "Pelznickol," a scary Nicholas dressed in furs. Pelznickol carried switches to frighten naughty youngsters, but he also carried a bag of toys and treats. These two personages eventually merged into "Kriss Kringle," a merry gift giver closely akin to Santa Claus, except that he tucked presents into the branches of the Christmas tree.

Writers and artists were also imprinting lively visions of Santa on nineteenth-century America. They saw him as a lovable jolly fellow, small in size but large at heart. For Washington Irving, "the good St. Nicholas" was a figure well known to the folks of New Amsterdam (later renamed New York). He could be seen riding over their treetops and roofs, "now and then drawing forth magnificent presents from his breeches pockets and dropping them down the chimneys of his favorites." This passage appeared in *A History of New York*, first published in 1809. The most famous literary image of Santa followed a few years later, in 1822, when Clement C. Moore wrote "The Night Before Christmas." That's when Santa became the twinkle-eyed, dimpled, plump, "right jolly old elf" everyone knows today.

As the frontier opened up and Americans moved westward, Santa Claus did his best to come along. Among their prized possessions, families carried Irving's book and Moore's poem. Pioneer children worried that Santa would not find them in the wilderness, especially in bad weather. Just in case, though, they left cakes for him by the fireplace and, outside, hay and salt for his reindeer. Often it was easier for Santa to make a single stop, perhaps at a Christmas Eve church supper or in the town hall. During the Civil War, children in Confederate states feared that Santa wouldn't come at all. What if he'd been detained at a blockade on his journey from the North or, worse, captured by Yankees? Happily, after the conflict ended, Santa resumed his annual visits without a hitch.

It was during the Civil War era that another important Santa Claus enthusiast appeared on the scene—this time with a pen and sketch pad in hand. Thomas Nast was a political cartoonist for the New York periodical *Harper's Weekly.* He drew his first Santa in 1863 and continued drawing them for another twenty-three years. The artist pictured Santa as a rotund elf, nearly as wide as he was tall, dressed in a furry suit and jaunty cap decorated with holly sprigs. Thanks

to Nast's drawings, Americans met a Santa Claus who looked and behaved like a real person. He had a home and workshop at the North Pole, busied himself year round making toys, studied letters from every good boy and girl to make up his gift list, and kicked off his boots to take a nap by the fire when his Christmas Eve journey was done.

By the turn of the century Nast-style drawings were cropping up everywhere. Santa's suit was now colored red, like Saint Nicholas' robes, and it was trimmed with white fur. But all other resemblance to his dignified ancestor was gone. Santa Claus appeared on cards, in songs, and in countless stories. He received so many letters from good boys and girls that special post offices were set up all over the country. At least two towns—one in Texas, another in Indiana—changed their names to "Santa Claus" to help distribute mail.

The American portrait of Santa Claus needed one final touch—the Santa first painted in 1931 for a Coca Cola advertising campaign. Created by artist Haddon Sundblom, this Santa was no longer a dwarf—in fact he seemed larger than life—but he was still an elf in spirit. He could be seen, year after year, in magazines and on billboards, until well into the 1970s.

The Santa Claus that we all know so well is recognized around the world. He has journeyed abroad with troops during wartime, and he now colors the language and customs of people everywhere. Wherever he appears, he radiates the warmth and good cheer that is Christmas. 🎄

Left: *Kriss Kringle's Christmas Tree* was a children's book published in 1845. This title page is believed to be the first time that a Santa Claus figure was shown with a Christmas tree in this country.

Father Christmas and his escorts—merry maidens and Punchlike jesters—celebrate the season with traditional food and drink. 1860s.

Modeled after the "Jolly St. Nick" described by Clement C. Moore in "The Night Before Christmas," Thomas Nast's classic nineteenth-century illustrations still provide the most familiar image of the American Santa Claus. Here Santa enjoys a leisurely pipe before descending the chimney with his sack full of toys.

Far left: Father Christmas with his staff reflects the continuing influence of St. Nicholas with his Archbishop's crozier. The turkey shows that the saint has found his way to the New World. Charles Goodall, London, 1860s.

Left: This portrait of Father Christmas is unusual because of the lifelike woolly beard and hair attached to the card. The holly wreath is symbolic of a much earlier pre-Christian Druidic tradition. Charles Goodall, London, 1860s.

SANTA CLAUS **121**

A heavily burdened Father Christmas struggles through the snow to deliver his gifts. Although horses and mules were common means of transportation on greeting cards during this period, it's unusual to see a goat pictured in this capacity. Raphael Tuck, London, 1870s.

St. Nicholas is shown here at his most monklike, making his way through the deep woods on a moonlit night, bringing presents to an isolated house. The caption on the card reads, "May the good Saint drawing near, Fill your cup with joy, my dear." Obpacher Brothers, Munich, 1880s.

Kate Greenaway was a popular illustrator of children's books and greeting cards from the 1860s through the 1890s. Her Father Christmas is engaged in a hilarious game of blind man's bluff.

Many of the most powerful images of Christmas are brought together in this lace-trimmed card. Drawn by a single reindeer, Father Christmas' laden sled spills toys and nuts. Perched behind, the Christ Child carries a blazing tree, while the tiny bird in the foreground symbolizes the Holy Spirit. 1880s.

This unusual card shows an early use of red and green as Christmas colors. Traditional greenery—holly, yew, and mistletoe—is a holdover from pre-Christian days. The owl stands for good luck. Of course, the stockings, Santa with his laden sack, and sleeping children are later themes. Louis Prang, Boston, 1878.

This popular image of St. Nicholas knocking at the door goes back to the original story of the generous saint giving to the poor. W. Hagelsberg, Berlin, 1880s.

This huge, black-furred Santa and sleeping children graced an early advertising card.

On this pre-World War I postcard, Santa and Uncle Sam join hands and offer a toast as if to celebrate not only Christmas, but also America's happy prosperity and growth as a nation.

This carved wood Santa Claus, dating to the late nineteenth century, is attributed to Charles Robb, a professional wood carver. The figure originally belonged to a Lutheran church located on Bleecker Street in New York City. For more than forty years, Santa's backpack held service programs and notices of interest to the congregation.

A truly American Santa, this nineteenth-century cloth doll is a three-dimensional representation of Thomas Nast's famous illustrations. In the days when parents still made most of the children's presents, Mother would buy the preprinted cloth, cut out the figure, and stuff it herself.

A Scrooge's-eye view shows Santa in a very different light: actively participating in a family mugging of poor Papa. *Puck Magazine*, 1892.

Humorous Christmas greetings depicting mischievous children are not a recent invention, as this pair of 1911 cards shows. J.J. Marks, New York.

A MERRY
CHRISTMAS TO YOU

His brown fur cap and pipe give this turn-of-the-century Santa a Russian appearance. He is using wax to leave his personal seal on every gift he wraps.

Christmas Greetings.

The religious and secular aspects of Christmas blend in this card, which shows St. Nicholas as Santa Claus, accompanied by an angel, and following a star.

Moving swiftly into the twentieth century, Santa takes on a dapper and stylized, "art deco" appearance around 1920.

A Happy CHRISTMAS

A MERRY CHRISTMAS
To wish you all the joys and toys that Santa Claus can carry.

Ellen Clapsaddle, one of the most popular card illustrators of her day, was noted for the cherubic children she painted. Today, her postcards are sought after by collectors of Christmas art. International Art Publishing Co., New York, 1910.

Above: By the 1970s, Santa and his reindeer had developed concerns and interests even more pressing than their traditional Christmas Eve journey.

Left: In this lithograph by artist N.C. Wyeth, Santa casts a quick glance over his shoulder at his faithful team as he prepares to descend into the sleeping house with his sack full of toys.

Left: Like the rest of the country, Santa in the sixties suffered a severe case of anxiety about the bomb.

Right: The thoroughly modern Santa of the eighties has apparently given up on the North Pole—sun, surf, and sand are more his style.

In his early days, Santa Claus got around on foot, with the aid of his trusty staff. As modes of transportation became more sophisticated, though, he kept up with the times.

Above left: Shadowed by his faithful reindeer, Santa tries out an early two-wheeler. Louis Prang, Boston, 1886.

Above: From his vantage point in a balloon high above the earth, Santa observes the opening of the Panama Canal.

Left: Alert guardian rabbits make sure that Santa-on-skis will successfully complete his rounds. Ca. 1910, Curt Tech Co., Chicago.

Right: In what is surely one of the most unusual modes of transportation ever devised, two white gobblers are harnessed to the overloaded sleigh.

Below: In 1913, artist John Winsch portrayed Santa taking to the skies to scatter gifts indiscriminately to eager children below.

A Joyous Christmas

Below: When all is said and done, though, there's nothing more satisfying for all concerned than the traditional means of transportation—a miniature sleigh and eight tiny reindeer.

Happy Christmas

Above: A jolly ride in an open automobile makes it a snap for Santa and his helper to deliver the goods.

The urge to play Santa is irresistible—how many roles are there that spread so much happiness and downright hilarity? On these two pages, celebrities and student Santas indulge that seasonal desire to dress up in red woolens and a long white beard.

At a taping of a 1974 Christmas television special, the temperature in Los Angeles was 100 degrees. No wonder Bing Crosby looks burned out inside that heavy wool suit!

Santa-on-a-cycle Bob Hope and motorcycle cop Phil Silvers clown it up for a 1967 television special.

Who is that crawling out of the chimney to be met by a crowd of adoring fans? Why, it's Santa Jimmy Durante!

Above: Can you guess the identities of these celebrity Santas? Left to right, they are Cybill Shepherd, William Shatner, and Mr. T with helper Nancy Reagan.

Not all would-be Santas start out famous. Here thirteen University of Santa Claus students, class of 1985, demonstrate the transforming power of curly beards and the classic red suit.

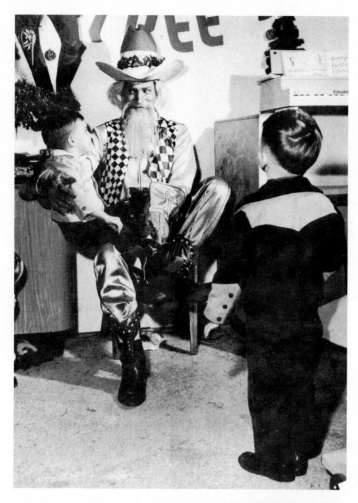

Ever since Santa started to come down from the North Pole for personal appearances in department stores, shopping malls, and parades, his relationship with the children of America has been intensely personal.

Left: A Texas-style Santa called Josh Jingle in a Dallas department store.

Below: In New York's Chinatown, Santa gives two youngsters a preview of what they can expect to find under the tree.

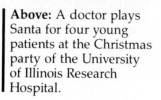
Above: A doctor plays Santa for four young patients at the Christmas party of the University of Illinois Research Hospital.

Below: Not every child loves Santa all the time. These little girls seem to be saying, "Mama! Get me out of here!"

Above: It's not every youngster who gets to meet the great Rudolph in person.

THE CHRISTMAS TREE

Choosing and bringing home the Christmas tree is a happy time for families all across America. The only thing that's more fun is decorating the tree once it's home.

For city dwellers, getting a tree usually means a trip to a nearby corner lot where fir, spruce, and pine trees cluster together under cheerful strings of colored lights. Or the family may go on a longer outing to a Christmas tree farm, where they can pick from acre upon acre of fragrant evergreens of every size. In some parts of the country, folks can still step out the front door, walk a little way into the woods, and help themselves.

Wherever they get it, almost every household in America puts up some kind of Christmas tree, for the tree and its trimmings are as much a part of the season as Santa Claus. Like Santa, the evergreen owes its special position today to the legends surrounding it in old-world traditions, both Christian and pagan.

In ancient times, evergreens were thought to possess almost mystical powers. This was because they continued to flourish when other trees stood bare and gray in December. The evergreen's winter fruits of cones and colorful berries were a sign of life, fertility, and the promise of spring. In some cultures, the thick protective boughs were thought to harbor friendly spirits hiding from winter storms.

The custom of decorating the tree, or using it in decorative ways, is a very old one. The Roman poet Virgil wrote of decorating pine trees to please the fertility god Bacchus. Another practice was to bring small trees or cut boughs indoors to act as lucky charms for the coming spring and to give shelter to the spirits. People held some of the same superstitions about evergreens as about fire—both were seen as symbols of renewed life. Evergreen and fire were joined in blazing bonfires, logs burning on the home hearth, and candles placed on or near the ceremonial tree.

During the Middle Ages, the evergreen took on a new role. The early Christian church held miracle and mystery plays at the Christmas season to teach its congregations about the Bible. In these plays, a fir tree hung with apples reminded people of Adam and Eve's expulsion from the Garden of Eden. Gradually it became the custom in Germany, England, and Scandinavia to build a wooden pyramid shaped like a fir. Some families kept the form simple, placing candles on the branchlike tiers and an apple at the top. Others stuffed real boughs into the triangular frame and piled them with fruits, candles, and trinkets. Germans often placed this decorated wooden pyramid and an unadorned fir tree side by side. Over time the two trees became one, the fresh and fragrant evergreen inheriting all the trimmings of the wooden candlestick—and more.

The custom of displaying a fully decorated tree in the home at Christmas began in the sixteenth century in Alsace, then a region of western Germany. Trees were trimmed as creatively as materials would allow—bright flowers of paper and cloth, wafer-thin cookies shaped as angels and stars, sugared fruits, and nuts. Slowly the custom moved north to Scandinavia and west to France and the British Isles. In France and England, though, it never took universal hold because firs were so scarce and other traditions so strong.

In America, the custom arrived with the earliest German immigrants. One of the first American Christmas trees appeared in 1747, in the German Moravian settlement at Bethlehem, Pennsylvania. Although firs were abundant in the area, this tree was a simply decorated wooden pyramid. A Revolutionary War story tells of George Washington and his troops surprising British-sent mercenary soldiers from Hesse, Germany, as they gathered around a candle-lit tree singing carols. That was in New Jersey. In Newport, Rhode Island, another group of homesick Hessians set up trees for the pleasure of the city's children. An 1842 report describes a table-top tree adorned with candles, popcorn, nuts, and homemade paper ornaments—the loving effort of a German-born teacher in Williamsburg, Virginia. Little by little, word of this delightful new custom from Germany spread across the country.

For German immigrants the celebration of Christmas was deeply religious—the *Christbaum*, or Christmas tree, was a symbol of Christ. It was also a time for the family to hold firm to their old-world traditions in this new and sometimes hostile land. Indoors, they decorated the tree with the few ornaments they had carried across the ocean, and with cookies, gingerbread, and candy made just for the occasion. Outdoors, they covered living trees with treats for the hungry birds and animals—cabbages, apples, raisins, popcorn, nuts, and bits of stale bread. Every living thing was meant to share in the celebration.

By 1850, even frontier towns knew about the Christmas tree. There, it was usually easy to find a suitable evergreen. The challenge and fun came in the decorating. Children and adults fashioned scraps of cloth, ribbon, paper, wood—even discarded bits of yellow soap—into ornaments. They made use of nature's gifts, too—straw, seed pods, and acorns.

Where conifers were rare, families came up with substitute trees. On the plains, sage and cedar brush wore red paper chains and nuts silvered with the foil peeled off cigars. On the Texas coast, a sawed-off limb of live oak carried little candles and colorfully wrapped presents on its gnarled branches. Southern families sometimes chose the common sassafras tree. Though bare of greenery and homely in the winter, it became a wonder with its branches full of apples, frosted cookies, toys, paper decorations, and clumps of cotton in place of snow. Just about any kind of vegetation would serve, as long as it could bear Christmas finery.

The decorated Christmas tree reached a splendid new high in America's Victorian households, especially in the cities of the Atlantic seaboard and in San Francisco. Families selected tall firs and, as is common today, placed them on the floor instead of the table top. Parents usually decorated the tree after the children went to bed, for many youngsters believed that Santa Claus brought the tree and its trimmings along with his gifts. These trees glowed with countless candles and shimmering glass ornaments imported from Germany. Small gifts were tied to the branches with bright ribbons. Sweets of many colors and shapes weighted down the thickly covered branches as well, and set children's mouths to watering in anticipation of a post-Christmas ritual that we no longer have. In those days, one of the best parts of the holiday celebration was dismantling the tree, when children got to sample the candies, gingerbread cookies, and nuts that had been used as decorations.

Since the threat of fire from the candles was so great, buckets of water were hidden in the room where the tree stood. Also, a wet sponge on a stick was kept handy right next to the tree to put out minor blazes. It was a good thing that Americans of that era still erected the tree to coincide with the Twelve Days of Christmas. They set it up on Christmas Eve and took it down on January 5, the eve of Epiphany, so the dangerous time was fairly short. Of course, all this changed when the electric light bulb came into use. Without the fire hazard presented by candles, the tree could be cut earlier and remain in place longer. Electric lights changed the look of the tree too, adding to the variety of colors and shapes. By the 1920s, candle-lit trees had all but disappeared.

At the same time as Christmas trees were becoming more popular, the American population was growing and moving to the cities. People began ordering their trees from farmers. Soon, the more enterprising farmers saw a good business opportunity. They began bundling up trees to peddle at city produce markets a few days before Christmas. New York's Washington Market saw its first corner lot in 1851, when a fellow from the Catskills brought spruces and firs down the Hudson on a steamboat. By the 1880s the market was buried in evergreens from all over the Northeast. On the Chicago lakefront, from 1884 until 1933, a family of German heritage brought trees from Minnesota by schooner to sell. When the Christmas Tree Ship arrived, Chicagoans knew the Christmas season had begun.

All of this interest in Christmas trees had its effect. By the end of the nineteenth century, the once-abundant fir was dwindling in numbers. Few tree farmers replanted where they had cut. The pleas of conservationists went largely unheeded until President Theodore Roosevelt added his voice to theirs. By the 1920s, efforts to reseed forests were under way. Shortly after that, Christmas tree farms became profitable ventures. New types of evergreens came on the market—the long-needled, long-lasting Scotch pine and the more traditionally shaped Douglas fir.

Today, these two varieties are the most popular of the Christmas evergreens.

There have been other changes, too. Some families prefer artificial trees for their fire safety, longevity, and convenience. In the 1980s, some of these trees are convincingly real-looking. And many Americans who have gardens buy live Christmas trees, decorating them year after year with strands of outdoor lights, and in the off-season admiring their wild sturdiness. These trees become like family friends.

In fact, few things are as friendly and inviting as the Christmas tree. Like so much else of the American Christmas, the tree is both old and new, linking Christmases past and present. It belongs to everyone, yet for each family it holds a very personal meaning. Knowing about its folklore and long history only adds to its magic. ✄

Below: Brisk winds and blowing snow speed a mother and daughter home with their tree and wreath. This richly colored lithograph appeared as a Christmas card in the late 1800s.

Right: A lull between customers gives the proprietors of this Washington, D.C., Christmas tree lot a chance to warm their hands on a cold December day in 1948.

Far right: In 1942, women supported the war effort by taking over jobs from men called into the service. In a stockyard near Tacoma, Washington, a woman trims tree butts to ready them for bundling and shipping.

Below: Neat bundles of fresh firs arrive in the city in this Ford truck ad that appeared in the December 20, 1930 *Saturday Evening Post*. With its sidewalk Santa and Christmas shoppers, the scene has not changed much since then.

Left: For families all across America, choosing and bringing home the Christmas tree is a special annual event. Their selection made, this Washington, D.C.,couple heads home, Christmas tree and baby son in tow. The photo was taken in December 1948.

Below: At the end of an afternoon's outing in the country in 1961, parents, grandparents, and kids return with trees for several households. The sleds double for transport duty as well as for play.

Right: Unaware of peeking eyes, a nineteenth-century mother hangs toys on a table-top evergreen. It was then common for parents to decorate late on Christmas Eve for the sake of youngsters who believed that Santa Claus brought the tree and trimmed it himself.

Far right: By the turn of the century the tree had increased in stature, often stretching from floor to ceiling. Candles lit its branches, so wise homeowners kept water-filled buckets nearby. This scene is from a typical ad card of the time.

Above: For many Europeans who immigrated to this country from the 1840s on, the celebration of Christmas was simple and sparse. The heavy glass ornaments and manger scene suggest that this family is of German heritage.

Left: Nearly every American community decorates an outdoor tree or two for Christmas. This small crowd of on-lookers will swell when the mayor turns on the switch to light up the tree.

New York City dedicated the nation's first municipal Christmas tree on December 23, 1912, in Madison Square Park. The event marked the birth of the "Community Christmas Tree," an American custom that has now been adopted all over the world.

On the night before Christmas, 1901, these Wisconsin parents put the finishing touches on their family tree. Toy-filled stockings hold such delights as a watch on a chain, stuffed animals, and a limberjack puppet. There are practical presents, too, like clothing and a broom.

Where conifers are scarce, ingenious Americans substitute other trees or even bushes as Christmas trees. This bristly limbed tumbleweed, trimmed with handmade paper decorations, was the center of attraction in a classroom in 1907 in Phoenix, Arizona.

A holiday homecoming can be the best present of all. In December 1945 a reunion on a Kansas farm was especially joyous because it was the first time in several years that the family's Navy sons were able to join the celebration. The family's Christmas traditions included a Santa to pass out presents, singing carols around the piano, and attending church. The finale was an old-fashioned dinner for fifteen—roast goose, rabbit, and home-grown vegetables. Here, everyone is involved in the intricate job of untangling the lights and stringing them around the tree.

Christmas wouldn't be the same without the annual challenge of putting the electric tree lights in working order. This dad in Mount Vernon, Ohio, gets moral support from his four-year-old son as he repairs the extension cord. The year is 1949.

Trimming the tree from top to bottom can have its shaky moments, but this couple has the situation under control. The final step will be to tuck the presents under the evergreen's branches.

Opposite: Glass fruits and vegetables adorn this multicolored floor-to-ceiling tree. Most of the ornaments were hand-blown in Lauscha, Germany, and brought to this country in the 1870s. They recall the old-world custom of hanging apples, nuts, and sugared fruits on trees. Cucumber and corn ornaments were made only for export because in Germany those vegetables were considered unfit for human consumption. Note the miniature farm village lying beneath the tree.

Right: A feather tree forms a delicate frame for embossed paper ornaments, cardboard "scrap," and tiny American flags. This nineteenth-century artificial tree was popular in areas with few evergreens. Goose feathers, left their natural color or dyed green, were stuck into the tiers of a wooden stand shaped like a fir. The tree's base was given special attention—in this case a parade of cardboard animals from Noah's Ark surrounds the tree.

Right: The decorative border and lacy edge of this late 1880s greeting card frame a typical scene from a merry Victorian Christmas—a splendid array of gifts, happy children, and, at the heart of the celebration, a candle-lit tree.

Lightly adorned with red bows, carved animals, and a few glass beads, this simple tree might have stood in a New England country parlor of the late 1800s. The china head of the bonneted doll in the foreground was made in Germany. American children used to cruder, homemade dolls of wood or rag were delighted to receive these finely crafted imports.

Above left: A dove looks for a place to perch on this extravagantly decorated tree. The molded glass figures were made in Germany between the 1880s and the Second World War. At the foot of the tree a wrought iron fence encloses a miniature town.

Above right: One-of-a-kind replicas of fancy Victorian paper decorations give this fir an opulent look. Gold braid, fringe, embossed paper, and bits of cloth and lace lend a three-dimensional quality. Turn-of-the-century toys line the base of the tree.

Right: Cheerful red and white ornaments brighten a tree in an 1840-built Vermont schoolhouse. Copying examples of traditional decorations, school-children made yarn dolls, paper cornucopias and rings, gingerbread men, popcorn and cranberry strings. The beribboned pine cones add a touch of nature.

Above: The splendor of the Christmas tree is not limited to evergreens. In Dallas, a magnificent lighted pecan tree, over a century old, resembles a burst of fireworks against a darkened sky.

Right: In Washington, D.C., the congressional Christmas tree outshines even the Capitol dome. In its spectacular finery, the tree takes on the grandeur of a public monument.

Right: The National Community Christmas Tree of 1980 stands tall and elegant on the White House grounds but carries no lights other than a lone star at the top. President Jimmy Carter decided to forego lights, as he had done the year before, as a reminder of the nation's continuing vigil for American hostages held captive in Iran.

In New York City's Rockefeller Center, a towering 65-foot Norway spruce serves as a breathtaking backdrop to a concert of carols and popular Christmas tunes led by the choir from La Guardia Community College. Hundreds of holiday shoppers join in.

Americans have never let a lack of traditional greenery lessen their enjoyment of the season. In the Arizona desert, a giant saguaro cactus brightens the landscape as gaily as any Christmas tree and welcomes weary holiday travelers to a roadside motel.

GIFTS AND TOYS

Everyone knows the story of the first Christmas, when the three wise kings traveled from afar to offer gifts to the Christ Child. They brought gold coins, the sweet spice frankincense, and aromatic myrrh. Shepherds and peasants offered gifts at the manger, too: a lamb, some doves, a flute, and food for the parents of the new-born baby. Today we carry on this custom of gift giving at Christmas, sometimes in simple ways, sometimes extravagantly.

The American tradition of gift giving has European roots. Our Santa with his bag of toys echoes the European St. Nicholas, who wandered about the continent with gifts for the deserving, coins for the needy, and treats for good children. The kinds of toys that European immigrants brought to this country a few hundred years ago weren't so very different from the favorite playthings of American youngsters today—dolls, toy soldiers, rocking horses, wooden animals, building blocks, puzzles, games.

In the mid-Atlantic region, where German settlers put up Nativity scenes every Christmas, children were allowed to play with the little figures. These tableaux grew from simple manger scenes to miniature worlds of people, animals, and buildings—even Noah's Ark, complete with animals lined up two by two. The ark, in fact, became one of the most popular children's Christmas presents. Sometimes little trains wound their way around the town set up beneath the Christmas tree, just as they do today.

Before the 1850s nearly every gift was made at home. Dolls were carved from wood and given movable joints, or sewn from old linens and stuffed with straw. A rag-doll body might wear a sculptured head of papier-mâché dipped in wax. Dolls in wealthy families might have an imported porcelain face, porcelain hands, and a fashionable wardrobe.

On the East Coast it was possible to order toys from Europe, but expensive and risky. George Washington sent for Christmas presents for his two young stepchildren in September 1759; a mechanical parrot, Prussian soldier, wax doll, and tea set were among the items he requested. But the presents didn't arrive until March of the following year!

Pioneer children received mostly homespun presents, but sometimes their fathers would shop for them in big towns. Then they would get writing slates and pencils, a new shotgun, a fancy toy or two from New York or Charleston, a shiny drum, or packets of firecrackers. In the South, boys and girls pulled from their stockings an assortment of "poppers" and whistles, tin horns, hand-carved toys, and holiday cakes—and an apple and orange, an old-world custom.

America's gift-giving frenzy started after the Civil War. Toy stores had sprouted up by the dozens. All manner of factory-produced items could be bought—wind-up boats and trains, music boxes topped with twirling ballerinas and dancing bears, Victorian doll-houses, and arks with precut, prepainted animals. Also the dry goods store, forerunner of today's department store, had come into its own, offering every gift imaginable under one roof.

It wasn't many years until the weeks preceding Christmas looked a lot like they do today, especially in large cities. Sleds and carriages sat side-by-side in traffic jams; sidewalks were crowded with shoppers, toy vendors, and bell-ringing Santa Clauses; long lines led to the cash register; and stores hung out banners proclaiming "Open 'til Midnight."

Over the last century nearly every year has seen a new type of gift, especially in the world of toys. The electric train arrived in the early 1900s, and so did another long-time favorite, the stuffed teddy bear. Named after President Theodore Roosevelt, the first bear was stitched by hand and put on display in a New York City candy store window. American and German toy manufacturers picked up the idea and produced thousands in time for the next Christmas season.

In the 1920s and '30s, boys might open packages containing hand-cranked dump trucks and matchbox-size cars. Girls growing up in the '40s found dolls modeled after celebrities waiting for them under the tree. In pre-styrofoam days, children of both sexes enjoyed creating a potato person with a Mr. Potato Head kit. And the whole family often got into the act assembling colorful insectlike "cooties" and building elaborate structures with erector sets.

Recent toys reflect the American love of technology. A host of battery-operated, electronic, and now computer-run toys and space-age games have joined more traditional playthings under the Christmas tree. Still, there's not a child of nine or ninety who doesn't smile with pleasure at the little bag of chocolate coins tucked in the stocking—a reminder of the very first Christmas gifts.

Far left and left: Early risers sound the note that Christmas Day is here. The color lithograph, titled "The Reveille," appeared in the supplement to *Harper's Weekly* on December 10, 1904. The modern music maker on her right proves that while trees have changed, Christmas morning hasn't.

Opposite: Suggestions for gift giving came with a moral message in Victorian times. It appears, though, that handkerchiefs as a gift idea have always been in style.

Left: Everybody loves a pretty face—even Santa Claus. In this 1913 greeting card, artist John Winsch dressed an armload of huggable dolls in the height of fashion and captured Santa's mixed feelings about parting with some of his favorites.

Right: Toys that end up under the tree start here in Santa's workshop. Intent on finishing the toys in time for his Christmas Eve delivery, he has rolled up his sleeves, put on his slippers, and set to work.

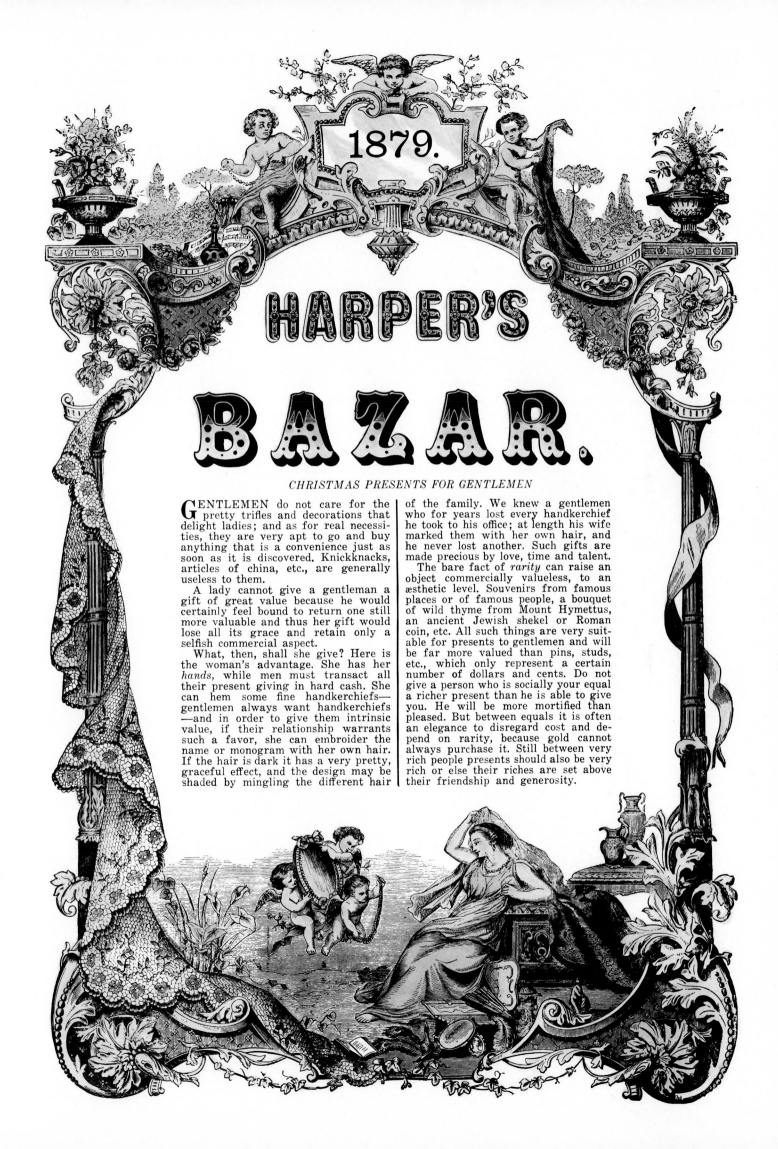

1879.

HARPER'S BAZAR.

CHRISTMAS PRESENTS FOR GENTLEMEN

GENTLEMEN do not care for the pretty trifles and decorations that delight ladies; and as for real necessities, they are very apt to go and buy anything that is a convenience just as soon as it is discovered. Knickknacks, articles of china, etc., are generally useless to them.

A lady cannot give a gentleman a gift of great value because he would certainly feel bound to return one still more valuable and thus her gift would lose all its grace and retain only a selfish commercial aspect.

What, then, shall she give? Here is the woman's advantage. She has her *hands*, while men must transact all their present giving in hard cash. She can hem some fine handkerchiefs—gentlemen always want handkerchiefs—and in order to give them intrinsic value, if their relationship warrants such a favor, she can embroider the name or monogram with her own hair. If the hair is dark it has a very pretty, graceful effect, and the design may be shaded by mingling the different hair

of the family. We knew a gentlemen who for years lost every handkerchief he took to his office; at length his wife marked them with her own hair, and he never lost another. Such gifts are made precious by love, time and talent.

The bare fact of *rarity* can raise an object commercially valueless, to an æsthetic level. Souvenirs from famous places or of famous people, a bouquet of wild thyme from Mount Hymettus, an ancient Jewish shekel or Roman coin, etc. All such things are very suitable for presents to gentlemen and will be far more valued than pins, studs, etc., which only represent a certain number of dollars and cents. Do not give a person who is socially your equal a richer present than he is able to give you. He will be more mortified than pleased. But between equals it is often an elegance to disregard cost and depend on rarity, because gold cannot always purchase it. Still between very rich people presents should also be very rich or else their riches are set above their friendship and generosity.

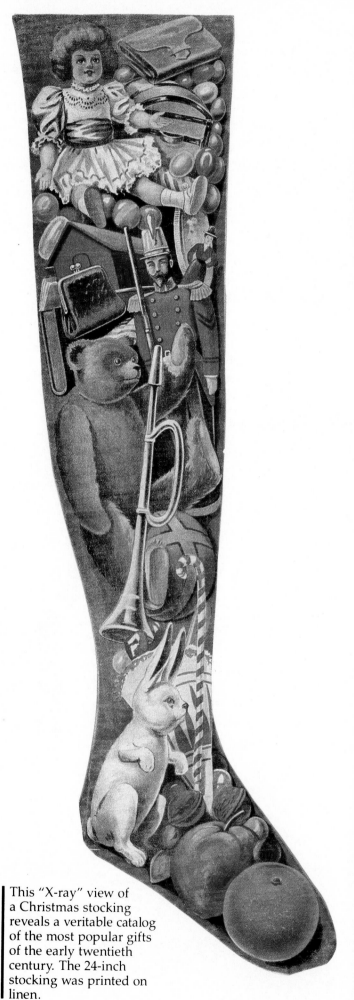

This "X-ray" view of
a Christmas stocking
reveals a veritable catalog
of the most popular gifts
of the early twentieth
century. The 24-inch
stocking was printed on
linen.

Sometimes the best gifts
are the simplest—for
a baby, as simple as
discovering its own toes.

Board games are
an ancient form of
entertainment that never
grows old. Parker
Brothers issued the
"Santa Claus Game" in
about 1910.

Left: An early football player, manufactured in 1915 by Albert Schoenhut of Philadelphia.

Right: Before the invention of batteries, wheeled pull-toys like this racehorse were very popular.

Above: The best loved gift—teddy bears often become like members of the family.

Left: An old-fashioned doll offers an old-fashioned treat of gingerbread and apples.

This endearing stuffed toy is the original "Teddy" bear, born in 1902 and named after President Theodore Roosevelt. Hand-sewn by a New York candy store owner, Morris Mitchom, who made toys as a hobby, this bright-eyed little fellow came into being thanks to a real bear cub encountered by the president. On a hunting expedition, Roosevelt came across a brown bear cub licking honey off its paws. He refused to shoot the defenseless little animal, and let it amble off into the woods. Captivated by the story, Mitchom made a bear from golden plush and displayed it in his store window with a sign labeling it "Teddy Bear." The toy was an instant hit, with the Roosevelt family as well as the rest of the country. Mitchom began producing teddy bears full time and eventually formed the Ideal Toy Company. This historic little golden bear now resides comfortably at the Smithsonian Institution.

Washington *Post* cartoonist Clifford Berryman commemorated Roosevelt's historic refusal in a series of drawings, one of which is shown here.

The gay events of the "HumptyDumptyCircus," pictured in full swing on the table above, and in detail on the left, took place on the pages of an illustrated catalog issued by Philadelphia toy-maker Albert Schoenhut. A few of the actual toys appear in the photo below.

Schoenhut began producing hand-painted wooden circus figures in 1903. Their size (the ringmaster is about 9 inches tall), sturdy construction, and movable joints made it easy for small hands to grasp and work the acrobats and animals into poses that only Big Top experts can perform in real life.

Above, this page and opposite: This turn-of-the-century show, called the "Santa Claus Panorama," employed a two-way crank and roller system to reveal a sequence of twenty-five colorful scenes, in which Santa Claus secretly watches children during the months and days before Christmas. One of many amusements and "social games" from Milton, Bradley & Company, this panorama came with props—including a poster to advertise the show, admission tickets, a read-along script—and advice that "curtains hung in a bay window or doorway and drawn around the case, concealing the operator, increase the effect."

Below: In this "Mechanical Life" picture, circa 1880, the family gathering comes alive with a little help from the clockwork mechanism at the back. As the little girl rocks her doll, one brother beats his drum, the other rides his hobbyhorse, and Grandfather bounces the baby on his knee. At the window, a spying Santa Claus can duck from view in the twinkling of an eye.

Below: Model train sets have ranked among the favorite presents to find under the tree since Lionel Trains produced its first electric locomotive in 1901.

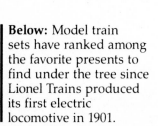

Above: This hard-working McCormick-Deering tractor and thresher set, measuring 19 inches in length, was produced in the 1930s by the Arcade Manufacturing Co.

Above: Colorful cardboard candy boxes were hung from the nineteenth-century tree, along with ornaments and little toys, or were given out as children's party favors. The cheerful scene on this church-shaped box combines several holiday motifs—the Christmas Eve service, a snowy setting, traditional ivy, and red-breasted birds. As midnight approaches, a toy-laden Santa Claus waits to descend the chimney—perhaps to leave a store of chocolates beneath the removable roof.

Above: The magic, noisy moment when the new puppy springs from the Christmas wrappings like a jack-in-the-box marks the start of a beautiful friendship.

Below: Christmas joy is measured in quiet moments, too.

Above: Sometimes the price (and size) of toys is no object, as shown in these 1955 photos. In the picture at the top, a six-foot stuffed bear dwarfs a little boy who perhaps is hoping that Santa Claus can afford the $299 price tag. In the photo below, a wistful young lady eyes a thousand-dollar doll dressed up in lace. What would these items cost today?

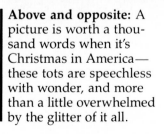

Above and opposite: A picture is worth a thousand words when it's Christmas in America— these tots are speechless with wonder, and more than a little overwhelmed by the glitter of it all.

CHRISTMAS CARDS

"Merry Christmas and Happy New Year!" Americans express this familiar sentiment—in all its variations, plain and fancy—on more than two billion Christmas cards every year. Like gifts, greeting cards are tokens of friendship and good will. They convey feelings that are sometimes difficult to put into words, and they help to span the miles between old friends and distant family members. Christmas cards are messengers of holiday cheer, and more: they provide a fascinating mirror of the times. From the lacy floral treasure that great-grandmother pressed into her scrapbook to the most contemporary humorous greetings, Christmas cards reflect and comment on the American scene—our national attitudes and regional interests, the faddish and the enduring.

Although the widespread sending of cards is recent, exchanging written greetings at the start of the new year is an age-old custom, practiced by the ancient Egyptians and later by the Romans. In medieval Europe, artists made new year's greetings by engraving on wood blocks. They combined pictures of the Nativity or other religious motifs with biblical phrases and expressions of good luck. By the eighteenth century it was customary in England to deliver written messages by hand or to leave cards behind after a visit with a new year's greeting penned in.

Unfortunately, sending these early expressions of good will to anyone farther than a few miles away was difficult and uncertain. Mail that could not be personally delivered had to be entrusted to a soldier or traveler going in the right direction. And the recipient had to pay whatever postage the carrier decided to charge. Fortunately for the future of Christmas cards, in 1840 England adopted the "penny post." With a one-penny stamp, greetings could be sent almost anywhere in the country.

The idea of sending seasonal greetings by mail caught on, and in 1860, a few companies began producing Christmas cards as a sideline to their main business of manufacturing playing cards, note papers, and valentines. In fact, many of these early holiday cards looked just like valentines, with paper lace, ribbons, embossed surfaces, and verses of love. In 1867 Marcus Ward & Company, a London firm, decided to put all its resources into Christmas card design. The company used the latest lithographic techniques and employed a number of fine artists, among them Kate Greenaway, who later became famous as an illustrator of children's books. By 1870, hundreds of Christmas scenes and sentiments were crossing the Atlantic for sale in the United States. But it took the vision and talent of Louis Prang to bring the American Christmas card into its own.

Louis Prang came to the United States from Germany in 1850. Settling in Boston, the young immigrant learned wood engraving, worked as an artist for a time, and then turned to lithography. At first he produced only business cards and novelty items, but then he grew interested in the reproduction of famous works of art. In 1874, Prang decided to print a selection of Christmas cards for export to England. The response was so positive that the following year he printed enough to sell in the home market as well.

The early cards from L. Prang & Co. were small, usually measuring two and a half by four inches, and they were printed on one side only. Many had flower motifs; some of the most striking ones displayed brightly colored bouquets or flowering plants on a black background. The sentiments were short, usually just a simple greeting, such as "Compliments of the Season," or "A Bright and Happy Christmas."

In 1880, Louis Prang initiated a yearly design competition, hoping to attract the most talented artists around. The prizes he offered were substantial—as much as $1,000 for first place. Among the better known winners of the Prang contest were artists Elihu Vedder, Thomas Moran, and Miss Lizbeth B. Humphrey. The entries were displayed at the American Art Gallery in New York. In this way, through the delightful medium of Christmas cards, Prang brought fine art to the attention of the general public.

As artists began to offer striking original designs, Prang enlarged his cards, often to seven by ten inches. One side was devoted to the design itself, and the other side carried the sentiment and a short biography of the artist. With more space for the greeting, rhyming verses and short prose pieces became more frequent. Great care went into creating these cards. Some of them required as many as twenty separate color plates to reproduce, though most were printed with just eight. Always excellent in color quality and finish, Prang's cards cost up to a dollar each. But the high price did not stop him from selling millions of cards in the decade following the first competition.

Between Prang's artistic cards and the inexpensive postcards imported from England and Germany lay an enormous variety of Christmas greetings. The Victorian passion for novelty items extended to paper cards with silk fringes, lace edges, and embossed centers; satin cards with jeweled designs, scented and hung with tassels; booklets filled with Christmas-inspired poetry and verse; and cards cut into holiday shapes—bells, candles, even plum puddings. Some cards folded out like maps; some fit together like a puzzle. Pop-up cards revealed a tiny manger or a tableau of skaters on a frozen pond; others, pressed in the right spot, chirped like a bird.

The motifs of Victorian Christmas cards were just as varied as the materials and shapes. Most did not relate to the holiday as a religious observance; then, as now, card giving was a social rather than a religious custom. Even dedicated churchgoers purchased cards with secular themes. Flowers and plants were favorite motifs, usually stylized, often with an Oriental touch.

The popularity of floral themes probably had to do with the original motive behind new year's greetings: every new year brings the promise of spring and its blossoms. Birds were popular, too, and seashells, butterflies, and bees. Another favorite subject was children, portrayed with a charm and daintiness bordering on the sentimental.

Among the early twentieth-century card makers, a few deserve mention. Rust Craft published Christmas "letters," cards filled with text and bearing only a single red decoration. The Gibson Art Company built a huge business in the 1880s distributing Prang cards, but by 1908 it was producing its own designs. About the same time, A. M. Davis introduced a series of postcards, then launched a line of full-sized greetings. All these card makers stressed sentiment over design.

In 1910 a young man named Joyce C. Hall began importing the same postcards that had competed with Prang's art cards. Selling to merchants in the quickly expanding area around Kansas City, Hall and two brothers were soon able to open their own specialty store. There they sold cards, gifts, and stationery, until in 1915 a fire wiped out their entire inventory. But the brothers turned adversity to advantage: they purchased an engraving firm and began creating their own products. With that decision, Hallmark Cards was born. Now the largest producer of greeting cards in the world, Hallmark offers 2,500 Christmas card designs to choose from every year. As Prang had done before him, Hall sponsored five International Art Award competitions between 1949 and 1960. The first three were restricted to Christmas themes, and many of the works were reproduced on Christmas cards.

The cards of the twentieth century, even more than their Victorian counterparts, function as a mirror of the times. With the world in a nearly constant state of conflict and besieged by the pressures of an ever-accelerating pace, humor—the most healing of qualities—has come to the forefront. And although most of the old themes are still popular, each year they are presented in new ways. A quick glance at the American Christmas card over the past few decades reveals many of society's trends and changes.

The First World War marked the end of the imported German postcard and the start of the industry's rapid growth in this country. War meant that families and friends were separated, and Christmas cards helped bring them together in spirit. Cards that sent hugs and kisses across the miles were in demand, as were cards that pictured soldiers with arms outstretched over the ocean.

The cards of the 1920s picked up on the good times, featuring roadster-driving Santas and stylish flappers, while those of the thirties made light of the bad times. They spoofed the poverty brought on by the Depression and good-naturedly looked forward to better days. The 1940s replayed the theme of separation by war, and patriotic symbols were displayed in humorous ways—Santa Claus carrying the American flag and Uncle Sam in Christmas settings.

In the 1950s, the Cold War advanced silently while television moved noisily into virtually every household. The success of the Russian satellite *Sputnik* accelerated the American space program. Santa Claus could be seen traveling round the globe in a space capsule rather than a sleigh, and relaxing after his rounds in front of the TV.

In the 1960s and '70s, the baby boomers born just after World War II came of age, bringing with them a sense of idealism and an active search for peace. Images of brotherhood and world peace emerged in the cards of the times: the dove, flower children, youngsters joining hands around the globe.

The Christmas cards of the 1980s include both the traditional and the modern. Humor is ever-popular, nostalgia is up, red and green are in, and the Victorian look is back, but tempered a bit. People are exchanging religious cards with a contemporary touch. And the familiar, universal symbols of Christmas are still strong—the brightly ornamented tree, stockings hanging by a blazing fire, Santa atop the chimney, and silent, snowy scenes of Anywhere, U.S.A.

The first known Christmas card was produced by English businessman Henry Cole in 1843 as a way to offer seasonal greetings without having to write out hundreds of personal messages. The three-by-five postcard was designed by Cole's friend, artist John Calcott Horsley. Cole had a thousand copies printed by lithograph on cardboard and water-colored by hand. Despite his good intentions, Cole was criticized for promoting drinking and for attempting "to wed art and manufacture."

Above: Richly colored and beautifully detailed, this 1881 religious card shows Prang's skill at color lithography.

Below: This delicately embossed and bordered card from the 1880s folds out to reveal church windows inscribed with the words and symbols of Christmas and Christianity.

Above: C.C. Coleman's rather busy still life earned third prize in Prang's 1881 competition.

Although Christmas cards of a religious nature were exchanged in the nineteenth century, they were not nearly as numerous as one might expect of the churchgoing Victorian society. Many card publishers, however, creatively combined scriptural subjects, such as the Nativity, the three wise men, and heavenly angels, with secular themes—the home and family, or beautiful flowers and birds. Louis Prang was a master at interweaving the religious side of the holiday into the celebration of hearth and home.

Like the rosy-cheeked innocents created by artist Ellen H. Clapsaddle on page 160, children on the cards of the Victorian era were almost always portrayed as pretty—with round faces, wide eyes, and red Cupid's-bow lips—healthy, well dressed even in nightgowns, and well mannered even at play. More often than not they were pictured as fashionable little adults, neat and good, mischievous sometimes, but never unruly. These youngsters also exhibited an air of innocence and purity that bordered on the sentimental.

A Merry Christmas.

A merry Christmas.

Above: This unusual card was designed in 1882 by Prang competition winner Lizbeth B. Humphrey, one of the first woman book illustrators in this country.

Top: The excitement of Christmas is captured in this 1910 greeting card designed by Frances Brundage. The New Jersey-born artist, who began her career illustrating children's books, went on to become a well-known painter of Christmas postcards.

Above: Tiny visiting cards like this one were designed especially for children. They were often attached to the envelope of a larger card containing a surprise pop-up, trick, or mechanical greeting.

Early Christmas cards were remarkable for the variety of subjects pictured. The message might convey the spirit of the season, but the art usually had little or nothing to do with Christmas and its traditional themes. The seashore was more popular than a snowy field; exotic plants more abundant than holly and mistletoe; melancholy women and wide-eyed children more common than Santa Claus. Flowers and birds rated at the top of the list as favorite subjects, with insects not far behind. Card publishers of the late 1800s often embellished these designs with fringes, tassels, lace, embossing, perfume, and even cut-glass "jewels."

Right: This fancy "Merwy Kissmas" card has it all: silk fringe and tassels, the innocent child, holiday greenery—plus a single rose—butterflies, and, of course, a bird. Designed by Alfred Fredericks, the card won fourth place in Louis Prang's 1882 competition.

Below: The hummingbird was a favorite motif on American cards, this one published by L. Prang & Co. in 1883. Except for the greeting itself, there's nothing at all to suggest Christmas.

Above: The robin enjoys a long association with Christmas in English folklore. This delightful card from the 1880s is one in a series called "The Robins' Tea Party."

Above: Novelty cards were a big hit in Victorian times, especially those that played a trick or worked mechanically. With a pull of the cord, this valentinelike paper bouquet blossoms with mottoes offering good wishes for the holiday season.

Below left: The traveling circus was at its most popular when Prang published this card celebrating baby's first Christmas in 1881.

Below: Monkeys are always up to mischief, it seems. This impish fellow adds a humorous twist to the old cat-and-mouse game.

Left: Elihu Vedder captured the $1,000 first prize in Prang's 1880 Christmas card competition with this portrait of his wife. Fringed and tasseled in gold silk, the card was meant to be displayed on the wall.

Below: Robinson Engraving Co., the publisher of this brightly fringed shamrock, was located in largely Irish Boston.

Below: This card from the 1860s, poked fun at moralistic groups that disapproved of holiday feasting. The illustration captures the essence of the "pagan" celebration: Father Christmas, holding a goblet of wine, is escorted by plum pudding and boar's head, and preceded by two more dinner traditions— the goose and the hare.

Below: Performing-animal cards entertained Victorians with their amusing designs and lighthearted verse. Frog motifs were faddish—painted on china, cast in bronze, and printed on Christmas cards. This one is a Prang design from 1885.

Above: Evocative of storybook illustrations, this lovely 1910 postcard was among the last Christmas cards to use the old color-lithography printing techniques.

Below: Stylized reindeer and block lettering show the influence of the Art Deco movement on this greeting card from 1929. The color-lined envelope adds a modern touch—postcards had gone out of style a decade before.

Top: The automobile brought changes everywhere, even to Christmas cards. This postcard was published by the International Art Co. in 1908.

Above: The gray tones and somber mood of this 1917 greeting card reflect the seriousness of the times. The outbreak of World War I spurred an increase in the volume of cards exchanged. Most of these cards focused not on the war, as this one does, but rather on friendship, family recollections of Christmases past, and hopes for a peaceful future.

From the beginning, Christmas cards have not only served as messengers of seasonal good will—they are also a mirror of the times. Each decade of the twentieth century has offered something new in Christmas cards.

Right: This card from 1934 depicts more than the latest improvements. It also uses some now-common themes: a mostly red and green design, poinsettias, and a cartoon character modeled after a real-life figure—President Franklin D. Roosevelt's Scottish terrier, Falah.

Below right: World War II fostered a large number of patriotic greetings, and the flag became a popular motif. Printed in 1942, just a year after the United States entered the war, this card reflects a commitment to victory. The only hint that it's a Christmas card lies in the word "Greeting."

Below: In this patriotic card from 1943 the flag, representing America and freedom, protectively encases three candles, traditional symbols of peace.

Above: A "Slim Jims" card from 1956 un-folds to wish a Merry Christmas and reveal a light and joyful interpretation of the journey to Bethlehem and the very first Christmas.

Below: After the launching of the Russian satellite, *Sputnik*, in 1957, American cards launched their own spaceships to rocket greetings around the world.

Above: Although the 1950s were years of prosperity, the escalation of the Cold War sparked a need for humor, as in this contemporary card from 1957.

Left: A pert young miss from 1968 is decked out for the season in an old-fashioned outfit that dazzles the eye.

Themes of peace and brotherhood have been popular since the late 1960s. Here an embossed gold and silver card from 1970, meant to be hung on the tree, shows the dove of peace with wings outstretched across the globe.

Elves and animals and candlelit evergreens have been a part of northern European Christmas folklore for centuries. This 1984 greeting captures the magic of a woodland ceremony.

Without a word, this pure white dove from 1980 expresses the universal message of peace on earth.

Ten clever elves, Santa's helpers no doubt, glee-fully apply themselves to the task of forming a greeting from their shadows.

THE NATIVITY

The story of the Nativity, the birth of Jesus, comes to us from the Gospels of Matthew and Luke, the first and third books of the New Testament. Luke's account relates the journey of Joseph and Mary to Bethlehem, where they must go to be counted in the census ordered by Caesar Augustus. Unable to find room in an inn, they take refuge in a stable used to shelter animals. Here Jesus is born and laid in a manger, a trough filled with hay. Nearby, in the hills overlooking the town, shepherds learn of the birth from an angel and rush to pay homage to the infant. In the Gospel according to Matthew, a new and brilliant star appears in the heavens, marking the birthplace, and three wise kings follow its light to the Christ Child.

Although many other stories and symbols have been gathered into the rich treasury of Christmas lore, the Nativity remains the central image of the holiday, the reason for its being. For centuries the scene described in the Gospels—the babe in his humble crib, the holy parents beside him, the shepherds and barnyard animals staring amazed while three resplendent kings kneel in adoration—has moved people of all faiths. No wonder it has long been customary to recreate this scene at Christmas time.

Over the years, the Nativity has been portrayed in many ways. In America, the most popular form is the *crèche*, a word meaning "manger" or "crib" in French. Carved from wood (although some makers use ceramics, glass, straw, fabric, or even plastic) and painted, a crèche usually depicts the entire Nativity scene: the manger, star, angels, shepherds, kings—and, of course, the Holy Family. Most are constructed on a miniature scale, although a few church crèches are almost life-size. Crèches originated in Europe with the Italian *presepio*, which used small carved figures in the eighteenth century. Many of the crèches made today are modeled after the Italian examples or after elaborate German crèches dating from the seventeenth century.

Americans of different ethnic heritages have developed interesting variations of the typical European crèches. In the Hispanic communities of the Southwest, for example, the scene is displayed with an enchanting simplicity, often consisting of only three or four figures on a platform board. Crafted by *santeros*, artists who specialize in portraying saints, these modest arrangements are prized as folk art.

Another variation is the *putz*, a term derived from the sixteenth-century Saxon word *putzen*, meaning "to decorate." This unique type of Nativity representation was brought to America by Moravian Protestants who emigrated from their homeland in central Europe during the eighteenth century. *Putzes* consist not only of a crèche but also of a miniature village complete with dozens of figures, animals, and houses, which add detail and a storylike background to the Nativity scene. The tradition of *putz* building contin-ues today in a number of communities, especially Bethlehem, Pennsylvania, site of an early Moravian settlement. Here each *putz* is highly individual, often combining the biblical scene with fantastic landscapes that may even include modern buildings.

The Nativity is a favorite subject for painters, illustrators, and other artists working in a variety of media, from stained glass windows in churches to Christmas card designs. Many American artists have drawn their inspiration from classic European paintings of the Nativity scene or, in the case of some of our early painters, found models in Bible illustrations brought from overseas. Other artists, however, dressed the characters and set the scene in a way that reflected their own time and locale, a practice shared by European painters during the Renaissance.

The Nativity is not only represented through sculptural models or through illustrations. Across America, the Nativity is literally brought to life by church and other groups who reenact the biblical story during the Christmas season. In Nativity plays and pageants children don colorful costumes and portray for their proud parents and neighbors the events surrounding the birth of Jesus. Sometimes their imaginative interpretations of the Nativity script provide highly original versions of the story.

A less dramatic but no less affecting enactment of the Nativity scene is called a *tableau vivant* ("living picture"). Held at night and usually outdoors, this type of performance centers around a manger built specially for the occasion. Beside it, a woman and man representing Mary and Joseph watch over the infant Jesus, sometimes portrayed by a real baby. Around them gather the adoring visitors—players dressed as shepherds and the three kings. Live animals may even take part.

In the southwestern states, the Christmas pageant follows a Mexican custom called *Las Posadas*, which commemorates the journey of Mary and Joseph to Bethlehem and their search for lodging (the word *posada* means "inn" in Spanish). In the night, a procession led by two children—who carry clay figures of Mary, Joseph, and an angel—winds its way through the streets of the town. Holding candles aloft and singing, the pilgrims continue until they finally arrive at the door of a house selected to represent the inn. Here the singers ask for lodging and are admitted. A manger has been set up inside, and upon entering, all kneel before it to pray and sing. This solemn moment is often followed by a festive party.

The Nativity scene is a source of beauty and fascination in both its artistic and spiritual aspects. It represents a momentous event, yet at its center is that most familiar sight: a mother and child. Its intimacy and simplicity allow all to share in its meaning and to experience the blessings of brotherhood, humility, and family symbolized by the birth of Christ.

Left: A detail from the annual display of The Metropolitan Museum of Art shows an opulently clad wise man and two members of his retinue. The figures average 12 to 15 inches in height, with pliable bodies of twine and wire, and limbs of carved wood. Their luxurious costumes are enriched with jewels, embroidery, and elaborate accessories.

Below: This traditional Nativity scene was set up on the Ellipse in Washington, D.C., for Christmas 1984.

Page 172: This eighteenth-century Neapolitan crèche is installed every year at Christmas in the Medieval Sculpture Hall of The Metropolitan Museum of Art in New York. Composed of a multitude of figures created by Italian artisans, the museum's crèche is arranged at the base of a 20-foot tree. The crèche has been part of the Christmas tradition at the museum every year since 1964.

Above: Children in costume portray the characters of the Nativity in this *tableau vivant*. They kneel in the stable to adore the Christ Child, whose presence is left to our imaginations.

Left: In California, a young boy sings to friends and neighbors who are enacting on stage the traditional Mexican pageant *Las Posadas*.

Artist Lauren Ford created the two etchings on this page out of her deep desire to bring the beauty of Christ's birth to the world of the 1930s and 1940s. In the familiar setting of her farm near Bethlehem, Connecticut, she depicted the timeless nature of the Nativity story. Miss Ford portrayed the Christ Child as if he had been born in her own barn, in her own town, surrounded by her own neighbors. In doing so, she followed the tradition of the great Renaissance artists, who painted the stories of Christ and his followers in the settings of their own times.

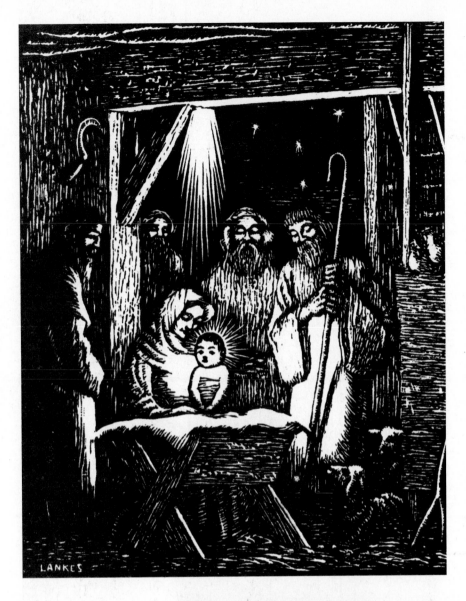

Left: The Gospel according to Luke tells us that an angel appeared to the shepherds who were watching over their flocks and told them about the birth in nearby Bethlehem. This wood engraving from 1922 by J. J. Lankes depicts the visit of the shepherds to the humble stable, which is illuminated by the glow from the Christ Child's halo and the light from the shining star overhead.

Below: This portrayal of the Adoration of the Magi was painted by an unknown New York artist around 1740. The inscription at the bottom of the painting refers to the second chapter of The Gospel according to Matthew, which describes the event. The soldiers with their bristling spears probably symbolize Herod's decree of slaughter for all the young male children of Bethlehem. The objects on the ground at the left are the kneeling magus' scepter and crowned hat.

THE GOSPEL ACCORDING TO MATTHEW

Now the birth of Jesus Christ was on this wise: When as his mother Mary was espoused to Joseph, before they came together, she was found with child of the Holy Ghost.

Then Joseph her husband, being a just man, and not willing to make her a publick example, was minded to put her away privily.

But while he thought on these things, behold, the angel of the Lord appeared unto him in a dream, saying, Joseph, thou son of David, fear not to take unto thee Mary thy wife: for that which is conceived in her is of the Holy Ghost.

And she shall bring forth a son, and thou shalt call his name Jesus: for he shall save his people from their sins.

Now all this was done, that it might be fulfilled which was spoken of the Lord by the prophet, saying,

Behold, a virgin shall be with child, and shall bring forth a son, and they shall call his name Emmanuel, which being interpreted is, God with us.

Then Joseph being raised from sleep did as the angel of the Lord had bidden him, and took unto him his wife:

And knew her not till she had brought forth her firstborn son: and he called his name Jesus.

Now when Jesus was born in Bethlehem of Judaea in the days of Herod the king, behold, there came wise men from the east to Jerusalem,

Saying, Where is he that is born King of the Jews, for we have seen his star in the east, and are come to worship him.

When Herod the king had heard these things, he was troubled, and all Jerusalem with him.

And when he had gathered all the chief priests and scribes of the people together, he demanded of them where Christ should be born.

And they said unto him, In Bethlehem of Judaea: for thus it is written by the prophet,

And thou Bethlehem, in the land of Juda, art not the least among the princes of Juda: for out of thee shall come a Governor, that shall rule my people Israel.

Then Herod, when he had privily called the wise men, enquired of them diligently what time the star appeared.

And he sent them to Bethlehem, and said, Go and search diligently for the young child; and when ye have found him, bring me word again, that I may come and worship him also.

When they had heard the king, they departed; and, lo, the star, which they saw in the east, went before them, till it came and stood over where the young child was.

When they saw the star, they rejoiced with exceeding great joy.

And when they were come into the house, they saw the young child with Mary his mother, and fell down, and worshipped him: and when they had opened their treasures, they presented unto him gifts; gold, and frankincense, and myrrh.

And being warned of God in a dream that they should not return to Herod, they departed into their own country another way.

And when they were departed, behold, the angel of the Lord appeareth to Joseph in a dream, saying, Arise, and take the young child and his mother, and flee into Egypt, and be thou there until I bring thee word: for Herod will seek the young child to destroy him.

When he arose, he took the young child and his mother by night, and departed into Egypt:

And was there until the death of Herod: that it might be fulfilled which was spoken of the Lord by the prophet, saying, Out of Egypt have I called my son.

THE GOSPEL ACCORDING TO LUKE

And it came to pass in those days, that there went out a decree from Caesar Augustus, that all the world should be taxed.

(And this taxing was first made when Cyrenius was governor of Syria.)

And all went to be taxed, every one into his own city.

And Joseph also went up from Galilee, out of the city of Nazareth, into Judaea, unto the city of David, which is called Bethlehem; (because he was of the house and lineage of David:)

To be taxed with Mary his espoused wife, being great with child.

And so it was, that, while they were there, the days were accomplished that she should be delivered.

And she brought forth her firstborn son, and wrapped him in swaddling clothes, and laid him in a manger; because there was no room for them in the inn.

And there were in the same country shepherds abiding in the field, keeping watch over their flock by night.

And, lo, the angel of the Lord came upon them, and the glory of the Lord shone round about them: and they were sore afraid.

And the angel said unto them, Fear not: for, behold, I bring you good tidings of great joy, which shall be to all people.

For unto you is born this day in the city of David a Saviour, which is Christ the Lord.

And this shall be a sign unto you; Ye shall find the babe wrapped in swaddling clothes, lying in a manger.

And suddenly there was with the angel a multitude of the heavenly host praising God, and saying,

Glory to God in the highest, and on earth peace, good will toward men.

And it came to pass, as the angels were gone away from them into heaven, the shepherds said one to another, Let us now go even unto Bethlehem, and see this thing which is come to pass, which the Lord hath made known unto us.

And they came with haste, and found Mary, and Joseph, and the babe lying in a manger.

And when they had seen it, they made known abroad the saying which was told them concerning this child.

And all they that heard it wondered at those things which were told them by the shepherds.

But Mary kept all these things, and pondered them in her heart.

And the shepherds returned, glorifying and praising God for all the things that they had heard and seen, as it was told unto them.

Opposite: Detail of the Madonna and Child from the crèche at The Metropolitan Museum of Art, shown on page 172. The lamb is symbolic of Christ's role as the Good Shepherd.

Left: This elegant angel is one of the multitude that adorn the 20-foot spruce above the Metropolitan's crèche. The angel's colorful costume is handmade from precious fabrics.

THE ART OF CHRISTMAS

For close to two thousand years, Christmas has been a source of inspiration for artists. In America as elsewhere, painters, illustrators, and printmakers have captured a wealth of holiday images, at once reflecting the many facets of our Christmas celebration and helping to define its character. Their depictions of holiday scenes and symbols are as varied as their own circumstances and backgrounds. Some have recorded Christmas as they observed or remembered it. Others have interpreted traditional ideas imaginatively, drawing on their sense of fantasy and fun. Still others, inspired by a particular holiday symbol or theme, have created works that express spiritual concerns, or that convey emotions evoked by Christmas experiences.

In depicting their Christmas images, American artists have used a wide range of materials and procedures, from simple wood carvings and hand-drawn cards to ambitious renderings in oil on canvas and complex printing processes. Over time, their views of Christmas have changed with the emergence of new artistic styles and techniques, as well as with the growth of the holiday itself. A contemporary picture is likely to reveal the influence of abstract art or other modern developments. Many of our best-loved Christmas images, however, date from the nineteenth century, when both life and art were simpler and the holiday was mainly a family affair. Pictures from this time show clearly and attractively the preparations and the fun, both indoors and out.

Nearly all of the artists represented here—those with advanced training as well as "primitive" painters—have enjoyed portraying the warmth and good cheer of the traditional family gathering. In times of national crisis, however, they have pictured Christmas in more somber tones. They have showed sadness and need as well as courage, hope, and kindness in the true spirit of the season. Some of the finest holiday images come to us on Christmas cards, many using original designs created especially for this medium, and some reproducing familiar paintings or other art work.

Whether old-fashioned or modern, humorous or poignant, real or imagined, the art of Christmas is pleasing and accessible. It delights us because we immediately recognize its images and sentiments. For the artists themselves, Christmas often has played an important role in their creative lives. They have found subject matter and inspiration in recording the holiday's history as well as their own Christmas experiences: a favorite memory, the delight of children, or moments of peace and happiness. Above all, their art makes visible the spirit of Christmas by showing us the beauty and joy that are special to this season.

Above: In nineteenth-century America, sleigh riding was a widely enjoyed part of the Christmas celebration. With rows of bells jingling on the harnesses it was a noisy, exciting, and sometimes romantic activity. In this artist's rendition, the driver of a swiftly traveling horse-drawn sleigh steals a kiss from his companion. (Anonymous artist, chromolithograph published by Hughes & Johnson, *Merry Christmas/Happy New Year,* National Museum of American Art, Smithsonian Institution)

Opposite: For children, finding the perfect Christmas tree is always a special delight. This little boy and girl, dressed in Pennsylvania Dutch costume, have found one exactly to their size and liking, and their faces shine with pleasure. H. Schile of New York published this brightly colored lithograph about 1870. (Anonymous, *Christmas Tree,* Division of Domestic Life, National Museum of American Art, Smithsonian Institution, Washington, D.C.)

In this wood engraving after a drawing by the Victorian
artist Alice Barber, a joyful group returns from the forest,
arms full of evergreen branches. The shy smile of the
young woman in the foreground suggests that she has a
special purpose in mind for the mistletoe she is carrying.
(*Gathering Christmas Greens,* published in *Harper's Weekly,*
November 30, 1889)

As Winslow Homer recorded in this 1865 wood engraving, finding the perfect Christmas tree in a snow-covered landscape is a task that everyone enjoys. While a strong man fells trees with his ax, other members of the expedition gather branches and weave them into wreaths on the spot. (*Christmas—Gathering Evergreens*, 5⅞″ × 9⅛″, published in *Harper's Weekly*, December 1858, courtesy of the Bowdoin College Museum of Art, Brunswick, Maine)

Even a hundred years ago, when cities were smaller and more people lived on the land, many families weren't able to make a winter excursion to the snow to collect their tree. So the firm of Currier & Ives published pictures that brought this pastime into the homes of thousands of Americans. This example dates from the late nineteenth century. (*Christmas Snow*, lithograph, undated, The Harry T. Peters Collection, Museum of the City of New York)

The tradition of portraying the search for the Christmas tree lives on in the art of the twentieth century. Anna Mary Robertson "Grandma" Moses (1860-1961) was well known for her paintings of holiday scenes, which were often reproduced on greeting cards. She began painting in her late seventies in a primitive style well suited to her subject matter. Here she depicts a scene from her own experience—a snowy New England landscape, and a group of people busily gathering Christmas trees. Most of the trees are so large that they must be transported by horse-drawn wagon, but one small boy has found a fir his own size that he can chop down and carry home unaided. (*Out for Christmas Trees*, oil and tempera on panel, 1946, copyright © 1961, Grandma Moses Properties Co., New York)

While sleigh riding was mainly a country pastime, building a snowman was something that even a New York City dweller could enjoy. In this etching by John Sloan, busy children equipped with pails and shovels construct a winter sculpture in a New York City park. (*Sculpture in the Square*, 1926, in the collection of The Corcoran Gallery of Art, Museum Purchase, Mary E. Maxwell Fund)

As much as American artists have enjoyed depicting winter fun and Christmas preparations outdoors, they take equal delight in showing how America celebrates indoors. In Winslow Homer's *The Christmas Tree*, the tree reaches to the ceiling. Wreaths and garlands decorate the rest of the room. You can almost hear the noise of the thirteen children gathered around the tree, while their elegantly dressed parents join more sedately in the festivities. (Wood engraving, 5⅞″ × 9⅛″, 1858, courtesy of the Bowdoin College Museum of Art, Brunswick, Me.)

Christmas wasn't always celebrated in a boisterous manner. The mood is more formal and restrained in this dark Victorian parlor painted by Eastman Johnson in 1864. The focus is on the little girl who stands entranced by the Christmas toy—a stick puppet—her brother is demonstrating. (*Christmas Time; The Blodgett Family,* oil on canvas, 30″ × 25″, The Metropolitan Museum of Art, Gift of Mr. and Mrs. Stephen Whitney Blodgett, 1983)

Charles Burchfield gives us a child's-eye view of Christmas morning at home in 1929. The interior is homely, with socks drying on a rack above an ungainly water cooler, but our eyes are held by the beautifully decorated tree and the gifts glimpsed through the kitchen door. (*Christmas Morning*, 1929, Christmas card from an original painting by Charles Burchfield, courtesy of the Burchfield Art Center, Buffalo, New York)

As a young boy in the late 1800s, Horace Pippin lived in humble but happy circumstances with his mother in Goshen, New York. In this painted recollection of a childhood Christmas, the simple homemade decorations and cheerful tree disguise the bleak interior of the home. At the time he painted this Christmas scene, Pippin was a well-known artist whose primitive paintings were much in demand. (*Christmas Morning, Breakfast*, oil on canvas, 1945, Cincinnati Art Museum, The Edwin and Virginia Irwin Memorial)

A young farm girl dreams of an elegant Christmas in this painting by primitive artist Edna Teall. Like Grandma Moses, Mrs. Teall began her painting career late in her life, in the 1950s. In this Christmas scene, she imagined herself as a little girl living in a grand house and receiving gifts from her mother. (Oil on canvas, photo by Herbert Orth for *Life* magazine)

Edna Teall's real Christmas was humbler than the one she imagined, but no less happy. This painting shows her grandmother's farmhouse, with the family gathered for the Christmas feast. When Aunt Hattie enters with the Christmas tree, the moment is too exciting for the children to remain politely seated. (*Christmas Meal*, oil on canvas, photo by Herbert Orth for *Life* magazine)

Sometimes an artist has to enlarge on reality to make it big enough to contain all of the Christmas bustle and cheer. In this painting by Grandma Moses, the farmhouse room is far larger than it really was—big enough to hold a huge Christmas tree, two dining tables, and twenty-four people celebrating in various ways, including Santa Claus bringing in the presents. (*Christmas at Home*, oil and tempera on panel, 1946, 18″ × 23″, copyright©1984, Grandma Moses Properties Co., New York)

Top: The economic hardships suffered by Americans during the Great Depression changed the way they celebrated Christmas. There's not much under the sparsely decorated tree in the laborer's shacklike home, but Virginia artist Palmer Hayden's message is about spiritual rather than material gifts. We are reminded that Christ himself was born in simple circumstances, and that the greatest gift of all is love. (*Christmas,* ca. 1939, oil on canvas, 57″ × 34½″, Collection of Evelyn N. Boulware, New York, NY. Photo by Chuck Stewart)

Left: World War I separated American soldiers from their loved ones at Christmas. In this Red Cross poster by renowned children's book illustrator Jessie Willcox Smith, a little boy is doing his part for the war effort. At the same time, he gazes hopefully out the window, as if looking for the father who can't be at home for Christmas. (*Have You a Red Cross Service Flag?* 1918, color lithograph, 28″ × 21″, The Fine Arts Museums of San Francisco, Achenbach Foundation for Graphic Arts, gift of Darwin Reidpath Martin)

Page 193: As one of America's best-loved artists, Norman Rockwell illustrated many facets of everyday life, and Christmas was one of his favorite subjects. The underlying theme of this painting is Christmas leave for service men and women during World War II. Among the bustling holiday travelers at Chicago's North Western Railway Station, couples pause to embrace. Notice also Harry Truman, America's vice president at the time, as one of the crowd. The painting was reproduced on the December 23, 1944 cover of *The Saturday Evening Post.* (Reprinted from *The Saturday Evening Post,* © 1944, The Curtis Publishing Co. Printed by permission of the estate of Norman Rockwell, copyright © 1944, Estate of Norman Rockwell)

In this painting by William Holbrook Beard, Santa flies through the air on a remarkable sleigh drawn by eight reindeer. But instead of jumping down the chimney himself, Beard's Santa drops the toys down, apparently assuming that they will magically find their way into the right stockings. (Oil on canvas, ca. 1862, 24″ × 36″, Museum of Art, Rhode Island School of Design, Jesse H. Metcalf Fund)

Santa Claus is one of the most recognizable figures in America, but one artist had great fun disguising him in this Christmas card of a winter landscape. Get ready for a surprise when you turn the picture on its side. This kind of trick image is called a *metamorphic* card. (Anonymous, chromolithograph, 4½″ × 2³⁄₁₆″. Photograph © 1987 John Grossman, Inc. From the John Grossman Collection of Antique Images)

The more familiar Santa became to the American public, the more artists took liberties with the way he could be pictured. He was not always the mysterious Christmas Eve visitor, invisible to children. In Horace Devitt Walsh's 1915 design, Santa is shown as the familiar gift giver surrounded by children made happy by his toys. (*Christmas 1915*, color halftone on white paper, 12⅞″ × 10″, The Pennsylvania Academy of the Fine Arts, gift of the artist, 1917)

Ever wonder what your friendly department store Santa Claus looks like the rest of the year? In this print by Gerald Gooch, we see an ordinary fellow dressed in a T-shirt and Bermuda shorts turning into Santa, one step at a time. (*Once a Year*, 1966, drypoint, 12″ × 18″, The Fine Arts Museums of San Francisco, Achenbach Foundation for Graphic Arts, gift of the artist)

This woodcut angel graced Rockwell Kent's 1938 Christmas card. Visiting the earth to light a star on the top of each tree, the angel seems to symbolize God's gift of peace on earth. (*Angel*, Christmas card from an original woodcut, courtesy American Artists Group, New York)

For artist Gary Bukovnik, red flowers convey the spirit of Christmas. Below, a pot of poinsettias, the traditional holiday choice. Right, a casual arrangement of a red amaryllis with a pinecone. (*Poinsettia*, watercolor 41½" × 29½", from the collection of Jon Riis and Richard Mafong, and *December Composition*, watercolor, 41" × 19½", courtesy of Staempfli Gallery, New York)

ON EARTH PEACE   GOOD WILL TOWARDS MEN

"The Sweet Story of Old"

Stirring the Pudding

Hark! The Bells

Snowballing

Looking Out for the Coach

THE LITERATURE OF CHRISTMAS

As Christmas draws near, bits and pieces of favorite Christmas stories start coming to mind—visions of sugarplums dancing, a child wanting "Christmas Every Day," a determined trek in search of fruitcake ingredients. At this time of remembering and sharing, family and friends gather to celebrate the season in their own special, traditional ways. Reading together is a simple pleasure of the day. Imagine a darkened room, a large fire throwing out light and warmth and flickering in the ornaments of the tree in the background. Someone brings out a cherished book, maybe one that's reread year after year, an eagerly awaited part of the Christmas ritual. Or it may be a new book each year—the choice of Christmas prose and poetry is that broad.

The mood of the literature varies, too, though wonder and awe, excitement and anticipation, generosity and love are prime ingredients. Some Christmas stories will make you laugh, while others will delight you with their whimsy and colorful descriptions of different times and places. Some will make you think. And as you read you will be getting a taste of America's history, for our Christmas literature has grown with the nation.

The stories included here have a distinctly American flavor, though it wasn't always so. In colonial times, Christmas stories came in the many styles and languages of the varied population—German, Scandinavian, Dutch, as well as English. As traditions mixed, an American form emerged.

In this selection you will find great Christmas literature and old favorites—pieces by Henry Wadsworth Longfellow and O. Henry—as well as such "lost" classics as Frances Hodgson Burnett's "Behind the White Brick" and Lincoln Steffens' "A Miserable, Merry Christmas." You will relive times when people were cheerful and optimistic; when the Civil War shattered the nation, altering images of Christmas and of life; when the hardships of war dampened but could not extinguish the spirit of the season; and when Americans took seriously the true meaning of Christmas.

Not all of the pieces are old. Modern names you will recognize include Robert Benchley, Truman Capote, and Garrison Keillor. There's also a humorous anecdote about W.C. Fields.

And, of course, you will meet Santa Claus many, many times. He has been a prominent figure on the Christmas literary scene in America since the early nineteenth century, when St. Nicholas—an import from the old country—caught the attention of writers.

Young and old will enjoy the stories and poems told here. Sharing them is one of the finest gifts of the Christmas season, because Christmas is not merely a place or a time—it is a reality that's created anew each season.

THE NIGHT BEFORE CHRISTMAS

What would Christmas Eve be without the annual reading of Clement C. Moore's beloved poem, "The Night Before Christmas"? Shared aloud in front of a crackling fire or read to wide-eyed youngsters tucked "snug in their beds," "A Visit from Saint Nicholas," as the poem is also known, is pure magic—rich in imagery, vividly descriptive, and just as lively and quick as Santa Claus himself.

This family classic came into being on Christmas Eve in 1822. Dr. Clement Moore, a dedicated husband and father of nine children, had promised his six-year-old daughter Charity a very special Christmas Eve gift. A New Yorker of Dutch descent, Moore was a professor of Oriental literature, Greek and Hebrew, a linguist, a devout clergyman, and a philanthropist. He enjoyed writing light prose and played the violin and organ as well—in short, a many-sided man.

Moore and the family handyman, Jan, set out early on the morning of the twenty-fourth to pick up some holiday supplies and last-minute gifts from downtown. Maybe it was the crispness of the newly fallen snow, or the companionable joviality of Jan, a short, round, white-bearded Dutchman. In any case, when they returned, the idea for the poem was firmly planted in Moore's mind. A few quiet hours in the study before dinner, and the now-famous verse was ready to be presented to a delighted Charity.

In writing his poem, Moore probably drew inspiration from the literature of the times, as well as from the mood of the day. He was thoroughly familiar with the descriptions of St. Nick sprinkled through Washington Irving's fun-poking *History of New York*.

He may also have borrowed from a little booklet called *The Children's Friend*. In this unusual tale, a bearded Santa Claus in brown furry garb arrived on New York rooftops in a sled drawn by a single reindeer. This Santa bore rewards for good children and carried a long black birch rod for anyone naughty, haughty, or rude. Moore apparently found him a bit harsh and omitted much of the imagery—but the reindeer remained and multiplied.

All influences aside, "The Night Before Christmas" is an original masterpiece. Can you imagine Moore's delight as he teamed up eight miniature reindeer, rather than one normal-sized beast, and gave them eight unforgettable names? Or his quiet laughter as he mentally guided the sleigh across the snowy lawn of the family house and up over the porch and onto the roof?

Not surprisingly, the entire Moore clan, especially Charity, treasured their father's Christmas Eve gift. The poem would probably have remained a family secret were it not for the visit of a friend a few months later. Charity proudly recited her verses to Harriet Butler, who shared them in turn with her Sunday School class and then sent a copy to the Troy (New York) *Sentinel*. The piece appeared the next Christmas, its author anonymous.

Moore, a private man, was embarrassed by the fuss, but he couldn't stop the tide of history. Within a few years, the poem began to crop up in periodicals everywhere, and in 1837 Moore reluctantly acknowledged its authorship. The *Sentinel* had offered the first illustrated version a few years earlier, crudely printing it on single news sheets. A decade later they published the poem on finer stock as a kind of Christmas greeting.

This was just the beginning. The illustrator T. C. Boyd, a wood engraver, introduced the flavor of Dutch New York to the tale. Boyd's St. Nick—like the earlier Dutchman, Jan—was a short, stocky fellow, full of whimsy. He had to climb on a chair to fill children's stockings. Eventually, in 1863, the popularity of the poem attracted the notice of the famous cartoonist Thomas Nast. His images of Moore's piece have lasted, and are the ones most of us still associate with the poem.

Clement C. Moore remained modest until the end. He spoke humbly of his poem as something "originally written many years ago." But there's little doubt that the world will remain grateful for years to come for his very special present. 🎄

THE NIGHT BEFORE CHRISTMAS OR A VISIT OF ST. NICHOLAS.

❧ THE NIGHT BEFORE CHRISTMAS

CLEMENT C. MOORE

'Twas the night before Christmas, when all
  through the house
Not a creature was stirring, not even a mouse;
The stockings were hung by the chimney with care,
In hopes that ST. NICHOLAS soon would be there;

The children were nestled all snug in their beds,
While visions of sugar-plums danced through their
  heads;
And Mamma in her 'kerchief, and I in my cap,
Had just settled our brains for a long winter's nap,—

When out on the lawn there arose such a clatter,
I sprang from my bed to see what was the matter;
Away to the window I flew like a flash,
Tore open the shutters and threw up the sash.

The moon on the breast of the new-fallen snow
Gave the lustre of midday to objects below;
When, what to my wondering eyes should appear,
But a miniature sleigh, and eight tiny reindeer,

With a little old driver, so lively and quick,
I knew in a moment it must be Saint Nick.
More rapid than eagles his coursers they came,
And he whistled, and shouted, and called them by
  name:

"Now, *Dasher!* now, *Dancer!* now, *Prancer* and *Vixen!*
On, *Comet!* on, *Cupid!* on, *Donder* and *Blitzen!*
To the top of the porch! to the top of the wall!
Now, dash away! dash away! dash away all!"

As dry leaves that before the wild hurricane fly,
When they meet with an obstacle, mount to the sky,
So up to the house-top the coursers they flew,
With a sleigh full of toys—and St. Nicholas too!

And then, in a twinkling, I heard on the roof,
The prancing and pawing of each little hoof.
As I drew in my head, and was turning around,
Down the chimney St. Nicholas came with a bound.

He was dressed all in fur, from his head to his foot,
And his clothes were all tarnished with ashes and
  soot!
A bundle of toys he had flung on his back,
And he looked like a pedlar just opening his pack;

His eyes—how they twinkled! his dimples, how
  merry!
His cheeks were like roses, his nose like a cherry!
His droll little mouth was drawn up like a bow,
And the beard of his chin was as white as the snow.

The stump of a pipe he held tight in his teeth,
And the smoke, it encircled his head like a wreath.
He had a broad face, and a little round belly,
That shook, when he laugh'd, like a bowlful of jelly.

He was chubby and plump; a right jolly old elf;
And I laughed, when I saw him, in spite of myself.
A wink of his eye, and a twist of his head,
Soon gave me to know I had nothing to dread.

He spoke not a word, but went straight to his work,
And filled all the stockings—then turned with a
  jerk,
And laying his finger aside of his nose,
And giving a nod, up the chimney he rose.

He sprang to his sleigh, to his team gave a whistle,
And away they all flew, like the down off a thistle.
But I heard him exclaim, ere he drove out of sight,
"Happy Christmas to all! and to all a good night!" ❧

In this 1862, pre-Nast edition, the artist has harnessed the reindeer four abreast, and pictures them galloping across the snow rather than flying off over the rooftops.

Anna Mary Robertson "Grandma" Moses (1860-1961), who became famous in old age, illustrated "The Night Before Christmas" in 1960 when she was almost a hundred years old. This painting, titled "So Long Till Next Year," is copyright© 1979, Grandma Moses Properties Co., New York.

A CHRISTMAS MEMORY

TRUMAN CAPOTE

New Orleans-born Truman Capote was a master at evoking a scene, a mood, a moment—or a memory. The story of how Buddy and his friend manage to scrape together the money and ingredients to bake thirty fruitcakes is one of the most moving and popular Christmas stories of recent years.

Imagine a morning in late November. A coming of winter morning more than twenty years ago. Consider the kitchen of a spreading old house in a country town. A great black stove is its main feature; but there is also a big round table and a fireplace with two rocking chairs placed in front of it. Just today the fireplace commenced its seasonal roar.

A woman with shorn white hair is standing at the kitchen window. She is wearing tennis shoes and a shapeless gray sweater over a summery calico dress. She is small and sprightly, like a bantam hen; but, due to a long youthful illness, her shoulders are pitifully hunched. Her face is remarkable—not unlike Lincoln's, craggy like that, and tinted by sun and wind; but it is delicate too, finely boned, and her eyes are sherry-colored and timid. "Oh my," she exclaims, her breath smoking the windowpane, "it's fruitcake weather!"

The person to whom she is speaking is myself. I am seven; she is sixty-something. We are cousins, very distant ones, and we have lived together—well, as long as I can remember. Other people inhabit the house, relatives; and though they have power over us, and frequently make us cry, we are not, on the whole, too much aware of them. We are each other's best friend. She calls me Buddy, in memory of a boy who was formerly her best friend. The other Buddy died in the 1880's, when she was still a child. She is still a child.

"I knew it before I got out of bed," she says, turning away from the window with a purposeful excitement in her eyes. "The courthouse bell sounded so cold and clear. And there were no birds singing; they've gone to warmer country, yes indeed. Oh, Buddy, stop stuffing biscuit and fetch our buggy. Help me find my hat. We've thirty cakes to bake."

It's always the same: a morning arrives in November, and my friend, as though officially inaugurating the Christmas time of year that exhilarates her imagination and fuels the blaze of her heart, announces; "It's fruitcake weather! Fetch our buggy. Help me find my hat."

The hat is found, a straw cartwheel corsaged with velvet roses out-of-doors has faded; it once belonged to a more fashionable relative. Together, we guide our buggy, a dilapidated baby carriage, out to the garden and into a grove of pecan trees. The buggy is mine; that is, it was bought for me when I was born. It is made of wicker, rather unraveled, and the wheels wobble like a drunkard's legs. But it is a faithful object; springtimes, we take it to the woods and fill it with flowers, herbs, wild fern for our porch pots; in the summer, we pile it with picnic paraphernalia and sugar-cane fishing poles and roll it down to the edge of a creek; it has its winter uses, too: as a truck for hauling firewood from the yard to the kitchen, as a warm bed for Queenie, our tough little orange and white rat terrier who has survived distemper and two rattlesnake bites. Queenie is trotting beside it now.

Three hours later we are back in the kitchen hulling a heaping buggyload of windfall pecans. Our backs hurt from gathering them: how hard they were to find (the main crop having been shaken off the trees and sold by the orchard's owners, who are not us) among the concealing leaves, the frosted, deceiving grass. Caaarackle! A cheery crunch, scraps of miniature thunder sound as the shells collapse and the golden mound of sweet oily ivory meat mounts in the milk-glass bowl. Queenie begs to taste, and now and again my friend sneaks her a mite, though insisting we deprive ourselves. "We mustn't, Buddy. If we start, we won't stop. And there's scarcely enough as there is. For thirty cakes." The kitchen is growing dark. Dusk turns the window into a mirror: our reflections mingle with the rising moon as we work by the fireside in the firelight. At last, when the moon is quite high, we toss the final hull into the fire and, with joined sighs, watch it catch flame. The buggy is empty, the bowl is brimful.

We eat our supper (cold biscuits, bacon, blackberry jam) and discuss tomorrow. Tomorrow the kind of work I like best begins: buying. Cherries and citron, ginger and vanilla and canned Hawaiian pineapple, rinds and raisins and walnuts and whiskey and oh, so much flour, butter, so many eggs, spices, flavorings: why, we'll need a pony to pull the buggy home.

But before these purchases can be made, there is the question of money. Neither of us has any. Except for skinflint sums persons in the house occasionally provide (a dime is considered very big money); or what we earn ourselves from various activities: holding rummage sales, selling buckets of hand-picked blackberries, jars of homemade jam and apple jelly and peach preserves, rounding up flowers for funerals and weddings. Once we won seventy-ninth prize, five dollars, in a national football contest. Not that we know a fool thing about football. It's just that we enter any contest we hear about: at the moment our hopes are centered on the fifty-thousand-dollar Grand Prize being offered to name a new brand of coffee (we suggested "A.M."; and, after some hesitation, for my friend thought it perhaps sacrilegious, the slogan "A.M.! Amen!"). To tell the truth, our only *really* profitable enterprise was the Fun and Freak Museum we conducted in a back-yard woodshed two summers ago. The Fun was a stereopticon with slide views of Washington and New York lent us by a relative who had been to those places (she was furious when she discovered why we'd borrowed it); the Freak was a three-legged biddy chicken hatched by one of our own hens. Everybody hereabouts wanted to see that biddy: we charged grownups a nickel, kids two cents. And took in a good twenty dollars before the museum shut down due to the decease of the main attraction.

But one way and another we do each year accumulate Christmas savings, a Fruitcake Fund. These moneys we keep hidden in an ancient bead purse under a loose board under the floor under a chamber pot under my friend's bed. The purse is seldom removed from this safe location except to make a deposit, or, as happens every Saturday, a withdrawal; for on Saturdays I am allowed ten cents to go to the picture show. My friend has never been to a picture show, nor does she intend to: "I'd rather hear you tell the story, Buddy. That way I can imagine it more. Besides, a person my age shouldn't squander their eyes. When the Lord comes, let me see him clear." In addition to never having seen a movie, she has never: eaten in a restaurant, traveled more than five miles from home, received or sent a telegram, read anything except funny papers and the Bible, worn cosmetics, cursed, wished someone harm, told a lie on purpose, let a hungry dog go hungry. Here are a few things she has done, does do: killed with a hoe the biggest rattlesnake ever seen in this county (sixteen rattles), dip snuff (secretly), tame hummingbirds (just try it) till they balance on her finger, tell ghost stories (we both believe in ghosts) so tingling they chill you in July, talk to herself, take walks in the rain, grow the prettiest japonicas in town, know the recipe for every sort of old-time Indian cure, including a magical wart-remover.

Now, with supper finished, we retire to the room in a faraway part of the house where my friend sleeps in a scrap-quilt-covered iron bed painted rose pink, her favorite color. Silently, wallowing in the pleasures of conspiracy, we take the bead purse from its secret place and spill its contents on the scrap quilt. Dollar bills, tightly rolled and green as May buds. Somber fifty-cent pieces, heavy enough to weight a dead man's eyes. Lovely dimes, the liveliest coin, the one that really jingles. Nickels and quarters, worn smooth as creek pebbles. But mostly a hateful heap of bitter-odored pennies. Last summer others in the house contracted to pay us a penny for every twenty-five flies we killed. Oh, the carnage of August: the flies that flew to heaven! Yet it was not work in which we took pride. And, as we sit counting pennies, it is as though we were back tabulating dead flies. Neither of us has a head for figures; we count slowly, lose track, start again. According to her calculations, we have $12.73. According to mine, exactly $13. "I do hope you're wrong, Buddy. We can't mess around with thirteen. The cakes will fall. Or put somebody in the cemetery. Why, I wouldn't dream of getting out of bed on the thirteenth." This is true: she always spends thirteenths in bed. So, to be on the safe side, we subtract a penny and toss it out the window.

Of the ingredients that go into our fruitcakes, whiskey is the most expensive, as well as the hardest to obtain: State laws forbid its sale. But everybody knows you can buy a bottle from Mr. Haha Jones. And the next day, having completed our more prosaic shopping, we set out for Mr. Haha's business address, a "sinful" (to quote public opinion) fish-fry and dancing café down by the river. We've been there before, and on the same errand; but in pre-

vious years our dealings have been with Haha's wife, an iodine-dark Indian woman with brassy peroxided hair and a dead-tired disposition. Actually, we've never laid eyes on her husband, though we've heard that he's an Indian too. A giant with razor scars across his cheeks. They call him Haha because he's so gloomy, a man who never laughs. As we approach his café (a large log cabin festooned inside and out with chains of garish-gay naked light bulbs and standing by the river's muddy edge under the shade of river trees where moss drifts through the branches like gray mist) our steps slow down. Even Queenie stops prancing and sticks close by. People have been murdered in Haha's café. Cut to pieces. Hit on the head. There's a case coming up in court next month. Naturally these goings-on happen at night when the colored lights cast crazy patterns and the victrola wails. In the daytime Haha's is shabby and deserted. I knock at the door, Queenie barks, my friend calls: "Mrs. Hah, ma'am? Anyone to home?"

Footsteps. The door opens. Our hearts overturn. It's Mr. Haha Jones himself! And he *is* a giant; he *does* have scars; he *doesn't* smile. No, he glowers at us through Satan-tilted eyes and demands to know: "What you want with Haha?"

For a moment we are too paralyzed to tell. Presently my friend half-finds her voice, a whispery voice at best: "If you please, Mr. Haha, we'd like a quart of your finest whiskey."

His eyes tilt more. Would you believe it? Haha is smiling! Laughing, too. "Which one of you is a drinkin' man?"

"It's for making fruitcakes, Mr. Haha. Cooking."

This sobers him. He frowns. "That's no way to waste good whiskey." Nevertheless, he retreats into the shadowed café and seconds later appears carrying a bottle of daisy yellow unlabeled liquor. He demonstrates its sparkle in the sunlight and says: "Two dollars."

We pay him with nickels and dimes and pennies. Suddenly, jangling the coins in his hand like a fistful of dice, his face softens. "Tell you what," he proposes, pouring the money back into our bead purse, "just send me one of them fruitcakes instead."

"Well," my friend remarks on our way home, "there's a lovely man. We'll put an extra cup of raisins in *his* cake."

The black stove, stoked with coal and firewood, glows like a lighted pumpkin. Eggbeaters whirl, spoons spin round in bowls of butter and sugar, vanilla sweetens the air, ginger spices it; melting, nose-tingling odors saturate the kitchen, suffuse the house, drift out to the world on puffs of chimney smoke. In four days our work is done. Thirty-one cakes, dampened with whiskey, bask on window sills and shelves.

Who are they for?

Friends. Not necessarily neighbor friends: indeed, the larger share are intended for persons we've met maybe once, perhaps not at all. People who've struck our fancy. Like President Roosevelt. Like the Reverend and Mrs. L. C. Lucey, Baptist missionaries to Borneo who lectured here last winter. Or the little knife grinder who comes through town twice a year. Or Abner Packer, the driver of the six o'clock bus

the chinaware; we giggle: as if unseen hands were tickling us. Queenie rolls on her back, her paws plow the air, something like a grin stretches her black lips. Inside myself, I feel warm and sparky as those crumbling logs, carefree as the wind in the chimney. My friend waltzes round the stove, the hem of her poor calico skirt pinched between her fingers as though it were a party dress: *Show me the way to go home*, she sings, her tennis shoes squeaking on the floor. *Show me the way to go home.*

Enter: two relatives. Very angry. Potent with eyes that scold, tongues that scald. Listen to what they have to say, the words tumbling together into a wrathful tune: "A child of seven! whiskey on his breath! are you out of your mind? feeding a child of seven! must be loony! road to ruination! remember Cousin Kate? Uncle Charlie? Uncle Charlie's brother-in-law? shame! scandal! humiliation! kneel, pray, beg the Lord!"

Queenie sneaks under the stove. My friend gazes at her shoes, her chin quivers, she lifts her skirt and blows her nose and runs to her room. Long after the town has gone to sleep and the house is silent except for the chimings of clocks and the sputter of fading fires, she is weeping into a pillow already as wet as a widow's handkerchief.

"Don't cry," I say, sitting at the bottom of her bed and shivering despite my flannel nightgown that smells of last winter's cough syrup, "don't cry," I beg, teasing her toes, tickling her feet, "you're too old for that."

"It's because," she hiccups, "I *am* too old. Old and funny."

"Not funny. Fun. More fun than anybody. Listen. If you don't stop crying you'll be so tired tomorrow we can't go cut a tree."

She straightens up. Queenie jumps on the bed (where Queenie is not allowed) to lick her cheeks. "I know where we'll find real pretty trees, Buddy. And holly, too. With berries big as your eyes. It's way off in the woods. Farther than we've ever been. Papa used to bring us Christmas trees from there: carry them on his shoulder. That's fifty years ago. Well, now: I can't wait for morning."

Morning. Frozen rime lusters the grass; the sun, round as an orange and orange as hot-weather moons, balances on the horizon, burnishes the silvered winter woods. A wild turkey calls. A renegade hog grunts in the undergrowth. Soon, by the edge of knee-deep, rapid-running water, we have to abandon the buggy. Queenie wades the stream first, paddles across barking complaints at the swiftness of the current, the pneumonia-making coldness of it. We follow, holding our shoes and equipment (a hatchet, a burlap sack) above our heads. A mile more: of chastising thorns, burs and briers that catch at our clothes; of rusty pine needles brilliant with gaudy fungus and molted feathers. Here, there, a flash, a flutter, an ecstasy of shrillings remind us that not all the birds have flown south. Always, the path unwinds through lemony sun pools and pitch vine tunnels. Another creek to cross: a disturbed armada of speckled trout froths the water round us, and frogs the size of plates practice belly flops; beaver workmen are building a dam. On the farther shore,

from Mobile, who exchanges waves with us every day as he passes in a dust-cloud whoosh. Or the young Wistons, a California couple whose car one afternoon broke down outside the house and who spent a pleasant hour chatting with us on the porch (young Mr. Wiston snapped our picture, the only one we've ever had taken). Is it because my friend is shy with everyone *except* strangers that these strangers, and merest acquaintances, seem to us our truest friends? I think yes. Also, the scrapbooks we keep of thank-you's on White House stationery, time-to-time communications from California and Borneo, the knife grinder's penny post cards, make us feel connected to eventful worlds beyond the kitchen with its view of a sky that stops.

Now a nude December fig branch grates against the window. The kitchen is empty, the cakes are gone; yesterday we carted the last of them to the post office, where the cost of stamps turned our purse inside out. We're broke. That rather depresses me, but my friend insists on celebrating—with two inches of whiskey left in Haha's bottle. Queenie has a spoonful in a bowl of coffee (she likes her coffee chicory-flavored and strong). The rest we divide between a pair of jelly glasses. We're both quite awed at the prospect of drinking straight whiskey; the taste of it brings screwed-up expressions and sour shudders. But by and by we begin to sing, the two of us singing different songs simultaneously. I don't know the words to mine, just: *Come on along, come on along, to the dark-town strutters' ball.* But I can dance: that's what I mean to be, a tap dancer in the movies. My dancing shadow rollicks on the walls; our voices rock

Queenie shakes herself and trembles. My friend shivers, too: not with cold but enthusiasm. One of her hat's ragged roses sheds a petal as she lifts her head and inhales the pine-heavy air. "We're almost there; can you smell it, Buddy?" she says, as though we were approaching an ocean.

And, indeed, it is a kind of ocean. Scented acres of holiday trees, prickly-leafed holly. Red berries shiny as Chinese bells: black crows swoop upon them screaming. Having stuffed our burlap sacks with enough greenery and crimson to garland a dozen windows, we set about choosing a tree. "It should be," muses my friend, "twice as tall as a boy. So a boy can't steal the star." The one we pick is twice as tall as me. A brave handsome brute that survives thirty hatchet strokes before it keels with a creaking rending cry. Lugging it like a kill, we commence the long trek out. Every few yards we abandon the struggle, sit down and pant. But we have the strength of triumphant huntsmen; that and the tree's virile, icy perfume revive us, goad us on. Many compliments accompany our sunset return along the red clay road to town; but my friend is sly and noncommittal when passers-by praise the treasure perched in our buggy: what a fine tree and where did it come from? "Yonderways," she murmurs vaguely. Once a car stops and the rich mill owner's lazy wife leans out and whines: "Giveya two-bits cash for that ol tree." Ordinarily my friend is afraid of saying no; but on this occasion she promptly shakes her head: "We wouldn't take a dollar." The mill owner's wife persists. "A dollar, my foot! Fifty cents. That's my last offer. Goodness, woman, you can get another one." In answer, my friend gently reflects: "I doubt it. There's never two of anything."

Home: Queenie slumps by the fire and sleeps till tomorrow, snoring loud as a human.

A trunk in the attic contains: a shoebox of ermine tails (off the opera cape of a curious lady who once rented a room in the house), coils of frazzled tinsel gone gold with age, one silver star, a brief rope of dilapidated, undoubtedly dangerous candy-like light bulbs. Excellent decorations, as far as they go, which isn't far enough: my friend wants our tree to blaze "like a Baptist window," droop with weighty snows of ornament. But we can't afford the made-in-Japan splendors at the five-and-dime. So we do what we've always done: sit for days at the kitchen table with scissors and crayons and stacks of colored paper. I make sketches and my friend cuts them out: lots of cats, fish too (because they're easy to draw), some apples, some watermelons, a few winged angels devised from saved-up sheets of Hershey-bar tin foil. We use safety pins to attach these creations to the tree; as a final touch, we sprinkle the branches with shredded cotton (picked in August for this purpose). My friend, surveying the effect, clasps her hands together. "Now honest, Buddy. Doesn't it look good enough to eat?" Queenie tries to eat an angel.

After weaving and ribboning holly wreaths for all the front windows, our next project is the fashioning of family gifts. Tie-dye scarves for the ladies, for the men a home-brewed lemon and licorice and aspirin syrup to be taken "at the first Symptoms of a Cold and after Hunting." But when it comes time for making each other's gift, my friend and I separate to work secretly. I would like to buy her a pearl-handled knife, a radio, a whole pound of chocolate-covered cherries (we tasted some once, and she always swears: "I could live on them, Buddy, Lord yes I could—and that's not taking His name in vain"). Instead, I am building her a kite. She would like to give me a bicycle (she's said so on several million occasions: "If only I could, Buddy. It's bad enough in life to do without something *you* want; but confound it, what gets my goat is not being able to give somebody something you want *them* to have. Only one of these days I will, Buddy. Locate you a bike. Don't ask how. Steal it, maybe"). Instead, I'm fairly certain that she is building me a kite—the same as last year, and the year before: the year before that we exchanged slingshots. All of which is fine by me. For we are champion kite-fliers who study the wind like sailors; my friend, more accomplished than I, can get a kite aloft when there isn't enough breeze to carry clouds.

Christmas Eve afternoon we scrape together a nickel and go to the butcher's to buy Queenie's traditional gift, a good gnawable beef bone. The bone, wrapped in funny paper, is placed high in the tree near the silver star. Queenie knows it's there. She squats at the foot of the tree staring up in a trance of greed: when bedtime arrives she refuses to budge. Her excitement is equaled by my own. I kick the covers and turn my pillow as though it were a scorching summer's night. Somewhere a rooster crows: falsely, for the sun is still on the other side of the world.

"Buddy, are you awake?" It is my friend, calling from her room, which is next to mine; and an instant later she is sitting on my bed holding a candle. "Well, I can't sleep a hoot," she declares. "My mind's jumping like a jack rabbit. Buddy, do you think Mrs. Roosevelt will serve our cake at dinner?" We huddle in the bed, and she squeezes my hand I-love-you. "Seems like your hand used to be so much smaller. I guess I hate to see you grow up. When you're grown up, will we still be friends?" I say always. "But I feel so bad, Buddy. I wanted so bad to give you a bike. I tried to sell my cameo Papa gave me. Buddy—" she hesitates, as though embarrassed—"I made you another kite." Then I confess that I made her one, too; and we laugh. The candle burns too short to hold. Out it goes, exposing the starlight, the stars spinning at the window like a visible caroling that slowly, slowly daybreak silences. Possibly we doze; but the beginnings of dawn splash us like cold water: we're up, wide-eyed and wandering while we wait for others to waken. Quite deliberately my friend drops a kettle on the kitchen floor. I tap-dance in front of closed doors. One by one the household emerges, looking as though they'd like to kill us both; but it's Christmas, so they can't. First, a gorgeous breakfast: just everything you can imagine—from flapjacks and fried squirrel to hominy grits and honey-in-the-comb. Which puts everyone in a good humor except my friend and I. Frankly, we're so impatient to get at the presents we can't eat a mouthful.

Well, I'm disappointed. Who wouldn't be? With socks, a Sunday school shirt, some handkerchiefs, a hand-me-down sweater and a year's subscription to

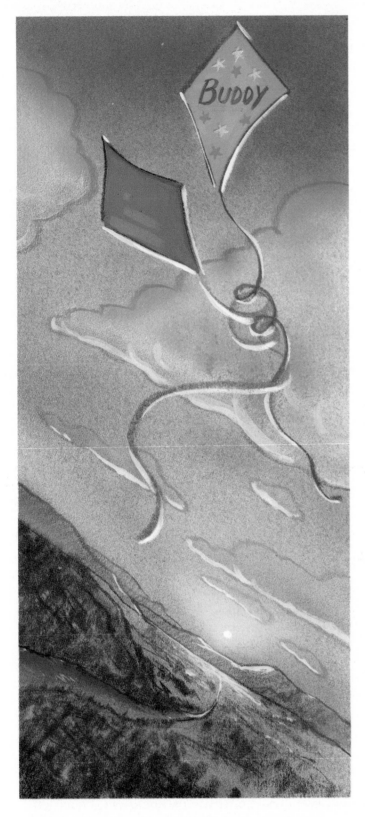

Queenie has scooted to bury her bone (and where, a winter hence, Queenie will be buried, too). There, plunging through the healthy waist-high grass, we unreel our kites, feel them twitching at the string like sky fish as they swim into the wind. Satisfied, sun-warmed, we sprawl in the grass and peel Satsumas and watch our kites cavort. Soon I forget the socks and hand-me-down sweater. I'm as happy as if we'd already won the fifty-thousand-dollar Grand Prize in that coffee-naming contest.

"My, how foolish I am!" my friend cries, suddenly alert, like a woman remembering too late she has biscuits in the oven. "You know what I've always thought?" she asks in a tone of discovery, and not smiling at me but a point beyond. "I've always thought a body would have to be sick and dying before they saw the Lord. And I imagined that when He came it would be like looking at the Baptist window: pretty as colored glass with the sun pouring through, such a shine you don't know it's getting dark. And it's been a comfort: to think of that shine taking away all the spooky feeling. But I'll wager it never happens. I'll wager at the very end a body realizes the Lord has already shown Himself. That things as they are"—her hand circles in a gesture that gathers clouds and kites and grass and Queenie pawing earth over her bone—"just what they've always seen, was seeing Him. As for me, I could leave the world with today in my eyes."

This is our last Christmas together.

Life separates us. Those who Know Best decide that I belong in a military school. And so follows a miserable succession of bugle-blowing prisons, grim reveille-ridden summer camps. I have a new home too. But it doesn't count. Home is where my friend is, and there I never go.

And there she remains, puttering around the kitchen. Alone with Queenie. Then alone. ("Buddy dear," she writes in her wild hard-to-read script, "yesterday Jim Macy's horse kicked Queenie bad. Be thankful she didn't feel much. I wrapped her in a Fine Linen sheet and rode her in the buggy down to Simpson's pasture where she can be with all her Bones . . ."). For a few Novembers she continues to bake her fruitcakes single-handed; not as many, but some: and, of course, she always sends me "the best of the batch." Also, in every letter she encloses a dime wadded in toilet paper: "See a picture show and write me the story." But gradually in her letters she tends to confuse me with her other friend, the Buddy who died in the 1880's; more and more thirteenths are not the only days she stays in bed: a morning arrives in November, a leafless birdless coming of winter morning, when she cannot rouse herself to exclaim: "Oh my, it's fruitcake weather!"

And when that happens, I know it. A message saying so merely confirms a piece of news some secret vein had already received, severing from me an irreplaceable part of myself, letting it loose like a kite on a broken string. That is why, walking across a school campus on this particular December morning, I keep searching the sky. As if I expected to see, rather like hearts, a lost pair of kites hurrying toward heaven. 🪁

a religious magazine for children. *The Little Shepherd.* It makes me boil. It really does.

My friend has a better haul. A sack of Satsumas, that's her best present. She is proudest, however, of a white wool shawl knitted by her married sister. But she *says* her favorite gift is the kite I built her. And it *is* very beautiful; though not as beautiful as the one she made me, which is blue and scattered with gold and green Good Conduct stars; moreover, my name is painted on it, "Buddy."

"Buddy, the wind is blowing."

The wind is blowing, and nothing will do till we've run to a pasture below the house where

THIS MUST WE KEEP

DOROTHY CANFIELD FISHER

Dorothy Canfield Fisher was a popular author of poetry, fiction, and commentaries on education, marriage, racism, and anti-Semitism from the outset of her career in the 1920s. Through the examples of her characters, she explored the dramas of every-day life, presenting challenges for her readers on controversial issues. Here she lists the historical threats to the reality and spirit of Christmas, and makes the reader face a contemporary threat—Christmas as nothing but a grab for gifts.

I have an overwhelming feeling of gratitude and ad-miration for one exquisite element in our human life which has been sacredly preserved for us by the con-servative instinct at its best—the ancient feast of joy and hope at the darkest period of each year. It was celebrated by man as long ago as we have the slight-est traces of human life; we celebrate it anew every year, deeply moved by a beautiful symbol of a mag-nificent truth which we inherit from all our ances-tors. We show our worthiness of it by preserving it and passing it on.

The celebration which to us is Christmas has been attacked again and again by one and another enemy. The Puritan radicals, confusing it with what seemed to them materialistic ceremoniousness, tried their best to throw it away as an outworn ancient piece of foolishness. The Romans, long before the coming of Christ, tried to lower a sacred festival to the level of a popular holiday with all license allowed. Our Scan-dinavian ancestors did their best, too, along the line. We ourselves are doing our best to cloud and darken its spiritual beauty by succumbing to the people who try to make Christmas only a shopping orgy.

But the perfect symbol of a mighty and radiant truth has always shone with a starlike beauty through the trash men heap around it. We moderns are irritated, weary and morose by the evening of December twenty-fourth because we half realize how shamelessly one of our most exquisite impulses is being exploited by the commercial instinct; and we sometimes think, "What a nuisance Christmas is! I wish we didn't have it—just a grab for presents." But on December twenty-fifth is there one of us who does not feel a pang, a shock of strange, secret, in-timate joy such as we know on no other day? There is something preserved from the past which has golden worth!

The ancient symbol grows more richly encrusted with poetry and spiritual meaning as the centuries go on. Our cave-men ancestors probably rejoiced

quite literally, quite materialistically, over the fact that the darkest days of the year were over, that they could turn their faces from blackness toward the hope of sunlight. The Romans felt the inner spiritual meaning of so turning from darkness to light—symbolizing it with their exchange of lighted candles and loving gifts, and with an even deeper piece of symbolism, only half understood but always a part of the joyous ceremony, when for a short time he who had been master and lord in the household became a servant, and he who had been a lowly servant put on fine garments and was humbly served by his master. Was not that a divination of a truth not yet expressed, and even now not grasped by us in its mystical significance, "For he that is least among you all, the same shall be great"?

And when Christianity came and found embedded in human life a symbol of such touching beauty, such unshakable hope, with what a profound wisdom did our faith lift this ancient vessel and pour it full of new wine! The coming of light after long darkness—that was the tenderness of the spirit of Jesus Christ. The old act of faith, to which man had clung with all his tortured, despairing, ever-hoping heart, of proclaiming with joy, at the very darkest period of the year, his sure and certain faith that light would come again—what better channel could be found along which to send forward the belief in the transformation of the world through the spirit of Christ? The new divination that men are to be valued for themselves, not for their outward place or class in society—what more popular expression of it than the ancient festival when servants became masters and masters servants—alas, that we have lost that!

Even the small oddities of custom found a place in this deepening of the meaning of one of the oldest of human institutions. The mistletoe of our Celtic ancestors under which, at Christmas, we still give and take harmless kisses, forbidden at other times—in its small corner this, too, is more than a harmless piece of gaiety; it reminds the meditative spirit of how much which is forbidden to the sensual and self-seeking can be safely done with a pure and loving heart.

Loftily mystical, homely, intimate, human, divine, wild with gaiety, solemn with the purest of thanksgivings for the best that God has given to man, Christmas is the exquisite universal expression of the faith which has kept us men and women alive through all errors and despairs—the faith that light will come again after darkness. That the celebration of this certainty that light will come again takes place at the very darkest of the year is for us, in our time of sorrow and anxiety, its most beautiful and moving aspect.

Let us keep this noble feast with joy and hope, and pass it on intact to those who come after us. ❧

NINETEEN STOCKINGS BY THE CHIMNEYPIECE

PEARL S. BUCK

Novelist and short-story writer Pearl Buck grew up in China, the daughter of missionary parents. The themes of reverence for life and of the human race as an international community are central to all of her work. In this thoughtful essay she considers the origin and significance of each small gift that goes into the stockings of her large family of "beautiful world children" on Christmas Eve.

This is the hour, unique in the whole year. Twenty-seven times the calendar has rolled around the circle of months to this hour of Christmas Eve. It is always the same and always different. The blessed sameness is in the old house which is our home and the Christmas tree, the gifts piled beneath it ready for tomorrow; it is in the quiet of the night when all are asleep except the two—or, as now, the one, myself; it is in the great stone chimneypiece by which I sit and the row of stockings hanging there. There have always been the stockings at this hour. The only difference has been in the number and the sizes.

They are limp and empty at this moment, but I shall fill them. And while I fill them, my mind, as always, goes back over the years when in this room, by this chimneypiece, we have filled the children's stockings. It is the final preparation for Christmas. Even when the children grew big enough to scoff at Santa Claus, even when they were big enough to go away to school and then to college, we never let them share this last hour of Christmas Eve and the filling of the stockings. This was our hour, the hour of recall and reflection, of private laughter and tenderness. We remembered, as I remember tonight, the incidents which made up the year so soon to be ended. We compared the children of this year with what they were the year before, the stockings bigger. How can boys have such enormous feet? Have we enough to fill them? These were annual cries. We always had enough, however big the feet were. And how small they were at first! There are still small ones, and the smallest now belongs to the newest baby, the tiny son of my daughter. And the row of stockings grows longer, five little stockings belonging to five little boys, and three little stockings belonging to three little girls, all the children of my children, hanging between the long stockings of their mothers and the big-footed socks of their fathers. Somehow each stocking looks like its owner, the boys ranging from the newborn baby to a couple of six-footers, and the girls—well, girls come in all sizes, too.

Here beside my chair are piled the gifts that I shall put into the stockings. The logs are blazing in the fireplace, and in the library next to the living room someone who should be in bed is playing Christmas carols softly, with the sweet intent, I am sure, of keeping me from being lonely. For I refuse to have anyone with me now for this hour. The tradition in our house has been that on Christmas Eve, for stockings, the parents are Santa Claus, and since I am now the only parent, I am Santa Claus. Nineteen piles of gifts on the floor beside me—each carefully wrapped, the size commensurate to the stocking. Inexpensive gifts, of course, amusing rather than valuable, but I like to put one unexpected gift into each stocking, something small enough to fit the toe, but unusual enough to inspire the last search. A ring for a girl who thought she would not get a ring this year, a pair of earrings for a young mother who lost an earring last summer that a baby tugged off and threw in the grass, a gold pencil for the young man with a new job, a silver spoon for the middle-sized baby who believes she can feed herself better than parent or grandparent can do it, widespread food notwithstanding, a watch for a little boy who has just learned to tell time—such things are the treasures.

Everything is wrapped and, if possible, my time permitting, that is, a nonsense verse or a message of love goes with each gift. Some years I am full of verse; on other years I cannot find a rhyme however I search my brain. The children, large and small, take me as I come and they are philosophical about it. Children learn to be philosophical about their parents, for which I am grateful. It is a holy experience to receive into one's arms a newborn human being, but sometimes I think that the highest experience of all is to look a full-grown man or woman in the face and recognize the mature human being that once was the newborn child. A new communication is established and upon equal terms. The satisfaction, the sheer human comfort of it! Next to the primary love between man and woman, I know of no other emotion as deep as that which parents feel when they know their children are grown men and women, ready to take their share in life's work.

The babies' stockings are full now. I have been busy all this while, half remembering, half thinking, and in between listening to the music from the other room.

"What Child is this—on Mary's breast—"

We sang the carols as every family does, every year, and we sang them again this year around the piano, the young mothers holding their babies, the young mothers, whose mother I am, and the babies listened, wide-eyed.

The middle-sized stockings next, and these belong to my three youngest daughters, those whom the world has given to me, one from Germany, two from Japan, fathers American soldiers, beautiful world-children who by some good fortune for me found their way to this house and to me as their mother. Sixteen, fourteen, and thirteen, and a ring goes into the toes of two stockings and a gold thimble into the toe of the third, for the one who likes to sew. "No candy this year, please, Mother"—and so no sweets to these fastidious three who are beginning to know they are pretty. I put in the lipstick for the eldest and next year I shall have to put in a lipstick for the next one. Fifteen is the beginning of such decorations in our family, but a necklace goes in for each one, a silver handwrought necklace bought in Darjeeling, India, when I was there visiting the Tibetan refugees

last spring. They are brave people, working hard to support themselves though exiled from their beloved and beautiful mountain country. I write a little message to go with the necklaces.

"Wear this with reverence for the pair of hands that worked so carefully to make something beautiful."

I am glad, too, that I bought the Tibetan jackets for the little boys and the gay Tibetan dresses for the tiny girls. I am glad I bought the handwrought brass candlesticks for the young married ones, I am glad I bought the two fine rugs for myself. I want to remember those noble people working to begin life again, anxious not to become a burden to their Indian hosts. Now at Christmas here in my home, in my country as yet undisturbed by war, I want to remember them. Let me never forget! Peace on earth, goodwill to men—

Ah, here is a treasure for my tall dark-eyed daughter, an emerald, rough cut, from India. She is clever with her crafts and she will set it into a gold ring or perhaps a clip. That goes into the toe of a very long stocking, so long that I wonder if I can fill it. A fan from Japan, that helps, and then the nonsense things, and last of all a paperback book for the top. It is of course essential that every stocking must appear to bulge and certainly to overflow at the top. Dolls, of course, for the tiny girls, little dolls, not competing with big ones under the Christmas tree, and small trucks for the small boys, not competing with large vehicles tomorrow, and for the older ones the paperback books that curl up nicely, or any other such objects that protrude pleasantly from stockings. Candy canes always, for what is a Christmas

stocking without a candy cane, red and white striped peppermint, harmless to all alike?

The value of stockings is apparent on Christmas morning when the older folk must get breakfast ready, a simple breakfast, remembering turkey and plum pudding later, ample in numbers, however, for while the table is set, orange juice and eggs and bacon and so forth in preparation, the stockings are unpacked. The little ones concentrate on the delightful task, and the older ones perform the same task en route between table and stove. By the time we sit down the stockings are limp again, and between sips and mouthfuls we exclaim and compare and the little boys swallow with dangerous haste so that they can get down on the floor and run their cars.

But that is tomorrow morning and it is still Christmas Eve. I finish the last stocking and hang it on the chimneypiece and sit down in the big chair to survey the noble work. A fine array, each year more stockings than the last, and peace descends. It is almost midnight. I wait as we always did, until I hear Big Ben from London. The logs are a mass of coals, crimson under the gray ash. The music comes to a close in the other room and the one who made it tiptoes in and curls up beside me on the floor. I put out my hand and she takes it. Mother and daughter we wait. Midnight. Across the ocean we hear the bells in London. Christmas Eve is ended again for another year. I refuse the mist of sadness that might envelope me if I allowed it. Tomorrow is Christmas Day. This silent room will be filled with life, new life, life renewed. Another Christmas, for this world in peril. A trembling peace and goodwill too scarce, but, thank God, another Christmas! 🎄

THE CHRISTMAS MIRACLE

ROBERT KEITH LEAVITT

Christmas miracles come in all sizes, as do Christmas essays. Like a tiny package that contains a pearl necklace, or a gold ring in the toe of a stocking, Robert Keith Leavitt presents a small jewel of a Christmas memory.

On the morning before the Christmas that fell when I was six, my father took my brother and me for a walk in the woods of the Old Colony town where we lived. Three times as we walked he stopped, and cut a small balsam tree. There was a very tiny one, hardly more than a seedling; a small one a foot or so high; and a youthful one of perhaps four feet. So we each had a tree to bear, flaglike, back to the house. It didn't occur to us single-minded larvae that this had the least connection with Christmas. Our father was a botanist Ph.D., given to plucking all manner of specimens whenever we walked, with the offhand explanation, "A fine *Tsuga canadensis*," or whatever it was. By nightfall we had forgotten all about the walk.

For this was Christmas Eve, and we were suddenly in a panic. Where was The Tree? On experience, we knew that it was usually delivered in the morning, that Father set it up in the afternoon and that Mother trimmed it at night, letting us help with the ornaments before she put us to bed in a fever of anticipation. But this year we had seen no tree arrive; look where we would, we could not find one; and even Mother turned aside our questions. Would there be no Tree? Would there, perhaps, be no Christmas at all for us? How we wished now, that we had not put the cat in the milk-pail!

But after supper Father and Mother took us into the sitting-room. In a cleared corner over by the big closet stood a jar of earth. "Christmas," said Father, "is a day of miracles, to remind us of the greatest Miracle of all. Perhaps we shall see one." Then Mother led us out, closing the door on Father and the jar of earth—and the closet.

"We can help," she said, "by learning this song." And she began, softly but very true, "O Little Town of Bethlehem." We tried hard in our shrill way. But even Mother had to admit it was only a good try. Yet when the door opened and we went again into the sitting-room, behold! A tiny Tree had appeared in the jar of earth! Hardly more than a seedling, to be sure, and not old enough yet to bear ornaments, but indubitably a Tree. Marveling, we went out again.

This time we did better—on the words, if not the tune. And when we re-entered the sitting-room, the Tree had grown—to perhaps a foot or so in height! A blaze of hope flashed upon us. We went out and tried harder on that song. And sure enough, this time the Tree was taller than either boy. Terrific! We could hardly wait to get outside and sing some more with Mother. For now hope was a rapture of certainty.

To this day I cannot hear "O Little Town of Beth-

lehem," from however a cracked a curbside organ, without hearing through and beyond it the clear, true voice of my mother. Nor hear that long-vanished sweetness without knowing that presently, somewhere, somehow a great door is going to open and disclose unearthly beauty. It is more than sixty years since our sitting-room door swung back for the fourth time, that night in the Old Colony of Massachusetts. But I can still see, sharp as life, the splendor of the Tree that towered to the ceiling in its glossy dark green, sparkling with silver tinsel, glowing with candles and half hiding in its crisp, fragrant needles, the incomparable perfection of spheres that shone like far-off other worlds, red and blue and green and gold . . .

Cynics say that miracles are all man-made—contrived, like a Christmas tree hidden in a closet and flashed upon wondering kids. That even the Christmas spirit is only a spell we work up to bemuse one another—and then fall for, ourselves, like so many simple children. What of it? So much the better! If mankind, by its own devoted labor, can induce in itself—if only for a day—an all-pervading spirit of friendship and cheer and good will and loving kindness, that alone is a very great miracle. It is the kind of miracle that must please above all others Him who knows how miracles are wrought. ✄

A MISERABLE, MERRY CHRISTMAS

LINCOLN STEFFENS

Lincoln Steffens was best known for his muckraking journalism, exposing corruption in business and government in the first decades of the twentieth century. He was also an accomplished writer with a keen eye for the telling detail, as this story of his boyhood in the Sacramento Delta in the 1870s shows. From Christmas despair to Christmas triumph—truly a miserable, merry day, excerpted from The Autobiography of Lincoln Steffens.

My father's business seems to have been one of slow but steady growth. He and his local partner, Llewelen Tozer, had no vices. They were devoted to their families and to "the store," which grew with the town, which, in turn, grew and changed with the State from a gambling, mining, and ranching community to one of farming, fruit-raising, and building. Immigration poured in, not gold-seekers now, but farmers, business men and home-builders, who settled, planted, reaped, and traded in the natural riches of the State, which prospered greatly, "making" the people who will tell you that they "made the State."

As the store made money and I was getting through the primary school, my father bought a lot uptown, at Sixteenth and K Streets, and built us a "big" house. It was off the line of the city's growth, but it was near a new grammar school for me and my sisters, who were coming along fast after me. This interested the family, not me. They were always talking about school; they had not had much of it themselves, and they thought they had missed something. My father used to write speeches, my mother verses, and their theory seems to have been that they had talents which a school would have brought to flower. They agreed, therefore, that their children's gifts should have all the schooling there was. My view, then, was that I had had a good deal of it already, and I was not interested at all. It interfered with my own business, with my own education.

And indeed I remember very little of the primary school. I learned to read, write, spell, and count, and reading was all right. I had a practical use for books, which I searched for ideas and parts to play with, characters to be, lives to live. The primary school was probably a good one, but I cannot remember learning anything except to read aloud "perfectly" from a teacher whom I adored and who was fond of me. She used to embrace me before the whole class and she favored me openly to the scandal of the other pupils, who called me "teacher's pet." Their scorn did not trouble me; I saw and I said that they envied me. I paid for her favor, however. When she married I had queer, unhappy feelings of resentment; I didn't want to meet her husband, and when I had to I wouldn't speak to him. He laughed, and she kissed me—happily for her, to me offensively. I never would see her again. Through with her, I fell in love immediately with Miss Kay, another grown young woman who wore glasses and had a fine, clear skin. I did not know her, I only saw her in the street, but once I followed her, found out where she lived, and used to pass her house, hoping to see her, and yet choking with embarrassment if I did. This fascination lasted for years; it was still a sort of super-romance to me when later I was "going with" another girl nearer my own age.

What interested me in our new neighborhood was not the school, nor the room I was to have in the house all to myself, but the stable which was built back of the house. My father let me direct the making of a stall, a little smaller than the other stalls, for my pony, and I prayed and hoped and my sister Lou believed that that meant that I would get the pony, perhaps for Christmas. I pointed out to her that there were three other stalls and no horses at all. This I said in order that she should answer it. She could not. My father, sounded, said that some day we might have horses and a cow; meanwhile a stable added to the value of a house. "Some day" is a pain to a boy who lives in and knows only "now." My good little sisters, to comfort me, remarked that Christmas was coming, but Christmas was always coming and grown-ups were always talking about it, asking you what you wanted and then giving you what they wanted you to have. Though everybody knew what I wanted, I told them all again. My mother knew that I told God, too, every night. I wanted a pony, and to make sure that they understood, I declared that I wanted nothing else.

"Nothing but a pony?" my father asked.

"Nothing," I said.

"Not even a pair of high boots?"

That was hard, I did want boots, but I stuck to the pony. "No, not even boots."

"Nor candy? There ought to be something to fill your stocking with, and Santa Claus can't put a pony into a stocking."

That was true, and he couldn't lead a pony down the chimney either. But no. "All I want is a pony," I said. "If I can't have a pony, give me nothing, nothing."

Now I had been looking myself for the pony I wanted, going to sales stables, inquiring of horsemen, and I had seen several that would do. My father let me "try" them. I tried so many ponies that I was learning fast to sit a horse. I chose several, but my father always found some fault with them. I was in despair. When Christmas was at hand I had given up all hope of a pony, and on Christmas Eve I hung up my stocking along with my sisters', of whom, by the way, I now had three. I haven't mentioned them or their coming because, you understand, they were girls, and girls, young girls, counted for nothing in my manly life. They did not mind me either; they were so happy that Christmas Eve that I caught some of their merriment. I speculated on what I'd get; I hung up the biggest stocking I had, and we all went reluctantly to bed to wait till morning. Not to sleep; not right away. We were told that we must not only sleep promptly, we must not wake up till seventhirty the next morning—or if we did, we must not go to the fireplace for our Christmas. Impossible.

We did sleep that night, but we woke up at six A.M. We lay in our beds and debated through the open doors whether to obey till, say, half-past six. Then we bolted. I don't know who started it, but there was a rush. We all disobeyed; we raced to disobey and get first to the fireplace in the front room downstairs. And there they were, the gifts, all sorts of wonderful things, mixed-up piles of presents; only, as I disentangled the mess, I saw that my stocking was empty; it hung limp; not a thing in it; and under and around it—nothing. My sisters had knelt down, each by her pile of gifts; they were squealing with delight, till they looked up and saw me standing there in my nightgown with nothing. They left their piles to come to me and look with me at my empty place. Nothing. They felt my stocking: nothing.

I don't remember whether I cried at that moment, but my sisters did. They ran with me back to my bed, and there we all cried till I became indignant. That helped some. I got up, dressed, and driving my sisters away, I went alone out into the yard, down to the stable, and there, all by myself, I wept. My mother came out to me by and by; she found me in my pony stall, sobbing on the floor, and she tried to

comfort me. But I heard my father outside, he had come part way with her, and she was having some sort of angry quarrel with him. She tried to comfort me; besought me to come to breakfast. I could not; I wanted no comfort and no breakfast. She left me and went on into the house with sharp words for my father.

I don't know what kind of a breakfast the family had. My sisters said it was "awful." They were ashamed to enjoy their own toys. They came to me, and I was rude. I ran away from them. I went around to the front of the house, sat down on the steps, and the crying over, I ached. I was wronged, I was hurt—I can feel now what I felt then, and I am sure that if one could see the wounds upon our hearts, there would be found still upon mine a scar from that terrible Christmas morning. And my father, the practical joker, he must have been hurt, too, a little. I saw him looking out of the window. He was watching me or something for an hour or two, drawing back the curtain never so little lest I catch him, but I saw his face, and I think I can see now the anxiety upon it, the worried impatience.

After—I don't know how long—surely an hour or two—I was brought to the climax of my agony by the sight of a man riding a pony down the street, a pony and a brand-new saddle; the most beautiful saddle I ever saw, and it was a boy's saddle; the man's feet were not in the stirrups; his legs were too long. The outfit was perfect; it was the realization of all my dreams, the answer to all my prayers. A fine new bridle, with a light curb bit. And the pony! As he drew near, I saw that the pony was really a small horse, what we called an Indian pony, a bay, with black mane and tail, and one white foot and a white star on his forehead. For such a horse as that I would have given, I could have forgiven, anything.

But the man, a disheveled fellow with a blackened eye and a fresh-cut face, came along, reading the numbers on the houses, and, as my hopes—my impossible hopes—rose, he looked at our door and passed by, he and the pony, and the saddle and the bridle. Too much. I fell upon the steps, and having wept before, I broke now into such a flood of tears that I was a floating wreck when I heard a voice.

"Say, kid," it said, "do you know a boy named Lennie Steffens?"

I looked up. It was the man on the pony, back again, at our horse block.

"Yes," I spluttered through my tears. "That's me."

"Well," he said, "then this is your horse. I've been looking all over for you and your house. Why don't you put your number where it can be seen?"

"Get down," I said, running out to him.

He went on saying something about "ought to have got here at seven o'clock; told me to bring the nag here and tie him to your post and leave him for you. But, hell, I got into a drunk—and a fight—and a hospital, and—"

"Get down," I said.

He got down, and he boosted me up to the saddle. He offered to fit the stirrups to me, but I didn't want him to. I wanted to ride.

"What's the matter with you?" he said, angrily. "What you crying for? Don't you like the horse? He's a dandy, this horse. I know him of old. He's fine at cattle; he'll drive 'em alone."

I hardly heard, I could scarcely wait, but he persisted. He adjusted the stirrups, and then, finally, off I rode, slowly, at a walk, so happy, so thrilled, that I did not know what I was doing. I did not look back at the house or the man, I rode off up the street, taking note of everything—of the reins, of the pony's long mane, of the carved leather saddle. I had never seen anything so beautiful. And mine! I was going to ride up past Miss Kay's house. But I noticed on the horn of the saddle some stains like rain-drops, so I turned and trotted home, not to the house but to the stable. There was the family, father, mother, sisters, all working for me, all happy. They had been putting in place the tools of my new business: blankets, currycomb, brush, pitchfork—everything, and there was hay in the loft.

"What did you come back so soon for?" somebody asked. "Why didn't you go on riding?"

I pointed to the stains. "I wasn't going to get my new saddle rained on," I said. And my father laughed. "It isn't raining," he said. "Those are not rain-drops."

"They are tears," my mother gasped, and she gave my father a look which sent him off to the house. Worse still, my mother offered to wipe away the tears still running out of my eyes. I gave her such a look as she had given him, and she went off after my father, drying her own tears. My sisters remained and we all unsaddled the pony, put on his halter, led him to his stall, tied and fed him. It began really to rain; so all the rest of that memorable day we curried and combed that pony. The girls plaited his mane, forelock, and tail, while I pitchforked hay to him and curried and brushed, curried and brushed. For a change we brought him out to drink; we led him up and down, blanketed like a race-horse; we took turns at that. But the best, the most inexhaustible fun, was to clean him. When we went reluctantly to our midday Christmas dinner, we all smelt of horse, and my sisters had to wash their faces and hands. I was asked to, but I wouldn't, till my mother bade me look in the mirror. Then I washed up—quick. My face was caked with the muddy lines of tears that had coursed over my cheeks to my mouth. Having washed away that shame, I ate my dinner, and as I ate I grew hungrier and hungrier. It was my first meal that day, and as I filled up on the turkey and the stuffing, the cranberries and the pies, the fruit and the nuts—as I swelled, I could laugh. My mother said I still choked and sobbed now and then, but I laughed, too; I saw and enjoyed my sisters' presents till—I had to go out and attend to my pony, who was there, really and truly there, the promise, the beginning, of a happy double life. And—I went and looked to make sure—there was the saddle, too, and the bridle.

But that Christmas, which my father had planned so carefully, was it the best or the worst I ever knew? He often asked me that; I never could answer as a boy. I think now that it was both. It covered the whole distance from broken-hearted misery to bursting happiness—too fast. A grown-up could hardly have stood it. ❧

CHRISTMAS IN LAKE WOBEGON

GARRISON KEILLOR

Garrison Keillor has created a new American classic—a town that's populated with characters who are at once strange and familiar, settings and situations that evoke a shock of recognition along with a good laugh. This short excerpt from Lake Wobegon Days *packs a wealth of detail about how ordinary church-going adults and small children shopping for presents really feel about Christmas.*

Baking begins in earnest weeks ahead of Christmas here in Lake Wobegon. Waves of cookies, enough to feed an army, enough to render an army defenseless, including powerful rumballs and fruitcakes soaked with spirits (if the alcohol burns off in the baking, as they say, then why does Arlene hide them from her mother?). And tubs of *lutefisk* appear at Ralph's meat counter, the dried cod soaked in lye solution for weeks to make a pale gelatinous substance beloved by all Norwegians, who nonetheless eat it only once a year. The soaking is done in a shed behind the store, and Ralph has a separate set of lutefisk clothes he keeps in the trunk of his Ford Galaxie. No dogs chase his car, but if he forgets to change his lutefisk socks, his wife barks at him. Ralph feels that the dish is a great delicacy, and he doesn't find lutefisk jokes funny. "Don't knock it if you haven't tried it," he says. Nevertheless, he doesn't offer it to the carolers who come by his house, because he knows it could kill them. You have to be ready for lutefisk.

Father Emil doesn't knock lutefisk; he thinks it may be the Lutheran's penance, a form of self-denial. His homily the Sunday before: We believe that we don't really know what's best for us, so we give up some things we like in the hope that something better might come, a good that we were not aware of, a part of ourselves we didn't know was there. We really don't know ourselves, our own life is hidden from us. God knows us. We obey His teaching, even when painful, entrusting our life to Him who knows best.

The faithful squirm when he says it. What comes next? they wonder. No Christmas this year? Just soup and crackers? Catholic children see Lutheran children eating candy that the nuns tell them they should give up until Christmas and think, "Ha! Easy for the nuns to talk about giving up things. Nuns do that for a living. But I'm twelve—things are just starting for me!"

Lutherans also get a sermon about sacrifice, which the late Pastor Tommerdahl did so well every year, entitling it "The True Meaning of Christmas." If you went to church with visions of sugarplums dancing in your head, he stopped the music. Santa Claus was not prominent in his theology. He had a gift for making you feel you'd better go home and give all the presents to the poor and spend Christmas with a bowl of soup—and not too many noodles in it, either. He preached the straight gospel, and as he

said, the gospel is meant to comfort the afflicted and afflict the comfortable. He certainly afflicted the Lutherans.

I heard his sermon one year, and I liked it, being afflicted by Christmas, knowing how much I was about to receive and how little I had to give. I was ten, my assets came to eight bucks, I had twelve people on my list and had already spent three dollars on one of them: my father, who would receive a Swank toiletries kit with Swank shaving lotion, Swank deodorant, Swank cologne, Swank bath soap on a rope and Swank hair tonic—an inspired gift. I walked into Detweiler's Drugstore, and there it was, the exotic Swank aroma that would complete his life and bring out the Charles Boyer in him. So I said,

"Wrap it up" and was happy to be bringing romance into his life, until the cash register rang and I realized I had five bucks left and eleven people to go, which came to forty-five cents apiece. Even back then forty-five cents was small change.

I imagined a man walking up and giving me fifty dollars. He was fat and old and had a kind face. "Here," he said, and he made me promise I wouldn't tell anyone. I promised. He gave me two crisp new twenty-five-dollar bills, a rarity in themselves and probably worth thousands. A Brink's truck raced through town and hit a bump, and a bag fell out at my feet. I called the Brink's office, and they said, "Nope. No money missing here. Guess it's your lucky day, son." I won the "Name the Lake Home" contest, and could choose between the lake home or the cash equivalent.

But there's nothing like a sermon against materialism to make a person feel better about having less. God watches over us no less for knowing what we can't afford. I took the five dollars and bought small bottles of Swank lotion for the others, which smelled as wonderful as his. If you splashed a few drops on your face, you left a trail through the house, and when you came to a room, they'd know you were coming. It announced you, like Milton Cross announced the opera. Dad was so moved by his gift, he put it away for safekeeping, and thanks to careful rationing over the years, he still has most of his Swank left.

BEHIND THE WHITE BRICK

FRANCES HODGSON BURNETT

Frances Hodgson Burnett is best known for her children's books, including The Secret Garden *and* Little Lord Fauntleroy, *although she also wrote novels and plays. "Behind the White Brick" is a charming, dreamy Christmas fantasy with a surprisingly sharp edge to it. Who would think that in Santa's workshop babies and dolls would speak with such a sarcastic tone!*

Jem knew what to expect when Aunt Hetty began a day by calling her "Jemima." It was one of the poor child's grievances that she had been given such an ugly name. In all the books she had read, and she had read a great many, Jem never had met a heroine who was called Jemima. But it had been her mother's

favorite sister's name, and so it had fallen to her lot. Her mother always called her "Jem," or "Mimi," which was much prettier, and even Aunt Hetty only reserved Jemima for unpleasant state occasions.

It was a dreadful day to Jem. Her mother was not at home, and would not be until night. She had been called away unexpectedly, and had been obliged to leave Jem and the baby to Aunt Hetty's mercies.

So Jem found herself busy enough. Scarcely had she finished doing one thing, when Aunt Hetty told her to begin another. She wiped dishes and picked fruit and attended to the baby; and when baby had gone to sleep, and everything else seemed disposed of, for a time, at least, she was so tired that she was glad to sit down.

And then she thought of the book she had been reading the night before—a certain delightful storybook, about a little girl whose name was Flora, and who was so happy and rich and pretty and good that Jem had likened her to the little princesses one reads about.

"I shall have time to finish my chapter before din-

nertime comes," said Jem, and she sat down snugly in one corner of the wide, old-fashioned fireplace.

But she had not read more than two pages before something dreadful happened. Aunt Hetty came into the room in a great hurry—in such a hurry, indeed, that she caught her foot in the matting and fell, striking her elbow sharply against a chair, which so upset her temper that the moment she found herself on her feet she flew at Jem.

"What!" she said, snatching the book from her. "Reading again, when I am running all over the house for you?" And she flung the pretty little blue-covered volume into the fire.

Jem sprang to rescue it with a cry, but it was impossible to reach it; it had fallen into a great hollow of red coal, and the blaze caught it at once.

"You are a wicked woman!" cried Jem, in a dreadful passion, to Aunt Hetty. "You are a very wicked woman."

Then matters reached a climax. Aunt Hetty boxed her ears, pushed her back on her little footstool, and walked out of the room.

Jem hid her face on her arms and cried as if her heart would break. She cried until her eyes were heavy, but just as she was thinking of going to sleep, something fell down the chimney and made her look up. It was a piece of mortar, and she bent forward and looked up to see where it had come from. The chimney was so very wide that this was easy enough. She could see where the mortar had fallen from the side and left a white patch.

"How white it looks against the black," said Jem, "it is like a white brick among the black ones. What a queer place a chimney is!"

And then a funny thought came into her fanciful little head. How many things were burned in the big fireplace and vanished in smoke or tinder up the chimney! Where did everything go? There was Flora, for instance. Where was she by this time? Certainly there was nothing left of her in the fire. Jem almost began to cry again at the thought.

"It was too bad," she said. "She was so pretty and funny, and I did like her so."

I dare say it scarcely will be credited by unbelieving people when I tell them what happened next . . . Jem felt herself gradually lifted off her little footstool.

"Oh!" she said, timidly, "how—how very light I feel! Oh, dear, I'm going up the chimney . . . I've heard Aunt Hetty talk about the draught drawing things up the chimney, but I never knew it was as strong as this."

She went up, up, up, quietly and steadily, and without any uncomfortable feeling at all; and then all at once she stopped, feeling that her feet rested against something solid. She opened her eyes and looked about her, and there she was, standing right opposite the white brick, her feet on a tiny ledge.

"Well," she said, "this is funny."

But the next thing that happened was funnier still. She found that, without thinking what she was doing, she was knocking on the white brick with her knuckles, as if it was a door and she expected somebody to open it. The next minute she heard footsteps, and then a sound, as if someone was drawing back a little bolt.

"It is a door," said Jem, "and somebody is going to open it."

The white brick moved a little, and some more mortar and soot fell; then the brick moved a little more, and then it slid aside and left an open space.

"It's a room!" cried Jem. "There's a room behind it!"

And so there was, and before the open space stood a pretty little girl, with long lovely hair and a fringe on her forehead. Jem clasped her hands in amazement. It was Flora herself, as she looked in the picture.

"Come in," she said. "I thought it was you."

"But how can I come in through such a little place?" asked Jem.

"Oh, that is easy enough," said Flora. "Here, give me your hand."

Jem did as she told her, and found that it was easy enough. In an instant she had passed through the opening, the white brick had gone back to its place, and she was standing by Flora's side in a large room—the nicest room she had ever seen. It was big and lofty and light, and there were all kinds of delightful things in it—books and flowers and playthings and pictures, and in one corner a great cage full of lovebirds.

"Have I ever seen it before?" asked Jem, glancing slowly round.

"Why," said Flora, laughing, "it's my room, the one you read about last night."

She led the way out of the room and down a little passage with several doors in each side of it, and she opened one door and showed Jem what was on the other side of it. That was a room, too, and this time it was funny as well as pretty. Both floor and walls were padded with rose color, and the floor was strewn with toys. There were big soft balls, rattles, horses, woolly dogs, and a doll or so; there was one low cushioned chair and a low table.

"You can come in," said a shrill little voice behind the door, "only mind you don't tread on things."

"What a funny little voice!" said Jem, but she had no sooner said it than she jumped back.

The owner of the voice, who had just come forward, was no other than Baby.

"Why," exclaimed Jem, beginning to feel frightened, "I left you fast asleep in your crib."

"Did you?" said Baby, somewhat scornfully. "That's just the way with you grown-up people. You think you know everything, and yet you haven't discretion enough to know when a pin is sticking into one. You'd know soon enough if you had one sticking into your own back."

"But I'm not grown up," stammered Jem; "and when you are at home you can neither walk nor talk. You're not six months old."

"Well, Miss," retorted Baby, whose wrongs seemed to have soured her disposition somewhat, "you have no need to throw that in my teeth; you were not six months old, either, when you were my age."

Jem could not help laughing.

"You haven't got any teeth," she said.

"Haven't I?" said Baby, and she displayed two beautiful rows with some haughtiness of manner.

"When I am up here," she said, "I am supplied with the modern conveniences, and that's why I never complain. Do I ever cry when I am asleep? It's not falling asleep I object to, it's falling awake."

"Wait a minute," said Jem, "Are you asleep now?"

"I'm what you call asleep. I can only come here when I'm what you call asleep. Asleep, indeed! It's no wonder we always cry when we have to fall awake."

"But we don't mean to be unkind to you," protested Jem, meekly.

She could not help thinking Baby was very severe.

"Don't mean!" said Baby. "Well, why don't you think more, then? How would you like to have all the nice things snatched away from you, and all the old rubbish packed off on you, as if you hadn't any sense? How would you like to have to sit and stare at things you wanted, and not be able to reach them, or, if you did reach them, have them fall out of your hand, and roll away in the most unfeeling manner? And then be scolded and called cross! It's no wonder we are bald. You'd be bald yourself. It's trouble and worry that keep us bald until we can begin to take care of ourselves; I had more hair than this at first, but it fell off, as well it might. No philosopher ever thought of that, I suppose!"

"Well," said Jem, in despair, "I hope you enjoy yourself when you are here."

"Yes, I do," answered Baby. "That's one comfort. There is nothing to knock my head against, and things have patent stoppers on them, so that they can't roll away, and everything is soft and easy to pick up."

There was a slight pause after this, and Baby seemed to cool down.

"I suppose you would like me to show you round?" she said.

"Not if you have any objection," said Jem, who was rather subdued.

"I would as soon do it as not," said Baby. "You are not as bad as some people, though you do get my clothes twisted when you hold me."

Upon the whole, she seemed rather proud of her position. It was evident that she regarded herself as hostess. She held her small bald head very high indeed, as she trotted on before them. She stopped at the first door she came to, and knocked three times. She was obliged to stand upon tiptoe to reach the knocker.

"He's sure to be at home at this time of year," she remarked. "This is the busy season."

"Who's he?" inquired Jem.

But Flora only laughed at Miss Baby's consequential air.

"S. C., to be sure," was the answer, as the young lady pointed to the doorplate, upon which Jem noticed, for the first time, "S. C." in very large letters.

The door opened, apparently without assistance, and they entered the apartment.

"Good gracious!" exclaimed Jem, the next minute. "Goodness gracious!"

She might well be astonished. It was such a long room that she could not see to the end of it, and it was piled up from floor to ceiling with toys of every description, and there was such bustle and buzzing

in it that it was quite confusing. The bustle and buzzing in it arose from a very curious cause too,—it was the bustle and buzz of hundreds of tiny men and women who were working at little tables no higher than mushrooms—the pretty tiny women cutting out and sewing, the pretty tiny men sawing and hammering and all talking at once. The principal person in the place escaped Jem's notice at first; but it was not long before she saw him, a little old gentleman, with a rosy face and sparkling eyes, sitting at a desk, and writing in a book almost as big as himself. He was so busy that he was quite excited, and had been obliged to throw his white fur coat and cap aside, and he was at work in his red waistcoat.

"Look here, if you please," piped Baby. "I have brought someone to see you."

When he turned round, Jem recognized him.

"Eh! Eh!" he said, "What! What! Who's this, Tootsicums?"

Baby's manner became very acid indeed.

"I shouldn't have thought you would have said that, Mr. Santa Claus," she remarked. "I can't help myself down below, but I generally have my rights respected up here."

"Come, come!" said S. C. chuckling comfortably and rubbing his hands. "Don't be too dignified—it's a bad thing. And don't be too fond of flourishing your rights in people's faces—that's the worst of all,

Miss Midget. Folks who make such a fuss about their rights turn them into wrongs sometimes."

Then he turned suddenly to Jem.

"You are the little girl from down below," he said.

"Yes, sir," answered Jem. "I'm Jem, and this is my friend Flora—out of the blue book."

"I'm happy to make her acquaintance," said S. C., "and I'm happy to make yours. You are a nice child, though a trifle peppery. I'm very glad to see you."

"I'm very glad indeed to see you, sir," said Jem. "I wasn't quite sure—"

But there she stopped, feeling that it would be scarcely polite to tell him that she had begun of late years to lose faith in him.

But S. C. only chuckled more comfortably than ever and rubbed his hands again.

"Ho, ho!" he said. "You know who I am, then?"

Jem hesitated a moment, wondering whether it would not be taking a liberty to mention his name without putting "Mr." before it; then she remembered what Baby had called him.

"Baby called you 'Mr. Claus,' sir," she replied; "and I have seen pictures of you."

"To be sure," said S. C. "S. Claus, Esquire, of chimneyland. How do you like me?"

"Very much," answered Jem; "very much indeed, sir."

"Glad of it! Glad of it! But what was it you were going to say you were not quite sure of?"

Jem blushed a little.

"I was not quite sure of that—that you were true, sir. At least I have not been quite sure since I have been older."

S. C. rubbed the bald part of his head and gave a little sigh.

"I hope I have not hurt your feelings, sir," faltered Jem, who was a very kind-hearted little soul.

"Well, no," said S. C. "Not exactly. And it is not your fault either. It is natural, I suppose; at any rate, it is the way of the world. People lose their belief in a great many things as they grow older; but that does not make the things not true, thank goodness! and their faith often comes back after a while. But, bless me!" he added briskly, "I'm moralizing, and who thanks a man for doing that? Suppose I show you my establishment, come with me."

It really would be quite impossible to describe the wonderful things he showed them. Jem's head was quite in a whirl before she had seen one-half of them, and even Baby condescended to become excited.

"There must be a great many children in the world, Mr. Claus," ventured Jem.

"Yes, yes, millions of 'em; bless 'em," said S. C., growing rosier with delight at the very thought. "We never run out of them, that's one comfort. There's a large and varied assortment always on hand. Fresh ones every year, too, so that when one grows too old there is a new one ready. I have a place like this in every twelfth chimney."

They were standing near a table where a worker was just putting the finishing touch to the dress of a large wax doll, and just at that moment, to Jem's surprise, she set the doll on the floor, upon its feet, quite coolly.

"Thank you," said the doll, politely.

Jem quite jumped.

"You can join the rest now and introduce yourself," said the worker.

The doll looked over her shoulder at her train.

"It hangs very nicely," she said, "I hope it's the latest fashion."

"Mine never talked like that," said Flora. "My best one could only say 'Mamma,' and it said it very badly, too."

"She was foolish for saying it at all," remarked the doll, haughtily. "We don't talk and walk before ordinary people; we keep our accomplishments for our own amusement, and for the amusement of our friends. If you should chance to get up in the middle of the night, some time, or should run into the room suddenly some day, after you have left it, you might hear—but what is the use of talking to human beings?"

"You know a great deal, considering you are only just finished," snapped Baby, who really was a Tartar.

"I was FINISHED," retorted the doll, "I did not begin life as a baby," very scornfully.

"Pooh!" said Baby. "We improve as we get older."

"I hope so, indeed," answered the doll. "There is plenty of room for improvement." And she walked away in a great state.

S. C. looked at Baby and then shook his head. "I shall not have to take very much care of you," he said, absent-mindedly. "You are able to take pretty good care of yourself."

"I hope I am," said Baby, tossing her head.

S. C. gave his head another shake.

"Don't take too good care of yourself," he said. "That's a bad thing, too."

He showed them the rest of his wonders, and then went with them to the door to bid them good-by.

"I am sure we are very much obliged to you, Mr. Claus," said Jem, gratefully. "I shall never again think you are not true, sir."

S. C. patted her shoulder quite affectionately.

"That's right," he said. "Believe in things just as long as you can, my dear. Good-by until Christmas Eve, I shall see you this year, if you don't see me."

"How kind he is!" exclaimed Jem, full of pleasure.

And then, suddenly, a very strange feeling came over Jem. Without being able to account for it at all, she found herself still sitting on her little stool, with a beautiful scarlet and gold book at her knee, and her mother standing by laughing at her amazed face. As for Miss Baby, she was crying as hard as she could in her crib.

"Mother!" Jem cried out, "have you really come home as early as this, and—and," rubbing her eyes in great amazement, "how did I come down?"

"Don't I look as if I was real?" said her mother, laughing and kissing her. "And doesn't your present look real? I don't know how you came down, I'm sure. Where have you been?"

Jem shook her head very mysteriously. She saw that her mother fancied she had been asleep, but she herself knew better.

"I know you wouldn't believe it was true if I told you," she said; "I have been

BEHIND THE WHITE BRICK." ❧

A CAROL FOR CHILDREN

OGDEN NASH

Ogden Nash was one of the most popular and often-quoted poets of his time. His offbeat, whimsical verses appeared in The New Yorker, The Saturday Evening Post, *and* Life *magazine. Written around the end of the First World War, "A Carol for Children" is somber, almost bitter in tone—quite unlike the poet's usual lighthearted style and outrageous rhymes.*

God rest you merry, Innocents,
Let nothing you dismay,
Let nothing wound an eager heart
Upon this Christmas day.

Yours be the genial holly wreaths,
The stockings and the tree;
An aged world to you bequeaths
Its own forgotten glee.

Soon, soon enough come crueler gifts,
The anger and the tears;
Between you now there sparsely drifts
A handful yet of years.

Oh, dimly, dimly glows the star
Through the electric throng;
The bidding in temple and bazaar
Drowns out the silver song.

The ancient altars smoke afresh,
The ancient idols stir;
Faint in the reek of burning flesh
Sink frankincense and myrrh.

Gaspar, Balthazar, Melchior!
Where are your offerings now?
What greetings to the Prince of War,
His darkly branded brow?

Two ultimate laws alone we know,
The ledger and the sword—
So far away, so long ago,
We lost the infant Lord.

Only the children clasp His hand;
His voice speaks low to them.
And still for them the shining band
Wings over Bethlehem.

God rest you merry, Innocents,
While Innocence endures.
A sweeter Christmas than we to ours
May you bequeath to yours.

CAROL OF THE BROWN KING

LANGSTON HUGHES

Black American writer Langston Hughes explored the topic of interracial tensions with considerable insight and sophisticated style. A prolific writer of novels, plays, poems, songs, and juvenile fiction, his writings were highly subjective, and often sarcastic in tone. "Carol of the Brown King," however, is a powerful and loving reminder that all people and all races are members of the human family.

Of the three Wise Men
Who came to the King,
One was a brown man,
So they sing.

Of the three Wise Men
Who followed the Star,
One was a brown king
From afar.

They brought fine gifts
Of spices and gold
In jeweled boxes
Of beauty untold.

Unto His humble
Manger they came
And bowed their heads
In Jesus' name.

Three Wise Men,
One dark like me—
Part of His
Nativity.

THE LESSER CHRISTMAS MIRACLE

JULIE McDONALD

How many children on how many farms have tried valiantly to stay awake until midnight on Christmas Eve so they could go down to the barn to see the animals kneel down and speak to worship the infant Jesus? In this short essay, Julie McDonald remembers the faith of a small child—a faith that she protects even as an adult.

It's easy for an Iowa child to believe what my Danish grandmother told me—that the farm animals celebrate the birth of Christ with human utterance at midnight on Christmas Eve. I first believed it on a farm near Fiscus, and it flowed like a sweet undercurrent beneath the many preparations for the holidays.

A piece had to be learned for the Christmas program at Merrill's Grove Baptist church, and I was admonished not to twist the hem of my skirt to immodest heights while delivering it. I performed without a lapse of memory and left my hemline alone, and when the program was over, we all got brown paper bags filled with hard candy. The bumpy raspberries with soft centers were my favorites, but I also admired the small rounds with a flower that remained visible until the candy was sucked to a sliver.

I had plans to visit the barn at midnight to hear what the cattle had to say to each other, but I kept them to myself, sensing that I would be thwarted should anyone find out. The paradoxically soft and stark light of the kerosene lamps shone on the clock face I could not yet read, and I asked again and again, "Is it midnight yet?" I had never experienced a midnight, and that prospect plus talking animals was almost too much excitement to bear.

My parents spoke of Santa Claus, which presented a problem. If I went to the barn at midnight to listen to the animals, Santa Claus would have to wait to bring my presents, and he might not be able to work me into his route. What to do?

Exhaustion solved my dilemma. I awoke in my own bed in the cold light of Christmas morning and hurried to the dining room to see what Santa had brought with no more than a fleeting regret about missing the animal conversation. There would be other years, other midnights. Now there was the joy of a small table painted bright orange and a sack of peanuts in the shell. The gifts seemed wonderful to me, and I had no notion of the thought and struggle that went into them in that Depression year. For years I did not know that my father made the table from an apple box, a broomstick and the core of a linoleum roll or that finding a few cents to buy peanuts involved looking through pockets and old purses for forgotten coins.

Later in the morning I went to the barn, hoping that the cattle still might have the power to speak, but they didn't. I had missed the moment, and now they only chewed and exhaled their grain-sweet breath in my face. "I'll come next year," I said, but I never did. That was my last Christmas on the farm and my father's last Christmas on earth. We moved to town.

In Harlan, Christmas meant colored lights strung from the Shelby County courthouse like a brilliant spider web, blue electric candles in Aunt Mary's window, and in Grandma's house (where we were living), a Christmas tree with wax candles—so lovely and so dangerous. We walked the streets of the town and admired the electric lights in other peoples' windows.

There were other Christmases in other houses, and for our family, hard times persisted, but they didn't seem so hard at the time. One year when we couldn't afford a Christmas tree, we cut a bough from the huge pine on the family cemetery plot and thrust it into a crock of sand. Then we punctured our fingers stringing popcorn and cranberries and made chains of paper loops to decorate it. The bough smelled as a Christmas tree should, but it also wept resin, recalling its funereal origin. That crying "tree" was banked with the best gifts we could manage, and I recall my delight with a glamorous milk glass flower pot filled with bath salts topped by a shiny and unnatural blue poinsettia.

In town, I could not go to the barn to listen to the animals talking, but I thought of them and wondered what they would say.

Many years later when I had children of my own, we were horse-sitting for my in-laws in Davenport at Christmas, and I was the last one up, filling stockings. As midnight struck with Westminster chimes, I considered going to the stable. I even reached for my coat, but I hung it up again. Mute horses would have stolen something precious from me. This dearest Christmas fancy of an Iowa child was something I wanted to keep, and I have. Surely the miraculous reason for Christmas can support this endearing lesser miracle.

EMMANUEL

A CHRISTMAS BALLAD FOR THE CAPTAIN

WILLIAM J. LEDERER

William Lederer is best known as the author, with Eugene Burdick, of The Ugly American. *When he was a naval officer stationed in Hawaii, his own three children and nine Samoan neighbor children demanded to know whether Santa Claus is real. Lederer answered their question with experiences from his own life, collected in* A Happy Book of Happy Stories.

I was the executive officer of the Navy destroyer in which the events of this story took place. It was in the early months of World War II. The rapidly expanding U.S. Navy desperately was seeking trained personnel to man the hundreds of new ships which were being built. The Navy took whoever was available—even the inmates of naval prisons.

There are five major characters in the story. One was our commanding officer—a very shy man who has requested that his real name not be used. The other four have no objections to being identified, and their real names are used.

Also, the names of the motion picture stars are real. They were stars forty years ago. Some of the young people reading this book might not be familiar with these stars. But, take my word for it, they were glamorous, beautiful, and, at that time, among the most famous people in the world.

I did not write this story. One of the men in our ship wrote it shortly after our ship was torpedoed and sunk on the way back from Anzio. He sent it to me and asked me to edit it, which I have done. His reason for writing the story was to send it to all surviving members of our ship as a small Christmas present.

After editing it, and revising it somewhat, I returned his manuscript. It appears in this book in the author's final revision—the way it was when he sent it to me on the following Christmas.

Captain Elias Stark, commanding officer of our destroyer, was a square-shouldered New Hampshireman, as quiet and austere as the granite mountains of his native state. About the only time the enlisted men heard him talk was when they reported aboard for the first time. He would invite them to his cabin for a one-minute speech of welcome, then question them about their families, and note, with pen and ink, the names and addresses of the sailors' next of kin.

That was the way he had first met the "Unholy K's"—Krakow, Kratch, Koenig, and Kelly. They had arrived with a draft of seventeen men from the naval prison at Portsmouth. Most of the prison group were bad eggs, but the worst were these four sailors from a small coal mining town in Pennsylvania. They had chests and shoulders like buffaloes, fists like sledgehammers, black stubble beards, and manners to match.

They had once been good kids, the mainstays of St. Stephen's choir in their hometown, but somehow they had gone astray. They seemed to specialize in getting into trouble together, as a quartet. All four went into the navy direct from reform school. Within six months they were in serious trouble again and had been sent to Portsmouth Naval Prison.

When they were called to the captain's cabin, they listened to his welcome speech with exaggerated expressions of boredom. Then the Old Man broke out his record book to note the names and addresses of the sailors' next of kin. He looked up inquiringly.

Krakow, the leader of the Unholy K's, took the initiative. Spreading his tremendous arms, he pulled Kelly, Kratch, and Koenig into a tight circle. "The four of us, sir, ain't got no family. We ain't got parents or wives or relatives." He paused. "All we got is girl friends, eh, fellas?"

Captain Stark simply puffed on his pipe. Patiently he asked, "Would you give me your best ladies' names and addresses for our records?"

The Unholy K's glanced at one another. Krakow said, "Sir, we don't feel like it's an officer's business who our girls are." He stopped as Kelly tugged his sleeve and whispered to him.

"Okay," continued Krakow sarcastically, "you want to know who our best girls are, I'll tell you. Mine's Rita Hayworth, Kelly's is Ginger Rogers, Kratch's is Lana Turner, and Koenig's is Paulette Goddard. They all got the same address: Hollywood, *sir.*"

"Very well," said the captain, "I will list those ladies' names in my records. Thank you, that will be all."

As soon as the Unholy K's got belowdecks they began bragging how they had made a fool out of the Old Man. Kelly started a bawdy song, and Krakow, Kratch, and Koenig joined in. Each man, in turn, made up a lyric while the other three harmonized. They had splendid voices, and with their choirboy training they formed a wonderful quartet. They sang four unprintable verses about the captain and why he wanted their girls' addresses.

Actually the captain had a good reason for obtaining personal information about the men. He strongly believed it was his duty to keep their families informed on how they were getting along. So, once every three months, in blunt New England fashion, he sent a personal note written in tiny, neat hand to everyone's next of kin.

For example:

> Dear Madam,
> Your son John is well—and as happy as can be expected in North Atlantic gales. If he shaved more often and cleaned his clothes more meticulously he would be more popular with his division chief.
> I think highly of him as a gunner's mate and, with luck, you should see him in a few months. You will find he has put on 12 pounds, and the extra flesh hangs well on him.
> > Sincerely,
> > Elias Stark
> > Commander, U.S. Navy

In September, after a year in the combat zone, our

they sang their insidious songs about the ship's officers, the crew listened. Their lyrics were so catchy that a song rendered in the aftercrew's washroom would be repeated all over the ship within a half-hour. No officers ever heard the four men sing; but the results of their music were uncomfortably apparent.

The Unholy K's had one song about the hundreds of packages which the captain had locked in the forward peak tank. The lyrics said that the boxes contained silk stockings, cigarettes, whiskey, drugs, and other black-market goods which the captain was going to sell in England. They depicted the captain becoming a millionaire and retiring to a mansion in New Hampshire as soon as the war was over.

The crew began to ask questions: Why *should* the Old Man be hiding the parcels? Why *had* they been delivered with so much secrecy? It was even rumored that the Old Man was head of a black-market cartel and the cartons contained drugs stolen from navy supply depots. But when the crew saw Captain Stark, tall, quiet, dignified, they knew in their hearts that the rumors were impossible.

In mid-December we shoved off from Newfoundland with another convoy. There were sixty-two ships in the group, many of them tankers filled with high-octane aviation gas. Almost immediately we ran into a gale. The ships wallowed and floundered among mountainous waves. For nearly a week we had nothing to eat but sandwiches, and it was impossible to sleep. On top of this misery, we received an emergency alert and intelligence that the largest Nazi submarine wolf pack ever assembled was shadowing our convoy.

After a few days at sea, all grumbling and grousing stopped. We were too weary to do anything but stand watch-in-watch and strain our eyes and ears for the enemy. Finally the storm slackened and the submarines closed in. During the beginning of the second week, hardly a night went by without the sky lighting up with the explosions of torpedoed ships.

Then, at sunrise on the twenty-fifth of December, as we neared the southwest tip of Ireland, our protection arrived—Royal Navy planes. The seas calmed and we relaxed; for the first time in what had seemed ages, the men were able to get a hot meal and sleep. All hands, except those on watch, turned in thankfully, exhausted.

Suddenly at nine o'clock on this Christmas morning, the bosun's mate piped reveille. A wave of grumbling passed over the ship. We had all expected to be able to sleep in unless there were an attack. A few minutes later Captain Stark's voice came over the loudspeaker. "This is the captain speaking. Shipmates, I know you are tired and want to sleep. But today is Christmas. There are special surprise packages from your families. They have been unloaded from the forward peak tanks and have been distributed throughout the ship alphabetically."

He went on to describe precisely where each group of presents was.

The news exploded through the ship. Men scrambled for their packages. Sailors sat all over the decks cutting string, tearing paper, wiping away tears, and shouting to shipmates about what they had received.

destroyer went to the Brooklyn Navy Yard for a three-week overhaul. Almost all the officers and men went home on furloughs. Only the Old Man stayed on board the entire time, working alone, day and night. No one knew the nature of his apparently urgent business; but whenever we passed his cabin we saw him hunched over his desk, scratching away with an old-fashioned pen, while his cherrywood pipe sent up clouds of blue smoke.

We were puzzled also by the scores of parcels in plain wrappers that began coming to the Old Man before we sailed. It was not until much later that we found out what they contained.

Meanwhile, our destroyer had gone to sea again, protecting convoys through the North Atlantic to England. It was rough work. Icy gales battered us; ships were torpedoed almost every night. We had little sleep, and much physical discomfort. Everyone drooped with fatigue. Tempers became edgy, and there were fights. Captain Stark was constantly on the bridge, smoking his pipe and watching everything carefully. Despite the fact that his clear blue eyes became bloodshot from exhaustion and he stooped a bit from weariness, he remained calm and aloof.

If he knew how the Unholy K's were trying to destroy the ship's morale, he never mentioned it. It was their well-rendered ballads that did the dirty work. Everyone was afraid of these four bullies; but when

But the four Unholy K's found no presents. They stood together, watching the others sullenly.

"Christmas!" said Koenig. "That's only an excuse to get suckers to spend money."

"Don't show *me* your new wristwatch," sneered Krakow to a young sailor who proudly held it up. "If I need a new ticker, I'll buy me one."

One happy kid came jigging up with a huge box of fudge. "From my girl," he sang out. "Now I see why the Old Man wanted her name and address."

"Hey!" said Krakow, grabbing Kelly's arm. "Didn't we give the Old Man *our* girls' names and addresses?"

"Yeah," said Kratch, beginning to grin in a sly manner. "Rita Hayworth, Lana Turner, Paulette Goddard, and Ginger Rogers."

"Then how come we didn't get anything?"

"Let's go see the Old Man."

The Unholy K's, smiling evilly, went to the captain's cabin.

"Captain Stark, sir," said Krakow with mock respect, "we got a complaint. Everybody got presents from the names and addresses they gave you. . . ."

The captain looked at the four men gravely. "Don't you think that's pretty nice?"

"But we gave you names and addresses and we didn't get no presents."

"Oh, you didn't?" said the Old Man slowly.

"No, sir, everyone but us. That's discrimination, sir."

"By gum," said the captain, standing up, "there *are* four extra packages. Now I just wonder. . . ." He went to his bunk and pulled the blanket off a pile of parcels.

"There's one for me!" hollered Kelly, surging forward.

Captain Stark stood up to his full six feet and blocked the way. Reaching into the bunk, he handed out the packages to the four men, one at a time.

"Now, if you'll excuse me, I'll conduct yuletide services for all hands." He went out to the bridge.

The Unholy K's ripped the colored wrappings. Krakow couldn't open his fast enough and took his sheath knife to slash through the ribbon. Inside the fancy box was a pair of knitted woolen gloves. He tried them on his big red hands.

"Gee, the right size!"

There was something else in the box. It was a picture of a shapely woman in a low-cut dress; and there was writing on it.

> Dear Joe Krakow,
> I knitted these gloves especially for you because you are my best boyfriend in the U.S. Navy. I hope that they'll keep you warm and that you'll have a wonderful Christmas wherever you may be.
> > From your best gal,
> > Rita Hayworth

Joe Krakow felt around his pockets for a handkerchief but couldn't find one. "What did you guys get?" he said, sniffling.

"Me," said Koenig shrilly, "I got a wallet and a picture of Paulette Goddard! *From Paulette Goddard!*"

Kelly received a wristwatch and an autographed picture from Ginger Rogers; and Kratch's present from Lana Turner was a gold fountain pen and a sentimentally inscribed photograph.

The Unholy K's shuffled around to the bridge where Captain Stark, his Bible open, stood in front of the microphone.

Krakow said, "Captain, sir. . . ."

"Later," the captain replied bluntly, without even turning. He switched on the loudspeaker system, announced church services, and read the story of the Nativity to all hands. Below in the engine room men listened, and in the chiefs' quarters, in the galley, in the mess compartments—throughout the entire ship two hundred and fifty sailors listened as the Old Man read the story of Jesus.

When he finished, he said he hoped everyone would join him in a few carols.

The Unholy K's pushed in on the captain. "Let us help you, sir," said Krakow urgently.

"This is not your type of song," the captain replied.

"Please, sir, the least we can do is lead the singing."

"Please, sir, let this be *our* Christmas present to *you.*"

"A Christmas present for *me?*" mused the Old Man. "Why, yes, we'd all appreciate having a choir for the occasion. What shall we start with?"

The four sailors looked at the Old Man and then down at the photographs and presents clutched tightly under their arms. They gathered around the microphone. Krakow coughed; then in his deep bass he boomed, "Shipmates, this is Koenig, Kelly, Kratch, and me, Krakow—four no-good bums. Today is Christmas, and we want to sing you a special ballad." He paused, wiped his eyes and nose on his sleeve again.

Krakow raised his hand like a symphony conductor, and the quartet began to sing:

> *Silent night, holy night,*
> *All is calm, all is bright . . .*

The magic of the holy music spread. Everyone in the ship joined. The helmsman and the officer of the deck put their throats to the Christmas ballad. Even Captain Elias Stark, the granite man from New Hampshire, moved into the quartet, inclined his head and, in a reedy tenor, swelled the song.

> *Sleep in heavenly peace.*
> *Sleep in heavenly peace.*

The joyous music rose above the noise of the ocean and the destroyer's engines. During the third stanza an enormous bird soared in from the low-hanging clouds and landed in the after rigging. It flapped its great wings and made noises as if it, too, were singing our Christmas ballad. My shipmates said it was an albatross. But, even though my eyes were filled with tears, I'd swear that it was an angel.

Of course, that was many years ago when I was still a kid. But even then I could recognize an angel when I saw one. As sure as my name's Joe Krakow.

🌿 CHRISTMAS BELLS

HENRY WADSWORTH LONGFELLOW

One of the most popular poets of the nineteenth century, Henry Wadsworth Longfellow is best remembered for his handling of American themes, especially Indian legends in The Song of Hiawatha *and colonial history in* The Courtship of Miles Standish. *"Christmas Bells," written in 1863 after Longfellow's son was wounded in the Civil War, vividly evokes the tragedy of war.*

I heard the bells on Christmas Day
Their old, familiar carols play,
    And wild and sweet
    The words repeat
Of peace on earth, good-will to men!

And thought how, as the day had come,
The belfries of all Christendom
    Had rolled along
    The unbroken song
Of peace on earth, good-will to men!

Till, ringing, swinging on its way,
The world revolved from night to day
    A voice, a chime,
    A chant sublime
Of peace on earth, good-will to men!

Then from each black, accursèd mouth
The cannon thundered in the South
    And with the sound
    The carols drowned
Of peace on earth, good-will to men!

It was as if an earthquake rent
The hearth-stones of a continent,
    And made forlorn
    The households born
Of peace on earth, good-will to men!

And in despair I bowed my head;
"There is no peace on earth," I said;
    "For hate is strong
    And mocks the song
Of peace on earth, good-will to men!"

Then pealed the bells more loud and deep,
"God is not dead; nor doth He sleep!
    The Wrong shall fail,
    The Right prevail,
Of peace on earth, good-will to men!" 🌿

MR. EDWARDS MEETS SANTA CLAUS

LAURA INGALLS WILDER

Ever since it was first published in 1935, Little House on the Prairie *has been an abiding favorite. Laura Ingalls Wilder's autobiographical books offer a vivid picture of family life on the American frontier, from Wisconsin to the Dakota Territory. It's hard to imagine how a peppermint stick and a penny could seem like the most magnificent Christmas presents that Santa Claus ever gave to two little girls; but Mrs. Wilder makes it real in this selection about a Christmas that almost didn't happen.*

The days were short and cold, the wind whistled sharply, but there was no snow. Cold rains were falling. Day after day the rain fell, pattering on the roof and pouring from the eaves.

Mary and Laura stayed close by the fire, sewing their nine-patch quilt blocks, or cutting paper dolls from scraps of wrapping-paper, and hearing the wet sound of the rain. Every night was so cold that they expected to see snow next morning, but in the morning they saw only sad, wet grass.

They pressed their noses against the squares of glass in the windows that Pa had made, and they were glad they could see out. But they wished they could see snow.

Laura was anxious because Christmas was near, and Santa Claus and his reindeer could not travel without snow. Mary was afraid that, even if it snowed, Santa Claus could not find them, so far away in Indian Territory. When they asked Ma about this, she said she didn't know.

"What day is it?" they asked her, anxiously. "How many more days till Christmas?" And they counted off the days on their fingers, till there was only one more day left.

Rain was still falling that morning. There was not one crack in the gray sky. They felt almost sure there would be no Christmas. Still, they kept hoping.

Just before noon the light changed. The clouds broke and drifted apart, shining white in a clear blue sky. The sun shone, birds sang, and thousands of drops of water sparkled on the grasses. But when Ma opened the door to let in the fresh, cold air, they heard the creek roaring.

They had not thought about the creek. Now they knew they would have no Christmas, because Santa Claus could not cross that roaring creek.

Pa came in, bringing a big fat turkey. If it weighed less than twenty pounds, he said, he'd eat it, feathers and all. He asked Laura, "How's that for a Christmas dinner? Think you can manage one of those drumsticks?"

She said, yes, she could. But she was sober. Then Mary asked him if the creek was going down, and he said it was still rising.

Ma said it was too bad. She hated to think of Mr. Edwards eating his bachelor cooking all alone on Christmas day. Mr. Edwards had been asked to eat Christmas dinner with them, but Pa shook his head and said a man would risk his neck, trying to cross that creek now.

"No," he said. "That current's too strong. We'll just have to make up our minds that Edwards won't be here tomorrow."

Of course that meant that Santa Claus could not come, either.

Laura and Mary tried not to mind too much. They watched Ma dress the wild turkey, and it was a very fat turkey. They were lucky little girls, to have a good house to live in, and a warm fire to sit by, and such a turkey for their Christmas dinner. Ma said so, and it was true. Ma said it was too bad that Santa Claus couldn't come this year, but they were such good girls that he hadn't forgotten them; he would surely come next year.

Still, they were not happy.

After supper that night they washed their hands and faces, buttoned their red-flannel nightgowns, tied their night-cap strings, and soberly said their prayers. They lay down in bed and pulled the covers up. It did not seem at all like Christmas time.

Pa and Ma sat silent by the fire. After a while Ma asked why Pa didn't play the fiddle, and he said, "I don't seem to have the heart to, Caroline."

After a longer while, Ma suddenly stood up.

"I'm going to hang up your stockings, girls," she said. "Maybe something will happen."

Laura's heart jumped. But then she thought again of the creek and she knew nothing could happen.

Ma took one of Mary's clean stockings and one of Laura's, and she hung them from the mantelshelf, on either side of the fireplace. Laura and Mary watched her over the edge of their bedcovers.

"Now go to sleep," Ma said, kissing them good night. "Morning will come quicker if you're asleep."

She sat down again by the fire and Laura almost went to sleep. She woke up a little when she heard Pa say, "You've only made it worse, Caroline." And she thought she heard Ma say: "No, Charles. There's the white sugar." But perhaps she was dreaming.

Then she heard Jack growl savagely. The door-latch rattled and some one said, "Ingalls! Ingalls!" Pa was stirring up the fire, and when he opened the door Laura saw that it was morning. The outdoors was gray.

"Great fishhooks, Edwards! Come in, man! What's happened?" Pa exclaimed.

Laura saw the stockings limply dangling, and she scrooged her shut eyes into the pillow. She heard Pa piling wood on the fire, and she heard Mr. Edwards say he had carried his clothes on his head when he swam the creek. His teeth rattled and his voice shivered. He would be all right, he said, as soon as he got warm.

"It was too big a risk, Edwards," Pa said. "We're glad you're here, but that was too big a risk for a Christmas dinner."

"Your little ones had to have a Christmas," Mr. Edwards replied. "No creek could stop me, after I fetched them their gifts from Independence."

Laura sat straight up in bed. "Did you see Santa Claus?" she shouted.

"I sure did," Mr. Edwards said.

"Where? When? What did he look like? What did he say? Did he really give you something for us?" Mary and Laura cried.

"Wait, wait a minute!" Mr. Edwards laughed. And Ma said she would put the presents in the stockings, as Santa Claus intended. She said they mustn't look.

Mr. Edwards came and sat on the floor by their bed, and he answered every question they asked him. They honestly tried not to look at Ma, and they didn't quite see what she was doing.

When he saw the creek rising, Mr. Edwards said, he had known that Santa Claus could not get across it. ("But you crossed it," Laura said. "Yes," Mr. Edwards replied, "but Santa Claus is too old and fat. He couldn't make it, where a long, lean razor-back like me could do so.") And Mr. Edwards reasoned that if Santa Claus couldn't cross the creek, likely he would come no farther south than Independence. Why should he come forty miles across the prairie, only to be turned back? Of course he wouldn't do that!

So Mr. Edwards had walked to Independence. ("In the rain?" Mary asked. Mr. Edwards said he wore his rubber coat.) And there, coming down the street in Independence, he had met Santa Claus. ("In the daytime?" Laura asked. She hadn't thought that anyone could see Santa Claus in the daytime. No, Mr. Edwards said; it was night, but light shone out across the street from the saloons.)

Well, the first thing Santa Claus said was, "Hello, Edwards!" ("Did he know you?" Mary asked, and Laura asked, "How did you know he was really Santa Claus?" Mr. Edwards said that Santa Claus knew everybody. And he had recognized Santa at once by his whiskers. Santa Claus had the longest, thickest, whitest set of whiskers west of the Mississippi.)

So Santa Claus said, "Hello, Edwards! Last time I saw you you were sleeping on a corn-shuck bed in Tennessee." And Mr. Edwards well remembered the little pair of red-yarn mittens that Santa Claus had left for him that time.

Then Santa Claus said: "I understand you're living now down along the Verdigris River. Have you ever met up, down yonder, with two little young girls named Mary and Laura?"

"I surely am acquainted with them," Mr. Edwards replied.

"It rests heavy on my mind," said Santa Claus. "They are both of them sweet, pretty, good little young things, and I know they are expecting me. I surely do hate to disappoint two good little girls like them. Yet with the water up the way it is, I can't ever make it across that creek. I can figure no way whatsoever to get to their cabin this year. Edwards," Santa Claus said. "Would you do me the favor to fetch them their gifts this one time?"

"I'll do that, and with pleasure," Mr. Edwards told him.

Then Santa Claus and Mr. Edwards stepped across the street to the hitching-posts where the pack-mule was tied. ("Didn't he have his reindeer?" Laura asked. "You know he couldn't," Mary said. "There isn't any snow." Exactly, said Mr. Edwards. Santa Claus traveled with a pack-mule in the southwest.)

And Santa Claus uncinched the pack and looked through it, and he took out the presents for Mary and Laura.

"Oh, what are they?" Laura cried; but Mary asked, "Then what did he do?"

Then he shook hands with Mr. Edwards, and he swung up on his fine bay horse. Santa Claus rode well, for a man of his weight and build. And he tucked his long, white whiskers under his bandana. "So long, Edwards," he said, and he rode away on the Fort Dodge trail, leading his pack-mule and whistling.

Laura and Mary were silent an instant, thinking of that.

Then Ma said, "You may look now, girls."

Something was shining bright in the top of Laura's stocking. She squealed and jumped out of bed. So did Mary, but Laura beat her to the fireplace. And the shining thing was a glittering new tin cup.

Mary had one exactly like it.

These new tin cups were their very own. Now they each had a cup to drink out of. Laura jumped up and down and shouted and laughed, but Mary stood still and looked with shining eyes at her own tin cup.

Then they plunged their hands into the stockings again. And they pulled out two long, long sticks of candy. It was peppermint candy, striped red and white. They looked and looked at that beautiful candy, and Laura licked her stick, just one lick. But Mary was not so greedy. She didn't take even one lick of her stick.

Those stockings weren't empty yet. Mary and Laura pulled out two small packages. They unwrapped them, and each found a little heart-shaped cake. Over their delicate brown tops was sprinkled white sugar. The sparkling grains lay like tiny drifts of snow.

The cakes were too pretty to eat. Mary and Laura just looked at them. But at last Laura turned hers over, and she nibbled a tiny nibble from underneath, where it wouldn't show. And the inside of that little cake was white!

It had been made of pure white flour, and sweetened with white sugar.

Laura and Mary never would have looked in their stockings again. The cups and the cakes and the candy were almost too much. They were too happy to speak. But Ma asked if they were sure the stockings were empty.

Then they put their arms down inside them, to make sure.

And in the very toe of each stocking was a shining bright, new penny!

They had never even thought of such a thing as having a penny. Think of having a whole penny for your very own. Think of having a cup and a cake and a stick of candy *and* a penny.

There never had been such a Christmas.

Now of course, right away, Laura and Mary should have thanked Mr. Edwards for bringing those lovely presents all the way from Independence. But they had forgotten all about Mr. Edwards. They had even forgotten Santa Claus. In a minute they would have remembered, but before they did, Ma said, gently, "Aren't you going to thank Mr. Edwards?"

"Oh, thank you, Mr. Edwards! Thank you!" they said, and they meant it with all their hearts. Pa shook Mr. Edwards' hand, too, and shook it again. Pa and Ma and Mr. Edwards acted as if they were almost crying, Laura didn't know why. So she gazed again at her beautiful presents.

She looked up again when Ma gasped. And Mr. Edwards was taking sweet potatoes out of his pockets. He said they had helped to balance the package on his head when he swam across the creek. He thought Pa and Ma might like them, with the Christmas turkey.

There were nine sweet potatoes. Mr. Edwards had brought them all the way from town, too. It was just too much. Pa said so. "It's too much, Edwards," he said. They never could thank him enough.

Mary and Laura were too much excited to eat breakfast. They drank the milk from their shining new cups, but they could not swallow the rabbit stew and the cornmeal mush.

"Don't make them, Charles," Ma said. "It will soon be dinner-time."

For Christmas dinner there was the tender, juicy, roasted turkey. There were the sweet potatoes, baked in the ashes and carefully wiped so that you could eat the good skins, too. There was a loaf of salt-rising bread made from the last of the white flour.

And after all that there were stewed dried blackberries and little cakes. But these little cakes were made with brown sugar and they did not have white sugar sprinkled over their tops.

Then Pa and Ma and Mr. Edwards sat by the fire and talked about Christmas times back in Tennessee and up north in the Big Woods. But Mary and Laura looked at their beautiful cakes and played with their pennies and drank water out of their new cups. And little by little they licked and sucked their sticks of candy, till each stick was sharp-pointed on one end.

That was a happy Christmas. ✻

IS THERE A SANTA CLAUS?

FRANCIS P. CHURCH

In 1897, eight-year-old Virginia O'Hanlon asked the question that has been repeated—and answered— every Christmas season since then. At her father's suggestion Virginia wrote to the New York Sun *for authoritative information on the existence of Santa Claus. Columnist Francis P. Church replied to her letter on the editorial page, and the* Sun *ran that column every Christmas Eve for nearly fifty years, until the paper went out of business. Virginia's heartfelt question and Church's heartwarming reply will be reprinted and read for a long time to come.*

We take pleasure in answering at once and thus prominently the communication below, expressing at the same time our great gratification that its faithful author is numbered among the friends of *The Sun:*

> Dear Editor, I am 8 years old.
>   Some of my little friends say there is no Santa Claus.
>   Papa says "If you see it in *The Sun* it's so."
>   Please tell me the truth. Is there a Santa Claus?
>> Virginia O'Hanlon
>> 115 West Ninety-fifth Street

Virginia, Your little friends are wrong. They have been affected by the skepticism of a skeptical age. They do not believe except they see. They think that nothing can be which is not comprehensible by their little minds. All minds, Virginia, whether they be men's or children's, are little. In this great universe of ours man is a mere insect, an ant, in his intellect, as compared with the boundless world about him, as measured by the intelligence capable of grasping the whole of truth and knowledge.

Yes, Virginia, there is a Santa Claus. He exists as certainly as love and generosity and devotion exist, and you know that they abound and give to your life its highest beauty and joy. Alas! how dreary would be the world if there were no Santa Claus! It would be as dreary as if there were no Virginias. There would be no childlike faith then, no poetry, no romance to make tolerable this existence. We should have no enjoyment, except in sense and sight. The eternal light with which childhood fills the world would be extinguished.

Not believe in Santa Claus! You might as well not believe in fairies! You might get your papa to hire men to watch in all the chimneys on Christmas Eve to catch Santa Claus, but even if they did not see Santa Claus coming down what would that prove? Nobody sees Santa Claus but that is no sign that there is no Santa Claus. The most real things in the world are those that neither children nor men can see. Did you ever see fairies dancing on the lawn? Of course not, but that's no proof that they are not there. Nobody can conceive or imagine all the wonders there are unseen and unseeable in the world.

You tear apart the baby's rattle and see what makes the noise inside, but there is a veil covering the unseen world which not the strongest man, not even the united strength of all the strongest men that ever lived, could tear apart. Only faith, fancy, poetry, love, romance, can push aside that curtain and view and picture the supernal beauty and glory beyond. Is it all real? Ah, Virginia, in all this world there is nothing else real and abiding.

No Santa Claus! Thank God! he lives, and he lives forever. A thousand years from now, Virginia, nay, ten times ten thousand years from now, he will continue to make glad the heart of childhood. ❧

CHRISTMAS EVERY DAY

WILLIAM DEAN HOWELLS

William Dean Howells was a most prolific writer of the nineteenth and early twentieth centuries—his output of over a hundred volumes included novels, poems, literary criticism, and essays, as well as short stories. Here he presents an amusing cautionary tale about a little girl who wished that Christmas would never end. As she soon learns, there are good reasons for Christmas to come but once a year.

The little girl came into her papa's study, as she always did Saturday morning before breakfast, and asked for a story. He tried to beg off that morning, for he was very busy, but she would not let him. So he began:

"Well, once there was a little pig—"

She put her hand over his mouth and stopped him at the word. She said she had heard little pig stories till she was perfectly sick of them.

"Well, what kind of story *shall* I tell, then?"

"About Christmas. It's getting to be the season. It's past Thanksgiving already."

"It seems to me," argued her papa, "that I've told as often about Christmas as I have about little pigs."

"No difference! Christmas is more interesting."

"Well!" Her papa roused himself from his writing by a great effort. "Well, then, I'll tell you about the little girl that wanted it Christmas every day in the year. How would you like that?"

"First-rate!" said the little girl; and she nestled into comfortable shape in his lap, ready for listening.

"Very well, then, this little pig—Oh, what are you pounding me for?"

"Because you said little pig instead of little girl."

"I should like to know what's the difference between a little pig and a little girl that wanted it Christmas every day!"

"Papa," said the little girl, warningly, "if you don't go on, I'll *give* it to you!" And at this her papa darted off like lightning, and began to tell the story as fast as he could.

Well, once there was a little girl who liked Christmas so much that she wanted it to be Christmas every day in the year; and as soon as Thanksgiving was over she began to send postal cards to the old Christmas Fairy to ask if she mightn't have it. But the old Fairy never answered any of the postals; and, after a while, the little girl found out that the Fairy was pretty particular, and wouldn't even notice anything but letters, not even correspondence cards in envelopes; but real letters on sheets of paper, and sealed outside with a monogram—or your initial, any way. So, then, she began to send her letters; and in about three weeks—or just the day before Christmas, it was—she got a letter from the Fairy, saying she might have it Christmas every day for a year, and then they would see about having it longer.

The little girl was a good deal excited already, preparing for the old-fashioned, once-a-year Christmas that was coming the next day, and perhaps the Fairy's promise didn't make such an impression on her as it would have made at some other time. She just resolved to keep it to herself, and surprise everybody with it as it kept coming true; and then it slipped out of her mind altogether.

She had a splendid Christmas. She went to bed early, so as to let Santa Claus have a chance at the stockings, and in the morning she was up the first of anybody and went and felt them, and found hers all lumpy with packages of candy, and oranges and grapes, and pocket-books and rubber balls and all kinds of small presents, and her big brother's with nothing but the tongs in them, and her young lady sister's with a new silk umbrella, and her papa's and mamma's with potatoes and pieces of coal wrapped up in tissue paper, just as they always had every Christmas. Then she waited around till the rest of the family were up, and she was the first to burst into the library, when the doors were opened, and look at the large presents laid out on the library-table—books, and portfolios, and boxes of stationery, and breast-pins, and dolls, and little stoves, and dozens of handkerchiefs, and ink-stands, and skates, and snow-shovels, and photograph-frames, and little easels, and boxes of watercolors, and Turkish paste, and nougat, and candied cherries, and dolls' houses, and waterproofs—and the big Christmas-tree, lighted and standing in a waste-basket in the middle.

She had a splendid Christmas all day. She ate so much candy that she did not want any breakfast; and the whole forenoon the presents kept pouring in that the expressman had not had time to deliver the night before; and she went 'round giving the presents she had got for other people, and came home and ate turkey and cranberry for dinner, and plum-pudding and nuts and raisins and oranges and more candy, and then went out and coasted and came in with a stomach-ache, crying; and her papa said he would see if his house was turned into that sort of fool's paradise another year; and they had a light supper, and pretty early everybody went to bed cross.

Here the little girl pounded her papa in the back, again.

"Well, what now? Did I say pigs?"

"You made them *act* like pigs."

"Well, didn't they?"

"No matter; you oughtn't to put it into a story."

"Very well, then, I'll take it all out."

Her father went on:

The little girl slept very heavily, and she slept very late, but she was wakened at last by the other children dancing 'round her bed with their stockings full of presents in their hands.

"What is it?" said the little girl, and she rubbed her eyes and tried to rise up in bed.

"Christmas! Christmas! Christmas!" they all shouted, and waved their stockings.

"Nonsense! It was Christmas yesterday."

Her brothers and sisters just laughed. "We don't know about that. It's Christmas to-day, any way. You come into the library and see."

Then all at once it flashed on the little girl that the Fairy was keeping her promise, and her year of Christmases was beginning. She was dreadfully sleepy, but she sprang up like a lark—a lark that had overeaten itself and gone to bed cross—and darted into the library. There it was again! Books, and portfolios, and boxes of stationery, and breast-pins—

"You needn't go over it all, Papa; I guess I can remember just what was there," said the little girl.

Well, and there was the Christmas-tree blazing away, and the family picking out their presents, but looking pretty sleepy, and her father perfectly puzzled, and her mother ready to cry. "I'm sure I don't see how I'm to dispose of all these things," said her mother, and her father said it seemed to him they had had something just like it the day before, but he supposed he must have dreamed it. This struck the little girl as the best kind of joke; and so she ate so much candy she didn't want any breakfast, and went 'round carrying presents, and had turkey and cranberry for dinner, and then went out and coasted, and came in with a—

"Papa!"
"Well, what now?"
"What did you promise, you forgetful thing?"
"Oh! oh, yes!"

Well, the next day, it was just the same thing over again, but everybody getting crosser; and at the end of a week's time so many people had lost their tempers that you could pick up lost tempers everywhere; they perfectly strewed the ground. Even when people tried to recover their tempers they usually got somebody else's, and it made the most dreadful mix.

The little girl began to get frightened, keeping the secret all to herself; she wanted to tell her mother, but she didn't dare to; and she was ashamed to ask the Fairy to take back her gift, it seemed ungrateful and ill-bred, and she thought she would try to stand it, but she hardly knew how she could, for a whole year. So it went on and on, and it was Christmas on St. Valentine's Day, and Washington's Birthday just the same as any day, and it didn't skip even the First of April, though everything was counterfeit that day, and that was some *little* relief.

After a while, coal and potatoes began to be awfully scarce, so many had been wrapped up in tissue paper to fool papas and mammas with. Turkeys got to be about a thousand dollars apiece—

"Papa!"
"Well, what?"
"You're beginning to fib."
"Well, *two* thousand, then."

And they got to passing off almost anything for turkeys—half-grown humming-birds, and even rocs out of the "Arabian Nights"—the real turkeys were so scarce. And cranberries—well, they asked a diamond apiece for cranberries. All the woods and orchards were cut down for Christmas-trees, and where the woods and orchards used to be, it looked just like a stubble-field, with the stumps. After a while they had to make Christmas-trees out of rags, and stuff them with bran, like old-fashioned dolls; but there were plenty of rags, because people got so poor, buying presents for one another, that they couldn't get any new clothes, and they just wore their old ones to tatters. They got so poor that everybody had to go to the poor-house, except the confectioners, and the fancy store-keepers, and the picture-booksellers, and the expressmen; and *they* all got so rich and proud that they would hardly wait upon a person when he came to buy; it was perfectly shameful!

Well, after it had gone on about three or four months, the little girl, whenever she came into the room in the morning and saw those great ugly lumpy stockings dangling at the fire-place, and the disgusting presents around everywhere, used to just sit down and burst out crying. In six months she was perfectly exhausted; she couldn't even cry any more; she just lay on the lounge and rolled her eyes and panted. About the beginning of October she took to sitting down on dolls wherever she found them—French dolls, or any kind—she hated the sight of them so; and by Thanksgiving she was crazy, and just slammed her presents across the room.

By that time people didn't carry presents around nicely any more. They flung them over the fence, or through the window, or anything; and, instead of running their tongues out and taking great pains to write "For dear Papa," or "Mamma," or "Brother," or "Sister," or "Susie," or "Sammie," or "Billie," or "Bobby," or "Jimmie," or "Jennie," or whoever it was, and troubling to get the spelling right, and then signing their names, and "'Xmas, 188—," they used to write in the gift-books, "Take it, you horrid old thing!" and then go and bang it against the front door. Nearly everybody had built barns to hold their presents, but pretty soon the barns overflowed, and then they used to let them lie out in the rain, or anywhere. Sometimes the police used to come and tell them to shovel their presents off the sidewalk, or they would arrest them.

"I thought you said everybody had gone to the poor-house," interrupted the little girl.

"They did go, at first," said her papa; "but after a while the poor-houses got so full that they had to send the people back to their own houses. They tried to cry, when they got back, but they couldn't make the least sound."

"Why couldn't they?"

"Because they had lost their voices, saying 'Merry Christmas' so much. Did I tell you how it was on the Fourth of July?"

"No, how was it?" And the little girl nestled closer, in expectation of something uncommon.

Well, the night before, the boys stayed up to celebrate, as they always do, and fell asleep before twelve o'clock, as usual, expecting to be wakened by the bells and cannon. But it was nearly eight o'clock before the first boy in the United States woke up, and then he found out what the trouble was. As soon as he could get his clothes on, he ran out of the house and smashed a big cannon-torpedo down on the pavement; but it didn't make any more noise than a damp wad of paper, and, after he tried about twenty or thirty more, he began to pick them up and look at them. Every single torpedo was a big raisin! Then he just streaked it upstairs, and examined his firecrackers and toy-pistol and two-dollar collection of fireworks and found that they were nothing but sugar and candy painted up to look like fireworks! Before ten o'clock, every boy in the United States found out that his Fourth of July things had turned into Christmas things; and then they just sat down and cried—they were so mad. There are about twenty million boys in the United States, and so you can imagine what a noise they made. Some men got together before night, with a little powder that hadn't turned into purple sugar yet, and they said they would fire off *one* cannon, any way. But the cannon burst into a thousand pieces, for it was nothing but rock-candy, and some of the men nearly got killed. The Fourth of July orations all turned into Christmas carols, and when anybody tried to read the Declaration, instead of saying, "When in the course of human events it becomes necessary," he was sure to sing, "God rest you, merry gentlemen." It was perfectly awful.

The little girl drew a deep sigh of satisfaction. "And how was it at Thanksgiving?" she asked. Her papa hesitated. "Well, I'm almost afraid to tell you. I'm afraid you'll think it's wicked." "Well, tell, any way," said the little girl.

Well, before it came Thanksgiving, it had leaked out who had caused all these Christmases. The little girl had suffered so much that she had talked about it in her sleep; and after that, hardly anybody would play with her. People just perfectly despised her, because if it had not been for her greediness, it wouldn't have happened; and now, when it came Thanksgiving, and she wanted them to go to church, and have a squash-pie and turkey, and show their gratitude, they said that all the turkeys had been eaten up for her old Christmas dinners, and if she would stop the Christmases, they would see about the gratitude.

Wasn't it dreadful? And the very next day the little girl began to send letters to the Christmas Fairy, and then telegrams, to stop it. But it didn't do any good; and then she got to calling at the Fairy's house, but the girl that came to the door always said "Not at home," or "Engaged," or "At dinner," or something like that; and so it went on till it came to the old once-a-year Christmas Eve. The little girl fell asleep, and when she woke up in the morning—

"She found it was all nothing but a dream," suggested the little girl.

"No, indeed!" said her papa. "It was all every bit true!"

"Well, what *did* she find out then?"

"Why, that it wasn't Christmas at last, and wasn't ever going to be, any more. Now it's time for breakfast."

The little girl held her papa fast around the neck.

"You shan't go if you're going to leave it *so!*"

"How do you want it left?"

"Christmas once a year."

"All right," said her papa; and he went on again.

Well, there was the greatest rejoicing all over the country, and it extended clear up into Canada. The people met together everywhere, and kissed and cried for joy. The city carts went around and gathered up all the candy and raisins and nuts, and dumped them into the river; and it made the fish perfectly sick; and the whole United States, as far out as Alaska, was one blaze of bonfires, where the children were burning up their gift-books and presents of all kinds. They had the greatest *time!*

The little girl went to thank the old Fairy because she had stopped it being Christmas, and she said she hoped she would keep her promise, and see that Christmas never, never came again. Then the Fairy frowned, and asked her if she was sure she knew what she meant; and the little girl asked her, why not? and the old Fairy said that now she was behaving just as greedily as ever, and she'd better look out. This made the little girl think it all over carefully again, and she said she would be willing to have it Christmas about once in a thousand years; and then she said a hundred, and then she said ten, and at last she got down to one. Then the Fairy said that was the good old way that had pleased people ever since Christmas began, and she was agreed. Then the little girl said, "What're your shoes made of?" And the Fairy said, "Leather." And the little girl said, "Bargain's done forever," and skipped off, and hippity-hopped the whole way home, she was so glad.

"How will that do?" asked the papa.

"First-rate!" said the little girl; but she hated to have the story stop, and was rather sober. However, her mamma put her head in at the door, and asked her papa:

"Are you never coming to breakfast? What have you been telling that child?"

"Oh, just a moral tale."

The little girl caught him around the neck again.

"*We* know! Don't you tell *what*, Papa! Don't you tell *what!*" ✖️

A CHRISTMAS SPECTACLE

ROBERT BENCHLEY

Humorist Robert Benchley was a popular writer and actor in the 1920s and 1930s. He made or appeared in over ninety films, so it comes as no surprise that this selection reads like a script. The characters in this story are pure Benchley—beleaguered and often overwhelmed by everyday events, including the school Christmas play.

For Use in Christmas Eve Entertainments in the Vestry

At the opening of the entertainment the Superintendent will step into the footlights, recover his balance apologetically, and say: "Boys and girls of the Intermediate Department, parents and friends: I suppose you all know why we are here tonight. (At this point the audience will titter apprehensively.) Mrs. Drury and her class of little girls have been working very hard to make this entertainment a success, and I am sure that everyone here to-night is going to have what I overheard one of my boys the other day calling 'some good time.' (Indulgent laughter from the little boys.) And may I add before the curtain goes up that immediately after the entertainment we want you to file out into the Christian Endeavor room, where there will be a Christmas tree, 'with all the fixin's,' as the boys say." (Shrill whistling from the little boys and immoderate applause from everyone.)

There will then be a wait of twenty-five minutes, while sounds of hammering and dropping may be heard from behind the curtains. The Boys Club orchestra will render the "Poet and Peasant Overture" four times in succession, each time differently.

At last one side of the curtains will be drawn back; the other will catch on something and have to be released by hand; someone will whisper loudly, "Put out the lights," following which the entire house will be plunged into darkness. Amid catcalls from the little boys, the spotlights will at last go on, disclosing:

The windows in the rear of the vestry rather ineffectively concealed by a group of small fir trees on standards, one of which has already fallen over, leaving exposed a corner of the map of Palestine and the list of gold-star classes for November. In the center of the stage is a larger tree, undecorated, while at the extreme left, invisible to everyone in the audience except those sitting at the extreme right, is an imitation fireplace, leaning against the wall.

Twenty-five seconds too early little Flora Rochester will prance out from the wings, uttering the first shrill notes of a song, and will have to be grabbed by eager hands and pulled back. Twenty-four seconds later the piano will begin "The Return of the Reindeer" with a powerful accent on the first note of each bar, and Flora Rochester, Lillian McNulty, Gertrude Hamingham and Martha Wrist will swirl on, dressed in white, and advance heavily into the footlights, which will go out.

There will then be an interlude while Mr. Neff, the sexton, adjusts the connection, during which the four little girls stand undecided whether to brave it out or cry. As a compromise they giggle and are herded back into the wings by Mrs. Drury, amid applause. When the lights go on again, the applause becomes deafening, and as Mr. Neff walks triumphantly away, the little boys in the audience will whistle: "There she goes, there she goes, all dressed up in her Sunday clothes!"

"The Return of the Reindeer" will be started again and the showgirls will reappear, this time more gingerly and somewhat dispirited. They will, however, sing the following, to the music of the "Ballet Pizzicato" from "Sylvia":

> *"We greet you, we greet you,*
> *On this Christmas Eve so fine.*
> *We greet you, we greet you,*
> *And wish you a good time."*

They will then turn toward the tree and Flora Rochester will advance, hanging a silver star on one of the branches, meanwhile reciting a verse, the only distinguishable words of which are: *"I am Faith so strong and pure—"*

At the conclusion of her recitation, the star will fall off.

Lillian McNulty will then step forward and hang her star on a branch, reading her lines in clear tones:

> *"And I am Hope, a virtue great,*
> *My gift to Christmas now I make,*
> *That children and grown-ups may hope today*
> *That tomorrow will be a merry Christmas Day."*

The hanging of the third star will be consummated by Gertrude Hamingham, who will get as far as *"Sweet Charity I bring to place upon the tree—"* at which point the strain will become too great and she will forget the remainder. After several frantic glances toward the wings, from which Mrs. Drury is sending out whispered messages to the effect that the next line begins, *"My message bright—"* Gertrude will disappear, crying softly.

After the morale of the cast has been in some measure restored by the pianist, who, with great presence of mind, plays a few bars of "Will There Be Any Stars In My Crown?" to cover up Gertrude's exit, Martha Wrist will unleash a rope of silver tinsel from the foot of the tree, and, stringing it over the boughs as she skips around in a circle, will say, with great assurance:

> *"'Round and 'round the tree I go,*
> *Through the holly and the snow*
> *Bringing love and Christmas cheer*
> *Through the happy year to come."*

At this point there will be a great commotion and the jangling of sleigh-bells off-stage, and Mr. Creamer, rather poorly disguised as Santa Claus, will emerge from the opening in the imitation fireplace. A great popular demonstration for Mr. Creamer will follow. He will then advance to the footlights, and,

rubbing his pillow and ducking his knees to denote joviality, will say thickly through his false beard:

"Well, well, well, what have we here? A lot of bad little boys and girls who aren't going to get any Christmas presents this year? (Nervous laughter from the little boys and girls.) Let me see, let me see! I have a note here from Dr. Whidden. Let's see what it says. (Reads from a paper on which there is obviously nothing written.) 'If you and the young people of the Intermediate Department will come into the Christian Endeavor room, I think we may have a little surprise for you. . . .' Well, well, well! What do you suppose it can be? (Cries of "I know, I know!"

from sophisticated ones in the audience.) Maybe it is a bottle of castor-oil! (Raucous jeers from the little boys and elaborately simulated disgust on the part of the little girls.) Well, anyway, suppose we go out and see? Now if Miss Liftnagle will oblige us with a little march on the piano, we will all form in single file—"

At this point there will ensue a stampede toward the Christian Endeavor room, in which chairs will be broken, decorations demolished, and the protesting Mr. Creamer badly hurt.

This will bring to a close the first part of the entertainment. ✄

A CHRISTMAS SPECTACLE **243**

THE NIGHT *AFTER* CHRISTMAS

ANONYMOUS

This parody of "The Night Before Christmas" was written in 1861, thirty-nine years after Clement C. Moore wrote his classic poem. The unknown writer replaces the charming images of children with visions of sugarplums dancing in their heads with the maladies of a household that has overindulged at the Christmas table.

'Twas the night after Christmas, when all through
    the house
Every soul was abed, and as still as a mouse;
The stockings, so lately St. Nicholas's care,
Were emptied of all that was eatable there.
The Darlings had duly been tucked in their beds—
With very full stomachs, and pains in their heads.

I was dozing away in my new cotton cap,
And Nancy was rather far gone in a nap,
When out in the nurs'ry arose such a clatter,
I sprang from my sleep, crying—"What is the
    matter?"
I flew to each bedside—still half in a doze—
Tore open the curtains, and threw off the clothes;
While the light of the taper served clearly to show
The piteous plight of those objects below;
For what to the fond father's eyes should appear
But the little pale face of each sick little dear?
For each pet that had crammed itself full as a tick,
I knew in a moment now felt like Old Nick.

Their pulses were rapid, their breathings the same,
What their stomachs rejected I'll mention by name—
Now Turkey, now Stuffing, Plum Pudding, of
    course,
And Custards, and Crullers, and Cranberry sauce;
Before outraged nature, all went to the wall,
Yes—Lollypops, Flapdoodle, Dinner, and all;
Like pellets which urchins from popguns let fly,
Went figs, nuts and raisins, jam, jelly and pie,
Till each error of diet was brought to my view,
To the shame of Mamma and Santa Claus, too.

I turned from the sight, to my bedroom stepped
    back,
And brought out a phial marked "Pulv. Ipecac.,"
When my Nancy exclaimed—for their sufferings
    shocked her—
"Don't you think you had better, love, run for the
    Doctor?"
I ran and was scarcely back under my roof,
When I heard the sharp clatter of old Jalap's hoof.
I might say that I hardly had turned myself round,
When the Doctor came into the room with a bound.
He was covered with mud from his head to his foot,
And the suit he had on was his very worst suit;
He had hardly had time to put *that* on his back,
And he looked like a Falstaff half fuddled with sack.

His eyes, how they twinkled! Had the Doctor got
    merry?
His cheeks looked like *Port* and his breath smelled
    of *Sherry.*
He hadn't been shaved for a fortnight or so,
And the beard on his chin wasn't white as the snow.
But inspecting their tongues in despite of their
    teeth,
And drawing his watch from his waistcoat beneath,
He felt of each pulse, saying—"Each little belly
Must get rid"—here he laughed—"of the rest of
    that jelly."
I gazed on each chubby, plump, sick little elf,
And groaned when he said so, in spite of myself;
But a wink of his eye when he physicked our Fred
Soon gave me to know I had nothing to dread.
He didn't prescribe, but went straightway to work
And dosed all the rest, gave his trousers a jerk,
And, adding directions while blowing his nose,
He buttoned his coat; from his chair he arose,
Then jumped in his gig, gave old Jalap a whistle,
And Jalap dashed off as if pricked by a thistle;
But the Doctor exclaimed, ere he drove out of sight,
"They'll be well by tomorrow—good night, Jones,
    good night!"

🌿 "SLEIGH BELLS GIVE ME DOUBLE NAUSEA"

WILL FOWLER

Strange as it may seem, not everyone loves Christmas. In the Bah, Humbug department, no Scrooge could ever beat the outrageous, acerbic W. C. Fields. But writer Will Fowler, who knew Fields as "Uncle Claude," seems to have discovered a small chink in that anti-Christmas armor.

A holiday visit with W. C. Fields

Whenever palm trees come alight with multicolored globes, and Salvation Army Santa Clauses tinkle bells on Hollywood Boulevard, I remember Christmas Day of 1940 when my father and I called upon our 61-year-old Uncle Claude, known to the world as W. C. Fields. Having declined all invitations to celebrate the season, Uncle Claude was at home, alone, when we arrived, sunning himself in the yard of his residence on De Mille Drive.

The house was hidden behind overgrown bushes and hedges not far from the center of Hollywood, a town which supported him but which he scorned both philosophically and emotionally. "Hollywood," Uncle Claude once said in his crackling voice, "is the gold cap on a tooth that should have been pulled out years ago." His aversion to holidays was equal to his dislike of the film capital.

By some mischance a servant switched on the radio, and there came floating over it a Noel chorale. "Turn it off! Cease!" Fields screamed. "Give me an ax, a heavy tomahawk! The royal mace of England! I'll smash the thing and its illegitimate fugue!" Then he added menacingly, "I'm changing my will. Nobody who observes Christmas will be mentioned in my last testament. Not a farthing for them, man or boy!"

"Uncle Claude," said my father (we called him Uncle Claude because he greatly disliked his middle name), "do you really hate Christmas? Or is it just another one of your well-advertised cantankerous poses?"

For a while Uncle Claude chewed a toothpick, a technique he claimed was of great help in curing him of the cigarette habit, then said deliberately: "I used to believe in Christmas until I was eight years old. While carrying ice in Philadelphia, I had saved several pennies and nickels to purchase my dear mother a clothes boiler for Christmas . . . the kind with a copper bottom. I hid the coins in a mason jar in the basement. One black day I caught my father stealing my money. Beginning then, I have remembered nobody on Christmas, and I want nobody to remember me, either."

"Is that the real reason you hate Christmas?" pursued my father. "You're always faking stories to cover yourself when someone hits on a sore spot."

Uncle Claude sat silent for a few moments, studying his admittedly closest friend. With his spindly legs and portly "dropped goiter" stomach, he resem-

bled a Micawber illustration from the pages of *David Copperfield*. He waved his small, shapely hands. Perhaps he had the most graceful hands in the world. He had been a great juggler; the arthritic condition which later hampered his swift fingers had not yet become painfully manifest. "You're a nosy bastard," he said.

"I wouldn't discuss noses," Pop replied. "Not when yours is, shall we say, the beak of the century."

"Don't make fun of a man's affliction," said Uncle Claude, selecting another toothpick with the grace of a conductor about to summon his orchestra to attention. "All you newspapermen are nosy. A pack of poltroons who laugh at heartaches. A murder sends them cheering to the nearest saloon. Scandal makes them glow all over. And you, you supposedly tough Hearst reporter, and that whippersnapper son of yours. You all love Christmas." He ceremoniously placed the wooden stick in the center of his mouth.

"At least," Fields muttered, "they don't serve the tainted day here with snow. Sleigh bells give me double nausea!"

He arose and retreated to the shade, carrying his wrought-iron garden chair. "All right," he said, "I suppose you'll go blatting to all the world about it, but I'm going to tell you why I eschew Christmas and other silly holidays. It's because those days point up a thing called loneliness. An actor on the road—as I was for so long—finds himself all alone on days when everyone else has friends and companionship. It's not so good to be in Australia, or in Scotland, or in South Africa, as I was on tour, all alone on a Christmas Day, and to see and hear a lot of happy strangers welcoming that two-faced merriment-monger Santa Claus, who passes you by.

"We're all lonely enough as it is. By God, I was *born* lonely!"

Now Fields slowly started rocking on his stationary chair, one eye on the gin bottle atop his portable bar constructed from a red, four-wheeled child's wagon. Some weeks earlier he had been at Soboba Hot Springs, a California health resort, where he was compelled to partake only of the native waters. He had imbibed nothing more powerful than ginger ale ever since the repair job.

"But Christmas and New Year's and Thanksgiving and all the rest," he eventually said, "make me even *more* lonely. So I observe only one day—April First. That's *my* day. It's Adam's birthday, too. If I remember correctly, the Holy Writ relates that Adam was created on April First. It explains a lot of things, especially politics and psychoanalysis."

Uncle Claude's gaze returned to the bottle of gin. "I've just reached a momentous decision," he announced. "I've either got to take a drink or shoot all the Santa Clauses infesting the boulevards." He made himself a triple martini. "It may interest you to know," he added, after a few sips, "that tomorrow I am removing both your names from my will. It was a hefty bequest, too. Oh well, if you prefer mistletoe. . . ."

When we started to leave, Uncle Claude asked us to "wait one minute. I have something for you." Each year, he gave us a gag Christmas present. The previous Christmas, it had been a large morocco-bound volume embossed with gold letters declaring:

"Places Where I Am Not Wanted, W. C. Fields."
When opened, it was discovered to be the thick Los
Angeles phone book.

He returned from inside the house carrying an envelope. "Open this later," he ordered.

That evening, we opened the envelope. His customary vulgar hand-drawn sketch of "Christmas Hated"
did not fall out. Instead, this was a small Christmas
card bearing a watercolor by Uncle Claude, showing
him as a red-and-white-bearded Santa Claus, puff-
ing on a very large cigar. A trail of smoke messaged,
"Merry Xmas."

Somehow I think that the man who died six years
later—on December 25, 1946—secretly had a small
soft spot for Christmas. ❧

THE GIFT OF THE MAGI

O. HENRY

O. Henry was the pseudonym of short-story writer, poet, newspaperman, and editor William Sidney Porter. "The Gift of the Magi," first published in 1905, is perhaps his most famous work, and demonstrates clearly why the name "O. Henry" is virtually synonymous with the surprise ending. In spite of the author's slightly sardonic style, the true spirit of Christmas shines through in this story.

One dollar and eighty-seven cents. That was all. And sixty cents of it was in pennies. Pennies saved one and two at a time by bulldozing the grocer and the vegetable man and the butcher until one's cheeks burned with the silent imputation of parsimony that such close dealing implied. Three times Della counted it. One dollar and eighty-seven cents. And the next day would be Christmas.

There was clearly nothing to do but flop down on the shabby little couch and howl. So Della did it. Which instigates the moral reflection that life is made up of sobs, sniffles, and smiles, with sniffles predominating.

While the mistress of the home is gradually subsiding from the first stage to the second, take a look at the home. A furnished flat at $8 per week. It did not exactly beggar description, but it certainly had that word on the lookout for the mendicancy squad.

In the vestibule below was a letter-box into which no letter would go, and an electric button from which no mortal finger could coax a ring. Also appertaining thereunto was a card bearing the name "Mr. James Dillingham Young."

The "Dillingham" had been flung to the breeze during a former period of prosperity when its possessor was being paid $30 per week. Now, when the income was shrunk to $20, the letters of "Dillingham" looked blurred, as though they were thinking seriously of contracting to a modest and unassuming D. But whenever Mr. James Dillingham Young came home and reached his flat above he was called "Jim" and greatly hugged by Mrs. James Dillingham Young, already introduced to you as Della. Which is all very good.

Della finished her cry and attended to her cheeks with the powder rag. She stood by the window and looked out dully at a grey cat walking a grey fence in a grey backyard. To-morrow would be Christmas Day, and she had only $1.87 with which to buy Jim a present. She had been saving every penny she could for months, with this result. Twenty dollars a week doesn't go far. Expenses had been greater than she had calculated. They always are. Only $1.87 to buy a present for Jim. Her Jim. Many a happy hour she had spent planning for something nice for him. Something fine and rare and sterling—something just a little bit near to being worthy of the honour of being owned by Jim.

There was a pier-glass between the windows of the room. Perhaps you have seen a pier-glass in an $8 flat. A very thin and very agile person may, by observing his reflection in a rapid sequence of longitudinal strips, obtain a fairly accurate conception of his looks. Della, being slender, had mastered the art.

Suddenly she whirled from the window and stood before the glass. Her eyes were shining brilliantly, but her face had lost its colour within twenty seconds. Rapidly she pulled down her hair and let it fall to its full length.

Now, there were two possessions of the James Dillingham Youngs in which they both took a mighty pride. One was Jim's gold watch that had been his father's and grandfather's. The other was Della's hair. Had the Queen of Sheba lived in the flat across the airshaft, Della would have let her hair hang out the window some day to dry just to depreciate Her Majesty's jewels and gifts. Had King Solomon been the janitor, with all his treasures piled up in the basement, Jim would have pulled out his watch every time he passed, just to see him pluck at his beard from envy.

So now Della's beautiful hair fell about her, rippling and shining like a cascade of brown waters. It reached below her knee and made itself almost a garment for her. And then she did it up again nervously and quickly. Once she faltered for a minute and stood still while a tear or two splashed on the worn red carpet.

On went her old brown jacket; on went her old brown hat. With a whirl of skirts and with the brilliant sparkle still in her eyes, she fluttered out the door and down the stairs to the street.

Where she stopped the sign read: "Mme. Sofronie. Hair Goods of All Kinds." One flight up Della ran, and collected herself, panting. Madame, large, too white, chilly, hardly looked the "Sofronie."

"Will you buy my hair?" asked Della.

"I buy hair," said Madame. "Take yer hat off and let's have a sight at the looks of it."

Down rippled the brown cascade.

"Twenty dollars," said Madame, lifting the mass with a practised hand.

"Give it to me quick," said Della.

Oh, and the next two hours tripped by on rosy wings. Forget the hashed metaphor. She was ransacking the stores for Jim's present.

She found it at last. It surely had been made for Jim and no one else. There was no other like it in any of the stores, and she had turned all of them inside out. It was a platinum fob chain simple and chaste in design, properly proclaiming its value by substance alone and not by meretricious ornamentation—as all good things should do. It was even worthy of The Watch. As soon as she saw it she knew that it must be Jim's. It was like him. Quietness and value—the description applied to both. Twenty-one dollars they took from her for it, and she hurried home with the 87 cents. With that chain on his watch Jim might be properly anxious about the time in any company. Grand as the watch was, he sometimes

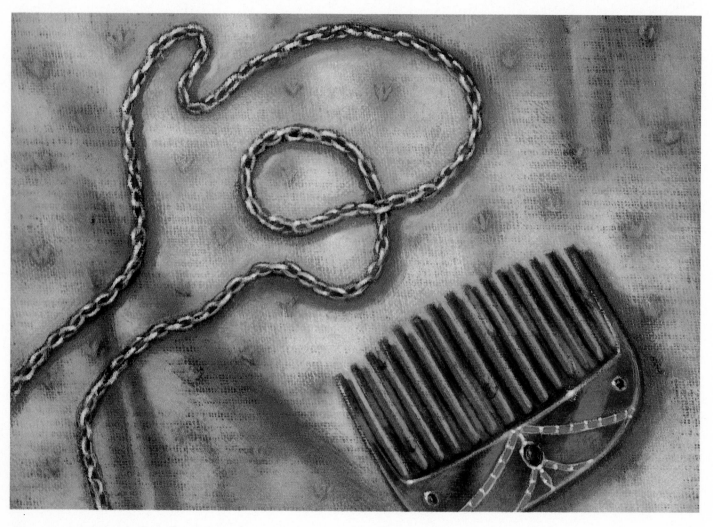

looked at it on the sly on account of the old leather strap that he used in place of a chain.

When Della reached home her intoxication gave way a little to prudence and reason. She got out her curling irons and lighted the gas and went to work repairing the ravages made by generosity added to love. Which is always a tremendous task, dear friends—a mammoth task.

Within forty minutes her head was covered with tiny close-lying curls that made her look wonderfully like a truant schoolboy. She looked at her reflection in the mirror long, carefully, and critically.

"If Jim doesn't kill me," she said to herself, "before he takes a second look at me, he'll say I look like a Coney Island chorus girl. But what could I do—oh! what could I do with a dollar and eighty-seven cents?"

At 7 o'clock the coffee was made and the frying-pan was on the back of the stove hot and ready to cook the chops.

Jim was never late. Della doubled the fob chain in her hand and sat on the corner of the table near the door that he always entered. Then she heard his step on the stair away down on the first flight, and she turned white for just a moment. She had a habit of saying little silent prayers about the simplest every-day things, and now she whispered: "Please God, make him think I am still pretty."

The door opened and Jim stepped in and closed it. He looked thin and very serious. Poor fellow, he was only twenty-two—and to be burdened with a family! He needed a new overcoat and he was without gloves.

Jim stopped inside the door, as immovable as a setter at the scent of quail. His eyes were fixed upon Della, and there was an expression in them that she could not read, and it terrified her. It was not anger, nor surprise, nor disapproval, nor horror, nor any of the sentiments that she had been prepared for. He simply stared at her fixedly with that peculiar expression on his face.

Della wriggled off the table and went for him.

"Jim, darling," she cried, "don't look at me that way. I had my hair cut off and sold it because I couldn't have lived through Christmas without giving you a present. It'll grow out again—you won't mind, will you? I just had to do it. My hair grows awfully fast. Say 'Merry Christmas!' Jim, and let's be happy. You don't know what a nice—what a beautiful, nice gift I've got for you."

"You've cut off your hair?" asked Jim, laboriously, as if he had not arrived at that patent fact yet even after the hardest mental labour.

"Cut it off and sold it," said Della. "Don't you like me just as well, anyhow? I'm me without my hair, ain't I?"

Jim looked about the room curiously.

"You say your hair is gone?" he said, with an air almost of idiocy.

"You needn't look for it," said Della. "It's sold, I tell you—sold and gone, too. It's Christmas Eve, boy. Be good to me, for it went for you. Maybe the hairs of my head were numbered," she went on with a sudden serious sweetness, "but nobody could ever count my love for you. Shall I put the chops on, Jim?"

Out of his trance Jim seemed quickly to wake. He enfolded his Della. For ten seconds let us regard with discreet scrutiny some inconsequential object in the other direction. Eight dollars a week or a million a year—what is the difference? A mathematician or a wit would give you the wrong answer. The magi brought valuable gifts, but that was not among them. This dark assertion will be illuminated later on.

Jim drew a package from his overcoat pocket and threw it upon the table.

"Don't make a mistake, Dell," he said, "about me. I don't think there's anything in the way of a haircut or a shave or a shampoo that could make me like my girl any less. But if you'll unwrap that package you may see why you had me going a while at first."

White fingers and nimble tore at the string and paper. And then an ecstatic scream of joy; and then, alas! a quick feminine change to hysterical tears and wails, necessitating the immediate employment of all the comforting powers of the lord of the flat.

For there lay The Combs—the set of combs, side and back, that Della had worshipped for long in a Broadway window. Beautiful combs, pure tortoise shell, with jeweled rims—just the shade to wear in the beautiful vanished hair. They were expensive combs, she knew, and her heart had simply craved and yearned over them without the least hope of possession. And now, they were hers, but the tresses that should have adorned the coveted adornments were gone.

But she hugged them to her bosom, and at length she was able to look up with dim eyes and a smile and say: "My hair grows so fast, Jim!"

And then Della leaped up like a little singed cat and cried, "Oh, oh!"

Jim had not yet seen his beautiful present. She held it out to him eagerly upon her open palm. The dull precious metal seemed to flash with a reflection of her bright and ardent spirit.

"Isn't it a dandy, Jim? I hunted all over town to find it. You'll have to look at the time a hundred times a day now. Give me your watch. I want to see how it looks on it."

Instead of obeying, Jim tumbled down on the couch and put his hands under the back of his head and smiled.

"Dell," said he, "let's put our Christmas presents away and keep 'em a while. They're too nice to use just at present. I sold the watch to get the money to buy your combs. And now suppose you put the chops on."

The magi, as you know, were wise men—wonderfully wise men who brought gifts to the Babe in the manger. They invented the art of giving Christmas presents. Being wise, their gifts were no doubt wise ones, possibly bearing the privilege of exchange in case of duplication. And here I have lamely related to you the uneventful chronicle of two foolish children in a flat who most unwisely sacrificed for each other the greatest treasures of their house. But in a last word to the wise of these days let it be said that of all who give gifts these two were the wisest. Of all who give and receive gifts, such as they are wisest. Everywhere they are wisest. They are the magi. ✲

SPECIAL THANKS

Ruth Asawa and Family, San Francisco, California
Rachel Bolton, Product Information Coordinator, Hallmark Cards Inc., Kansas City, Missouri
Andreas Brown, Gotham Book Mart, New York, New York
Jean Byrne, Editor, *The Green Scene*, Pennsylvania Horticultural Society
Dolph Gotelli, Professor of Design, University of California at Davis, expert on and collector of Christmas antiques
John Grossman, The Gifted Line, Sausalito, California
David Haberstich, Museum Specialist, Photographics Collections, Archive Center, National Museum of American History, Smithsonian Institution
Virginia Herz, Novato, California
Midd Hunt, Photographer, Washington, D.C.
Lorene Mayo, Museum Specialist, Archive Center, National Museum of American History, Smithsonian Institution
Ink Mendelsohn, Smithsonian News Service
Betty Monkman, Associate Curator, The White House, Washington, D.C.
James Morrison, Christmas expert and collector, Georgetown, Maryland
Dane Penland, Photographer, Washington, D.C.
Richard E. Presha, Worldly Possessions, Philadelphia, Pennsylvania
Anne Serio, Museum Specialist, Divison of Domestic Life, National Museum of American History, Smithsonian Institution
Katie Lazar Sinnes, Kansas City, Missouri
Eliza Sweetman, Newell Color Labs, San Francisco, California
Leslie Tilley, editcetera, Berkeley, California
Jeff Tinsley, Photographer, Washington, D.C.
Sharron Uhler, Curator of the Hallmark Historical Collection, Hallmark Cards Inc., Kansas City, Missouri
John Wells, Photographer, San Francisco, California
Frederick Yost, lighting engineer, and Jessie Yost, Philadelphia, Pennsylvania

CREDIT LINES

IMAGES

1 A. Pierce Bounds/UNIPHOTO
3 Norman Rockwell, cover of *The Literary Digest*, December 18, 1920. Copyright © 1920 Funk & Wagnalls Company. Courtesy Library of Congress.
4 © R.C. Paulson/H. Armstrong Roberts
7 © Jon Riley/Folio Inc.
8–9 © Ira Block/The Image Bank
10 © Peter Ralston, 1985
12–13 © CLI Colour Library International
14 © Ernst Haas
15 (top) © Barry Staver
15 (bottom) © Russ Davies/ Stockphotos Inc.
16 © John McDermott
16–17 (top) Courtesy J. C. Nichols Company, Kansas City
16–17 (bottom) Steve Hansen/ TIME Magazine
18 © Cecile Brunswick
19 © H. Armstrong Roberts
20 Courtesy Frederick Yost
21 © Steve Hansen/Stock Boston
22–23 © Joe Grossinger/ Stockphotos Inc.
23 (top) © Craig Blouin/f/Stop Pictures
23 (bottom) © Wally McNamee/Folio Inc.
24 © Herb and Dorothy McLaughlin
25 © J. Anderson/H. Armstrong Roberts
26 © Michael Skott
28–29 Myron Davis for LIFE
30–31 Courtesy Leonard McCombe
32 The Collection of Advertising History, National Museum of American History, Smithsonian Institution, Washington, D.C.
34 Courtesy of the New-York Historical Society, New York City
35 (top) Peter Stackpole for LIFE
35 (bottom) The National Archives
36 (top) Library of Congress
36 (bottom left) Photoworld/ FPG International
36 (bottom right) The National Archives
37 (top) The National Archives
37 (bottom) Free Library of Philadelphia, Print and Picture Department
40 © Nathan Benn, Woodfin Camp & Associates
41 The Collection of Advertising History, National Museum of American History, Smithsonian Institution, Washington, D.C.
44 The Collection of Advertising History, National Museum of American History, Smithsonian Institution, Washington, D.C.

44 Recipe for Orange Stuffing from GREAT DINNERS FROM LIFE, © 1969 Time-Life Books Inc.
45 Recipe for Spiced Acorn Squash from FOODS OF THE WORLD: AMERICAN COOKING, © 1968 Time-Life Books Inc.
45 Recipe for Braised Brussels Sprouts from THE GOOD COOK: VEGETABLES, © 1979 Time-Life Books Inc. Reprinted by permission of Edward J. Acton, Inc.
46 The Collection of Advertising History, National Museum of American History, Smithsonian Institution, Washington, D.C.
46 Recipe for Red Cabbage with Apples from FOODS OF THE WORLD: THE COOKING OF GERMANY, © 1969 Time-Life Books Inc.
48 From the collection of K. Burke
48 Recipe for Dresdner Stollen from THE FOODS OF THE WORLD: THE COOKING OF GERMANY, © 1969 Time-Life Books Inc.
49 Photo by Henry Groskinsky, © 1969 Time-Life Books Inc., from FOODS OF THE WORLD: THE COOKING OF GERMANY
51 Photo by Anthony Blake, © 1969 Time-Life Books Inc., from FOODS OF THE WORLD: THE COOKING OF THE BRITISH ISLES
51 Recipes for Plum Pudding and Brandy Butter from FOODS OF THE WORLD: THE COOKING OF THE BRITISH ISLES, © 1969 Time-Life Books Inc.
52–53 Photo by Mark Kauffman, © 1971 Time-Life Books Inc., from FOODS OF THE WORLD: AMERICAN COOKING, SOUTHERN STYLE
53 The Collection of Advertising History, National Museum of American History, Smithsonian Institution, Washington, D.C.
53 Recipe for White Fruit Cake from FOODS OF THE WORLD: AMERICAN COOKING, SOUTHERN STYLE, © 1971 Time-Life Books Inc.
54–55 Photo and recipe for Jewelled Croquembouch courtesy of the California Milk Advisory Board
55 Photo and recipe for Heirloom Fruit Cake courtesy of the California Raisin Advisory Board. Photo by Alan Krosnick.
56 Photo by Richard Jeffrey, © 1970 Time-Life Books Inc., from FOODS OF THE WORLD: AMERICAN COOKING, THE EASTERN HEARTLAND
56 Recipe for Pfeffernüsse from FOODS OF THE WORLD: THE COOKING OF GERMANY, © 1969 Time-Life Books Inc.
56 Recipe for Bourbon Balls from FOODS OF THE WORLD: AMERICAN COOKING, SOUTHERN STYLE, © 1971 Time-Life Books Inc.

56–57 Photo and recipes for Miller's Mocha Morsels and Gingerbread Cookies courtesy of the California Raisin Advisory Board. Photo by Alan Krosnick.
57 Recipe for Moravian Animal Cookies from FOODS OF THE WORLD: AMERICAN COOKING, THE EASTERN HEARTLAND, © 1970 Time-Life Books Inc.
59 Recipe for Chocolate Brownies from THE TIME-LIFE HOLIDAY COOKBOOK, © 1976 Time-Life Books Inc.
61 Recipe for Divinity Candies from THE TIME-LIFE HOLIDAY COOKBOOK, © 1976 Time-Life Books Inc.
61 Recipe for Christmas Almond Brittle from THE GOOD COOK: CANDY, © 1981 Time-Life Books Inc. Reprinted by permission of Trident Press Limited.
63 Photo and recipe for Fireside Glögg courtesy of the California Raisin Advisory Board. Photo by Alan Krosnick.
63 Recipe for Traditional Eggnog from THE TIME-LIFE HOLIDAY COOKBOOK, © 1976 Time-Life Books Inc.
64 © Brian R. Tolbert/brt Photo
66 © Alyce B. Gambal
67 © Brian R. Tolbert/brt Photo. Ornaments from the collection of James Morrison, Georgetown, Maryland.
68 Photographs © 1987 The Gifted Line, John Grossman, Inc. From the John Grossman Collection of Antique Images.
69 (top left, top right, middle left, middle right, bottom right) Courtesy Phillip Snyder. Photographed by Steven Mays, © 1978 Time-Life Books Inc. From THE ENCYCLOPEDIA OF COLLECTIBLES.
69 (bottom left) Hallmark Historical Collection, Hallmark Cards, Inc.
70 (top left) © Brian R. Tolbert/ brt Photo. Ornaments from the collection of Bruce Catts, New York City.
70 (top right) Photograph © 1987 The Gifted Line, John Grossman, Inc. From the John Grossman Collection of Antique Images.
70 (bottom) Courtesy Shelburne Museum, Shelburne, Vermont
71 (top) Courtesy Gerald R. Ford Library
71 (bottom) © Brian R. Tolbert/ brt Photo. Ornaments from the collection of James Morrison, Georgetown, Maryland.
72–73 Photograph by John Edwards. Bubble lights from the collection of James Morrison, Georgetown, Maryland.
74 © Brian R. Tolbert/brt Photo. Pine Cone Santa from the collection of James Morrison, Goergetown, Maryland. Constructed by Susan Shroyer.

75 (left) Photo and text courtesy of Hagley Museum and Library, Delaware, and *The Green Scene*, Pennsylvania Horticultural Society. Art adapted from drawings by Barbara French.

75 (right) Photo by Peter Ralston. Courtesy of Brandywine River Museum, Chadds Ford, Pennsylvania.

76 © Rick Buettner/Folio Inc.

77 (top) Photo by Anne Cunningham, courtesy of *The Green Scene*, Pennsylvania Horticultural Society

77 (bottom left, bottom right) Photos by John T. Chew, Jr., courtesy of Jane Lennon and *The Green Scene*, Pennsylvania Horticultural Society

78 Photos by John Gouker, courtesy of Rose Kosta and *The Green Scene*, Pennsylvania Horticultural Society

79 Photos by Peter Ralston. Courtesy of Brandywine River Museum, Chadds Ford, Pennsylvania, and The Green Scene, Pennsylvania Horticultural Society

80 Photos and text courtesy of the Henry Francis du Pont Winterthur Museum, Winterthur, Delaware

82–83 Photos by Tom Belshaw, © 1982 Time-Life Books Inc., from THE GOOD COOK: COOKIES AND CRACKERS

84–85 Photos Fil Hunter, recipes Maribeth Warfield

86–91 Photos by Fred Lyon

92, 93 Hallmark Historical Collection, Hallmark Cards, Inc.

95 (top) Hallmark Historical Collection, Hallmark Cards, Inc.

95 (bottom) The Collection of Advertising History, National Museum of American History, Smithsonian Institution, Washington, D.C.

96 (top left) All rights reserved, the Mystic Seaport Museum, Inc. Mary Ann Stets, photographer.

96 (top right) The Research Libraries, The New York Public Library, Special Collections Office

96 (bottom) Myron Davis for LIFE

97 (top) Steve Hansen/TIME Magazine

97 (bottom) Ralph Crane for LIFE

98 Hallmark Historical Collection, Hallmark Cards, Inc.

100 Photograph © 1987 The Gifted Line, John Grossman, Inc. From the John Grossman Collection of Antique Images.

101 Rudolph the Red-Nosed Reindeer, ® and © The Robert L. May Company, 1987. Original Rudolph manuscript courtesy of Dartmouth College Archives.

102 The Collection of Advertising History, National Museum of Amrican History, Smithsonian Institution, Washington, D.C.

103 (top left, top right, middle left, bottom) The Collection of Advertising History, National Museum of American History, Smithsonian Institution, Washington, D.C.

103 (middle right) Hallmark Historical Collection, Hallmark Cards, Inc.

104–105 The Collection of Advertising History, National Museum of American History, Smithsonian Institution, Washington, D.C.

106 (top) Courtesy of Eastman Kodak Company

106 (bottom) Photograph by Ralph Steiner. Courtesy State Historical Society of Wisconsin.

107 Courtesy of Lionel Trains, Inc.

108 Ralph Crane for LIFE

109 Courtesy of The Coca-Cola Company

110 © Kathleen Hennessy

113 (top) Courtesy Franklin D. Roosevelt Library

113 (bottom) George Skadding/ AP

114 (top left) UPI/Bettmann Newsphotos

114 (right) Hallmark Corporate Archives, Hallmark Cards, Inc.

114 (bottom) Courtesy Dwight D. Eisenhower Library

115 (top) Courtesy John F. Kennedy Library, Photo. No. ST-C72-40-62

115 (left) Hallmark Corporate Archives, Hallmark Cards, Inc.

115 (right) Courtesy John F. Kennedy Library, Photo. No. KN-C 19677

116 (top) Courtesy Lyndon Baines Johnson Library, photo by Frank Wolfe

116 (left) Nixon Papers, The National Archives

116 (right) Courtesy Gerald R. Ford Library

117 (top left) Courtesy Jimmy Carter Library

117 (top right) Courtesy American Greetings

117 (bottom left) Hallmark Corporate Archives, Hallmark Cards, Inc.

117 (bottom right) Courtesy The White House

118 Hallmark Historical Collection, Hallmark Cards, Inc.

120 (left) Library of Congress. Photo courtesy Smithsonian News Service.

120 (right) Hallmark Historical Collection, Hallmark Cards, Inc.

121 (bottom left, bottom right) Hallmark Historical Collection, Hallmark Cards, Inc.

122 Hallmark Historical Collection, Hallmark Cards, Inc.

123 (top left, top right) Hallmark Historical Collection, Hallmark Cards, Inc.

123 (bottom) The Collection of Advertising History, National Museum of American History, Smithsonian Institution, Washington, D.C.

124 (top) Photograph © 1987 The Gifted Line, John Grossman, Inc. From the John Grossman Collection of Antique Images.

124 (left) Abby Aldrich Rockefeller Folk Art Center, Williamsburg, Virginia

124 (bottom) Division of Domestic Life, National Museum of American History, Smithsonian Institution, Washington, D.C.

125 Photographs © 1987 The Gifted Line, John Grossman, Inc. From the John Grossman Collection of Antique Images.

126 Hallmark Historical Collection, Hallmark Cards, Inc.

127 (top left) N. C. Wyeth Santa, *Christmas Day*. 1921 Bank Holiday poster commissioned by the Treasury Department of the United States. © 1921 by Charles Daniel Frey Co., New York and Chicago. Published by the Canterbury Co., Inc., Chicago.

127 (top right, bottom left, bottom right) Hallmark Corporate Archives, Hallmark Cards, Inc.

128 (top left) Hallmark Historical Collection, Hallmark Cards, Inc.

128 (top right, bottom) Photographs © 1987 The Gifted Line, John Grossman, Inc. From the John Grossman Collection of Antique Images.

129 (top) Library of Congress

129 (middle left) Photograph © 1987 The Gifted Line, John Grossman, Inc. From the John Grossman Collection of Antique Images.

129 (bottom left, bottom right) The Collection of Advertising History, National Museum of American History, Smithsonian Institution, Washington, D.C.

130 (top left) Stanley Tretick/ PEOPLE WEEKLY

130 (top right) Julian Wasser/ TIME Magazine

130 (bottom) Courtesy of the New-York Historical Society, New York City. Photograph by Edwin Levick.

131 (top left) © Yani Begakis

131 (top center) © Columbia Pictures

131 (top right) Diana H. Walker/TIME Magazine

131 (middle, bottom) © Marc Romanelli

132 (top left) Ed Miley

132 (bottom left, bottom right) The National Archives

133 (left) Free Library of Philadelphia, Print and Picture Department

133 (top right, bottom right) Santa-Graf Corp., Chicago

134 © George Schwartz/FPG

136 The Collection of Advertising History, National Museum of American History, Smithsonian Institution, Washington, D.C.

137 (top left) The National Archives

137 (top right, bottom) Free Library of Philadelphia, Print and Picture Department

138 (top) The National Archives

138 (bottom) Robert W. Kelley for LIFE

139 (top left, top right, bottom right) The Collection of Advertising History, National Museum of American History, Smithsonian Institution, Washington, D.C.

139 (bottom left) Painting by Steven Dohanos, reprinted from *The Saturday Evening Post*, © 1948 The Curtis Publishing Company

140 (top) Library of Congress, Bain Collection

140 (middle) State Historical Society of Wisconsin, Kreuger Collection. Alex Kreuger, photographer.

140 (bottom) © Arizona Photographic Associates, Inc.

141 (top) Myron Davis for LIFE

141 (bottom left, bottom right) The National Archives

142 © Brian R. Tolbert/brt Photo. Ornaments from the collection of James Morrison, Georgetown, Maryland.

143 (top) © Brian R. Tolbert/brt Photo. Ornaments from the collection of James Morrison, Georgetown, Maryland.

143 (bottom) Hallmark Historical Collection, Hallmark Cards, Inc.

144 Courtesy Shelburne Museum, Shelburne, Vermont

145 (top left, top right) © Brian R. Tolbert/brt Photo

145 (bottom) Courtesy Shelburne Museum, Shelburne, Vermont

146 (top left) Jack Caspary/ TIME Magazine

146 (top right) Diana H. Walker/TIME Magazine

146 (bottom) © Dennis Brack/ Black Star

147 (top) © William A. York

147 (bottom) Tom Story/TIME Magazine

148 © Brian R. Tolbert/brt Photo

150 (top left) Free Library of Philadelphia, Print and Picture Department

150 (top right) The National Archives

150 (middle, bottom) Photographs © 1987 The Gifted Line, John Grossman, Inc. From the John Grossman Collection of Antique Images.

151 Free Library of Philadelphia, Print and Picture Department

152 (left, bottom) Photographs © 1987 The Gifted Line, John Grossman, Inc. From the John Grossman Collection of Antique Images.

152 (top) Hallmark Historical Collection, Hallmark Cards, Inc.

LITERATURE

INDEX

(Number in italics refer to captions.)